Choice Matters

Choice Matters

*How Healthcare Consumers Make Decisions
(and Why Clinicians and Managers Should Care)*

GORDON MOORE
JOHN A. QUELCH
EMILY BOUDREAU

OXFORD
UNIVERSITY PRESS

OXFORD
UNIVERSITY PRESS

Oxford University Press is a department of the University of Oxford. It furthers
the University's objective of excellence in research, scholarship, and education
by publishing worldwide. Oxford is a registered trade mark of Oxford University
Press in the UK and certain other countries.

Published in the United States of America by Oxford University Press
198 Madison Avenue, New York, NY 10016, United States of America.

Library of Congress Cataloging-in-Publication Data
Names: Moore, Gordon, author. | Quelch, John A., author. | Boudreau, Emily, author.
Title: Choice matters: how healthcare consumers make decisions (and why clinicians
and managers should care) / edited by Gordon Moore, John A. Quelch, Emily Boudreau.
Description: New York, NY : Oxford University Press, [2018] |
Includes bibliographical references and index.
Identifiers: LCCN 2018000070 | ISBN 9780190886134 (softcover : alk. paper)
Subjects: | MESH: Consumer Behavior | Decision Making | Delivery of Health Care
Classification: LCC RA395.A3 | NLM W 85.2 | DDC 362.1—dc23
LC record available at https://lccn.loc.gov/2018000070

This material is not intended to be, and should not be considered, a substitute for medical or other
professional advice. Treatment for the conditions described in this material is highly dependent on the
individual circumstances. And, while this material is designed to offer accurate information with
respect to the subject matter covered and to be current as of the time it was written, research
and knowledge about medical and health issues is constantly evolving and dose schedules for medications
are being revised continually, with new side effects recognized and accounted for regularly. Readers must
therefore always check the product information and clinical procedures with the most up- to- date
published product information and data sheets provided by the manufacturers and the most recent
codes of conduct and safety regulation. The publisher and the authors make no representations or
warranties to readers, express or implied, as to the accuracy or completeness of this material.
Without limiting the foregoing, the publisher and the authors make no representations or
warranties as to the accuracy or efficacy of the drug dosages mentioned in the material. The authors
and the publisher do not accept, and expressly disclaim, any responsibility for any liability, loss,
or risk that may be claimed or incurred as a consequence of the use and/ or application
of any of the contents of this material

1 3 5 7 9 8 6 4 2

Printed by Webcom, Inc., Canada

CONTENTS

PREFACE

This book is about healthcare consumers and their choices. It concerns how individuals make decisions and how increased consumer choice in healthcare may not only aid and empower American consumers but also improve the overall healthcare system. This is a critical issue in healthcare today as our nation struggles to provide excellent care that is affordable and accessible to all Americans.

Consumer choice is growing as a force for change. Social norms are changing as consumers take on increased responsibility across industries. They are sharing their experiences on social media and expecting better service from companies competing for their business. Online tools, apps, and reviews of services are starting to improve price and quality transparency in many markets, giving individuals more control and choice.

There is a rising tide of interest in more consumer choice in medical care. Healthcare costs are growing, and public policy is shifting expenses to consumers, thus motivating them to assume a larger role in their care and analyze costs most closely. Individuals want a say in how they consume care.

Change is already happening in response. Innovative models of care and new medical treatments are changing the range of choices available. It is becoming clear that, for many if not all health conditions, consumers want more convenient, less costly provider options—without sacrificing care quality. To fill this need, new retail care options have emerged and become mainstream. What is more, new technology has made virtual care and telehealth services a reality—making it possible to diagnose remotely many common infections and skin conditions. Meanwhile, payers and providers alike are talking increasingly about the importance of "patient-centered care." Some major medical centers have begun to segment their markets and specialize; most have sought to establish preeminent centers of excellence to become the preferred destinations for conditions requiring the most complicated surgeries. And, of course, consumer preferences don't just differ by health condition—they are influenced by myriad other factors, including insurance type, convenience, and demographics, such as age, socioeconomic status, gender, and ethnicity. The key takeaway here is that consumer preferences differ, and, as consumer autonomy continues to increase, individuals will seek out or be called upon to make more, and different, decisions about when, where, and how to buy health insurance, access primary care services, consult with clinical specialists, and undertake treatments.

How are providers responding? Most healthcare provider organizations, individual doctors, and health insurers remain woefully underprepared to navigate this transition from passive patient to active customer. Traditionally, they have not needed to adopt the consumer-focused strategies characteristic of other industries. Referral networks among providers have sustained their business models, while individual consumers have struggled to find information to inform them about services and provider alternatives. Though healthcare organizations have—for the most part—realized that new "patient-centered" strategies are necessary, many have faltered when it comes to implementation. To achieve success, organizations must take the time to understand consumers, their decision-making processes, and what they want and need from healthcare organizations.

Provider organizations aren't alone in struggling to adapt in a changing environment. Too many consumers remain reticent, unwilling to engage actively with the healthcare system or advocate for themselves, even when new tools make information more available than before. Consumers, for their part, need to reconsider how they think about and use healthcare services to take full advantage of the choices available and to stimulate new services targeting what they need and want.

This book is intended for managers, clinical leaders, and policy makers from health delivery organizations, healthcare companies, and government agencies that deliver products, services, and information to consumers. We also hope it will be useful for many at the front lines of medical care, including patients and their families and clinicians. We have all interacted with the healthcare system at some point in our lives, or we have helped family members or friends as they have made difficult healthcare decisions. Perhaps you are in the midst of one right now; making your child's yearly preventive appointment is on your to-do list or you are helping an aging parent plan a transition to an assisted living community. Maybe you have recently reconsidered your health insurance options, or perhaps you are dealing with a chronic health issue. Even if you are a skilled physician manager, you can—and should—draw on your personal experience as a healthcare consumer throughout our discussion. We'll consider how consumers make decisions across a range of situations—from choosing a physician or a hospital to selecting a health insurance provider. We'll consider short-term decisions, such as whether to receive a flu shot, and long-term challenges, such as how one selects an assisted living community.

Clearly, there are many characteristics of the healthcare market that make it difficult to change—both for healthcare organizations and for consumers. We'll address a range of questions in this domain: How is healthcare different from other consumer-driven markets? Can a person be a patient and consumer at the same time? How and why do consumers make the decisions they do? How can consumers improve how they engage with the healthcare system? What information do individuals use to make decisions about their health and healthcare services? What does all this mean for healthcare organizations, doctors, and other medical providers? How can healthcare organizations collect actionable data on their patients? How can organizations tailor their offerings to the wants and needs of multiple consumer segments? And finally, how can consumer choice improve the healthcare system's efficiency and effectiveness?

These questions raise controversial issues. Many people are deeply skeptical that market forces and consumer choice belong in medical care. Others take the polar opposite view that consumer forces are no different or less appropriate in healthcare than elsewhere. In this debate, we take a nuanced position that the same person can indeed be a patient and consumer simultaneously. Sometimes in healthcare people are only patients while at other times they are only consumers. Most frequently, we propose that they can be both at the same time.

The authors bring different perspectives to this issue. Dr. Moore was a front line primary care doctor for 40 years and understands and empathizes with the perspective of practicing doctors as well as patients. As a long-time researcher, business consultant, and professor of marketing at Harvard Business School, John Quelch understands the strengths and limitations of marketing methods as well as the management of business enterprises.

We address these questions across seven chapters. In Section 1 we discuss the drivers behind increasing consumer choice and address the nagging question of whether market forces are appropriate, or even work, in healthcare. The remainder of the book will be divided into three main sections, each with two chapters.

In Section 2, we focus on the relationship between consumer choice and the broader healthcare system. In this endeavor, we address the following questions: Is it appropriate for patients to be called consumers? Are there special characteristics of medical care that tend to constrain the design of a system with greater consumer choice? Are there certain types of healthcare decisions where consumer choice could have a more positive impact? Are there decisions where consumer choice may be constrained or not work well? How does the government affect the healthcare system and consumer choice? Conversely, how does individual choice influence the collective healthcare system? And most important, how do we create a system in which consumers have the autonomy to exert positive influence on the healthcare market, while the collective good is also maintained? In Chapter 2, we cover the special characteristics of healthcare that affect how choice and market forces work. In Chapter 3, we balance individual consumer choice with other interests and ask, as well as answer, the question of whether and where consumer choice might not work so well in healthcare; for example, in a population-based insurance group that pays for medical services, how far can consumer choice go before it threatens the collective resource?

In Section 3, we discuss how consumers make healthcare choices and decisions. In Chapter 4, we discuss the typical consumer decision-making process and why it often breaks down in healthcare decision-making. In Chapter 5, we argue that almost all healthcare decisions require the consumer to make trade-offs between six elements. We call these the six Es of consumer choice: effectiveness, empathy, economy, efficiency, experience, and empowerment. We review how each of these elements is applicable in a healthcare context, and we address the heuristics that different consumers use to trade off these benefits when making healthcare decisions.

After understanding how consumers make decisions, we turn to how to manage choice in Section 4. We address how both the supply side of medical care and the consumers need to change. In Chapter 6, we examine the application of market segmentation techniques to healthcare consumers, stressing that no one-size-fits-all solution is viable, and that differences among consumer segments require that choices be personalized to make the healthcare marketplace work for everyone. In Chapter 7, we focus on how organizations and consumers can enable a consumer-centric system. We address the difficult tactical question of how the mindset and operations of different players within one of the most complex industries in our country must change. In this chapter, we highlight the roles that healthcare providers, insurers, and pharmaceutical companies—as well as consumers—can play in enacting these consumer-centered changes. We describe the work that government must do to make consumer choice work. Consumer-oriented changes in healthcare will only happen when organizations, and the caregivers within them, take purposeful steps to deliver a better product and experience, and when consumers speak up to demand change. Finally, we present our thoughts about charting a path forward to unleash consumers as a force to help improve our system. We describe some typically American options that could enhance consumer choice and stimulate market forces to make the system better, more affordable, and self-improving.

Americans have both the best and the worst of healthcare. We believe American healthcare can do better by amplifying the role of consumer choice in the system. This book will show how.

Gordon Moore
Cambridge, MA

John A. Quelch
Miami, FL

Emily Boudreau
New Haven, CT
February, 2018

ACKNOWLEDGMENTS

We would like to thank our publisher, Oxford University Press, and our editor, Chad Zimmerman, for helping us move our manuscript through to publication. In addition, we greatly appreciated the support of Harvard University, University of Miami, and Yale University. Thank you to Devin DiCristofaro, Alexander Mintz, and Elaine Shaffer, whose meticulous work made this book a reality. Finally, thank you to the researchers, healthcare organizations, and thought leaders who shared their stories and insights with us.

SECTION 1

INTRODUCTION

Consumer Forces in Healthcare

It all began when 29-year old Sheila* woke up with a severe sore throat. She took her temperature and realized she also had a low-grade fever. Busy at work and with a friend planning to visit the following weekend, she didn't have time to be sick. Having had strep throat a few times in the past, she knew that it tended to come on quickly without other cold symptoms. She also knew that, if it were strep, receiving antibiotics might rapidly improve her condition. Wanting to get ahead of the impending pain, she quickly looked up options for retail or urgent care in her neighborhood of Washington, D.C.

She found an urgent care center less than a mile from her home that seemed like the best bet. Plus, she could see online that there was an appointment slot available at 8 AM. Sheila figured this would be faster than scheduling an appointment with her primary care physician, so she checked the FAQ section of the urgent care website to see what the visit would cost. She knew that all she was likely to need was a rapid strep test and a prescription for antibiotics if it were positive. The website included information on cost. It said:

> What will your urgent care visit cost? This varies depending on the type of treatment required, but typically your co-pay will be similar to a visit to a physician or primary care. If you do not have insurance, it will depend on the type of treatment. On average, it is approximately 1/4th of the cost of an ER visit.

Though this was a bit unclear, she had a good employer-sponsored insurance plan, which the urgent care website showed they accepted, and she knew that her co-pay for a primary care visit was a fairly acceptable $25. So she hopped in an Uber and arrived at the center soon after. She was immediately impressed by the check-in process, which was done entirely on an iPad. She was even more impressed when

---

* All names used in the vignettes are fictionalized.

the woman at the front desk immediately wiped down the iPad with a Clorox wipe after she had used it. "Smart. Clean," Sheila thought.

However, what came next surprised her. The receptionist said, "Your co-pay will be $50. How would you like to pay?"

"Fifty dollars? I checked my insurance card and my co-pay for primary care is $25," Sheila said. The woman at the desk informed her that the center bills as a specialist, not as primary care. "If you look on your card here, see, it says $50 co-payment for a specialist visit," the woman quickly explained, pointing at Sheila's insurance card.

Of course, Sheila already knew that, as it was clearly stated on her insurance card. What she didn't understand was why the center was billing as a specialist and why the website had been misleading. When she asked about what she had seen online, the woman gave her a confused look and repeated the cost of the co-pay. Sheila begrudgingly paid it. Within a few minutes, she saw a nurse practitioner, who ran a rapid strep test and informed her it was negative—"No strep here. Probably just a virus—get lots of sleep and drink fluids!"

Everything was over within an efficient 30 minutes. However, as she left the facility, Sheila felt confused. Even though the clinic was inviting, convenient, and clean, she was frustrated by the confusing information when it came to cost. She had not seen a specialist physician, and she had received virtually no explanation as to why the cost was higher than what she was led to believe on the website. Knowing that she didn't have strep gave her peace of mind, but she wasn't sure that was worth $50 when she could have paid $25 at her primary care physician for the same outcome.

But how could Sheila have known? She thought she was an informed consumer, and she had done her homework. She knew what she needed, and she had checked her insurance card and the clinic's website.

A few days after her visit, the urgent care center sent Sheila an automated email with a survey link, soliciting her feedback on the visit. She was impressed by this, and she hoped that the corporate office would reply to her concerns about the co-pay amount if she completed the survey. Disappointingly, no one from the organization ever reached out to her about her responses.

Then, the ordeal continued into the following month, when she received a simple follow-up email stating that she owed the center an additional $25. The email gave no explanation for the additional charge. Driven by a mixture of feelings ranging from frustration to confusion to empowerment, she decided to follow up with the organization. She called the corporate billing number suggested in the email; however, she couldn't reach a person.

A few days later, Sheila finally spoke with several administrators at the corporate billing office, who simply repeated that her co-pay was determined by her insurance company and that they couldn't do anything else to help her. However, they did say they would ask a manager to look into the text on the website. Sheila frustratingly said, "Had I known it would cost me $75 to get a rapid strep test, I wouldn't have gone to this clinic! I would have made an appointment with my primary care physician. Though it might have been less convenient, I'm certain now that it would have cost me less."

After these somewhat discouraging conversations, Sheila decided to leave a review on Yelp. If nothing else, hopefully her experience could help other people who might find themselves in a similar situation. As she wrote her Yelp review, she read a few of the other reviews on the clinic. She realized that others had similar experiences around billing confusion and overcharges.

This anecdote is a true story, and it highlights several notable challenges in healthcare today. Though American consumers have access to more information than ever before, the healthcare system remains confusing and difficult to navigate for even the simplest of medical problems. This is for two main reasons. First, the purchasing experience is, for most consumers[†] of healthcare, infrequent; most don't go out of their way to engage with the healthcare system. Health insurance or treatment is a "grudge" purchase, to be avoided if at all possible. As a result, few people other than the chronically ill have much understanding of disease states or practice in navigating healthcare options. Consumers, therefore, invariably rely on their doctors or *ad hoc* advice from friends and family members to guide them.

Second, when consumers do need to engage with the healthcare system, they encounter a system that appears overly complicated and often misleading. They are met by a confusing array of payers and providers—not to mention a host of other companies that sell health-related products and services. Many of their claims of medical benefits are exaggerated. What's more, decision points often come at a time when they or someone they love is sick. In this case, Sheila knew a lot about her disease, and its diagnosis and treatment. In more medically complicated situations, patients neither have time nor the know-how. They are not in a position to scrutinize a myriad of options or to refuse or postpone service. And, too often, they lack access to accurate cost and quality information. Bills arrive afterward and lack specificity, but patients are expected to pay them without hesitation.

How could Sheila's situation have been improved? First, the urgent care center should change its website. It is misleading to claim similar pricing to consumers' primary care when the corporate billing office seemed well aware that health insurers

---

[†] The distinction between patient and consumer is an important one in this book: At times, medical consumers, such as when they choose an insurance plan, are not patients. At times they are a consumer and a patient simultaneously, such as when they are making a financially influenced choice about whether to pay for a test or treatment. And when a person is severely or urgently ill, individuals are almost always predominantly patients. In this book, we try to use the convention of referring to people as consumers in the first two categories, and patients in the dire circumstances of the latter or when the context is specifically only medical. We will discuss the distinction between consumer and patient in greater detail in Chapter 2.

do not consider their facilities as such. Instead, the corporate office could make it clear which types of ailments would be best served by the site. Because the co-pay is higher than primary care, the office could communicate that consumers should consider its site an emergency room alternative, directing simple ailments like a sore throat to a cheaper site of care such as a nurse-led service in drugstores. Though this might result in lower visit volumes, the urgent care brand might boost its reputation by being viewed as more trustworthy. In addition, every bill should include detailed information about the charges, but presented in a user-friendly way. Finally, the billing office should receive customer service training, since the responses Sheila received were anything but customer-oriented.

Sheila's problem was simple. She knew what she needed and only had to find it conveniently and at an affordable price. She learned that she needed to be more thoughtful about where she goes for care. Checking the organization's website was a good first step but, given that her condition was not life threatening, she could have called the urgent care center to confirm the co-pay amount before she arrived, or even contacted her insurance company to inquire about her portion of the costs. After thoroughly reading the Yelp reviews, she realized that others had experienced similar billing challenges and confusion; had she read these beforehand, she might have been better equipped to handle the issues around cost, or she might have been motivated to select a different provider of care.

Consumers and the U.S. Healthcare System

Sheila's urgent care center is by no means unique. The entire medical care industry displays these symptoms. In fact, and in fairness, the facility Sheila went to might have been well intentioned, though ill prepared to respond to consumers' concerns. It's just that her care experience is more typical of healthcare than not. Whereas most industries have developed more consumer-driven strategies over the last half century, healthcare has been slow to make this shift. In almost every walk of life, consumers are demanding and being given more responsibility and control. Go into Starbucks and customize your drink. Go online with Vanguard and shape your own investment portfolio. Go to any Home Depot, choose what you want from the shelves, put back what you don't want, go through an automatic check-out aisle, and bag your own purchases. Organizations know that the importance of providing a meaningful customer experience is amplified in an age when consumers frequently share reviews online. Many businesses now actively solicit and respond to customer feedback—especially if it is negative. Order something as mundane as a water bottle or a phone case from Amazon, and you'll likely receive an email a week later asking you to evaluate not just the product purchased but also the purchase process.

All of these changes come from the fact that people have more choice today. Before the mass consumer market emerged in the 1950s, people bought most products and services locally. Distribution channels were narrower and consumers had fewer options. This all changed as a result of improved understanding of scale economies in large-scale production and distribution, trade agreements that motivated a freer global flow of goods and services, lower communications costs, and cheaper transportation by land, air, and sea. In developed economies, these changes have resulted in an oversupply of goods and services relative to demand that has, simply put, given consumers more control.

This mindset has encouraged companies to become consumer-centric. Businesses that have a pulse on consumer preferences are well positioned to introduce successful new products and services that fill unmet needs. And they are working to fill these needs faster than ever before. The speed with which potential customers can access information, compare options, and make decisions has increased. In response, these organizations are now collecting more and more information on their customers, using it not only to tailor marketing and communication strategies but also to inform research and development efforts. This strategy contrasts with a product-centric approach, which focuses on developing internal capabilities, ensuring efficient production of standard products, and prioritizing superior product development above all else.

In many cases, companies are delegating more work to the consumer to reduce costs and remain competitive. Many consumers are willing to take on these tasks because they value control. They believe the quality of service they receive from another human being would likely be poor or uneven, so why not do the job yourself? Other consumers value the lower prices they see in self-service, do-it-yourself settings. For example, the cost of making a stock trade or booking a flight online is less than going through a broker or customer service agent.

Healthcare falls into the product-centric approach. Our medical care system, in contrast to consumer-centric industries, talks a good game about being patient-centered but has difficulty seeing its work through the eyes of those it serves. Many providers seek to make the doctor or hospital more friendly, but often as an afterthought rather than modify the service and products that might truly change how care is delivered, how much it costs, and whether it could better satisfy patient needs. Furthermore, much of the decision-making responsibility has been relegated to business-to-business (so-called B2B) transactions. Insurance options are restricted by employer or government negotiations with payers. Payment policies have been negotiated by providers—hospitals, clinics, or other organizations representing doctors' interests.

Why is this the case? Over the past half century, our medical system has industrialized and consolidated, leaving the interests of consumers behind. Medical providers and healthcare companies, Medicare and other insurers, government, and self-insured businesses have primarily shaped the system. Instead of focusing on consumer preferences and needs, most market forces in healthcare have operated in a B2B environment, rather than one that is business to consumer (B2C).

For example, referral networks between primary care providers and specialists sustain their own business models. Furthermore, provider organizations have predominantly catered to the interests of health insurers to ensure that they are included in their networks. A health insurer's provider network consists of all the hospitals, doctors, and other healthcare providers that it has contracted with to provide medical care to its members. If a provider organization and treating clinician are "in network," the healthcare is delivered at a lower, contracted rate than it would be by an "out-of-network" provider. Consumers are pressured to go to providers that are within their health insurer's network, since they are less expensive.

The upshot of this is that there has been limited room for consumers to get what they want in price, quality, and service. Rather, they must accept what is available. Go to a medical appointment and you might spend longer in the waiting room than with your physician. An ambulatory medical appointment takes, on average, 121 minutes out of your day, of which only 20 minutes is face-to-face time with the physician.[1] Reimbursement and benefit restrictions focus providers on what has been agreed to by payers and insurers—to make money, they must produce reimbursable visits from large panels of patients. Similarly, insurers forgo service to reduce their costs; call your insurer, wade through tedious automation, and then wait to speak with someone before finding out you have called the wrong department. Want a copy of your medical records? Fill out a paper form and fax it to the office. Of course, there are some ways to escape these irritations. For example, you can pay for a concierge medical service; however, by and large, lack of service is the *status quo*.

At the heart of this dilemma is the fact that, over time, we have progressively reduced the use of consumer forces that might make the system better. The result in our view is that Americans have the worst of both approaches to the delivery and financing of healthcare—market and regulatory. They have expectations that they have choice and are in a market-based system; yet, because of powerful B2B relationships, they can find their choices even more strongly restricted than in other systems that are regulated. Americans rate their healthcare system unfavorably.[2] Despite offering some of the most advanced technology and highly skilled providers, most U.S. healthcare organizations lack a deep understanding of the people they ultimately serve—their consumers (or patients, when they seek care). And their patients are frustrated and confused.

A Historical Perspective

Choice Over Time

Our system is the result of actions and inactions over many years and at many hands. Our approach to healthcare is more a result of our inaction at the national, state, and employer levels to create a system that gives consumers choices than of a conscious decision to create a market-based system. Even advocates of consumer choice and market forces recognize that our system of care is patched together and that little conscious effort has been made to enhance consumer choice and market forces in ways that emulate its powerful application in other industries. How did we get where we are?

In her book *Remaking the American Patient: How Madison Avenue and Modern Medicine Turned Patients Into Consumers*, historian Nancy Tomes discusses how in the first half of the 1800s Americans had a vast number of options for medical care.[3] Medical choice was essentially an unconstrained open market, in which, for the most part, the industry was unregulated. There were different types of physicians with different types of training; some focused on homeopathic remedies, whereas others had more conventional training. If you wanted or needed care, you chose who would deliver it and where to get it. And you paid for it yourself. Quality was variable and difficult to assess. It was not difficult to hang out a shingle and call oneself a doctor. Many medical practitioners couldn't be trusted, and the consumer had to be hypervigilant to avoid selecting a fraudster. She wrote: "For both practical and ideological reasons, nineteenth-century Americans embraced a freewheeling approach to healthcare, characterized by enthusiastic self-medication and unapologetic questioning of medical authority."[3]

In 1847, a group of mainstream physicians banded together to form the American Medical Association (AMA), which immediately focused on improving the standing of the medical profession. It created new training requirements and adopted a code of ethics. Importantly, it supported more stringent licensing standards, and by 1900 such standards had been adopted by most states. Licensure would signal a certain level of competence to consumers. It would also help mainstream physicians elevate their standing. At the same time, the government began to enact greater levels of restrictions and limitations on medical treatments to protect patients. Tomes wrote:

> Underlying this restriction was a clear logic: patient-consumers would surrender the freedom to make certain kinds of choices in exchange for the guarantee of better goods and services. That logic met with fierce resistance from both providers and patients, neither of whom wanted their choices restricted. Progressive-era reformers eventually convinced enough voters and politicians to get legislation passed by emphasizing the promise of protection: seek out the licensed physician, use the drug as directed, and all will be well.[4]

Another important change occurred in the 1900s as well. Insurance to cover the costs of hospitals and then for doctors started in the 1930s, and by the mid-1960s, more than three-quarters of Americans had some form of medical insurance.[5] During this time, medical insurance evolved into large corporate businesses covering the approximately 50 percent of Americans who were employed while government provided insurance for the elderly and poor. About 15-25% of Americans had no insurance at all. The addition of Medicaid and Medicare by President Johnson in 1965 marked an important transition in the shift of medical care to an insured, largely unrestricted system, where many Americans paid little if anything for the healthcare they received. If you had insurance, and most did, you could go where you wanted and it was "free." Moreover, reimbursement to doctors and hospitals was fee for service and open ended; they were paid piecemeal for what they did, with few questions asked.

Comprehensive, full-choice insurance in this model couldn't last. Naturally, in such a system, costs rose, and along with them so did healthcare's share of gross domestic product (GDP), growing from about 5% of GDP in the 1970s to almost 20% today. To stem rising costs, payers raised premiums, then began to limit choice, and then restricted the services they covered. Personal insurance costs rose the most for those who wished to preserve open choice. Lower cost plans evolved in the early 1970s through what came to be called health maintenance organizations (HMOs), narrower networks of providers, and, in recent years, restricted benefits and high co-payments and deductibles.

Simply put, consumer choice was highly limited both by inability to pay for full coverage and by limited insurance benefit options defined by the big insurers and state and federal government. By the 21st century, B2B arrangements determined much of where patients could get care. If they wanted affordable premiums, their choices were limited and largely determined by the insurers either directly in the packages they offered or by contracting with delivery groups that bore medical costs themselves and thus had strong incentives to decide, for their patients, where they should go for care. The choice options were built into insurance (commercial or through government) by structuring benefits coverage, cost, and quality, with the tradeoffs in options largely being B2B decisions. Consumers had little choice but to accept these preset insurance packages.

The Healthcare Environment Changes

As we'll discuss in greater depth in the following section, there are consumer forces afoot that are forcing healthcare to change. Personal costs are rising and benefits are shrinking. Increasing premiums and cost-sharing mechanisms mean that individuals are financially responsible for a greater proportion of their own healthcare costs. Policy change—from both the political Left and Right—is motivating, and sometimes forcing, people to become more involved in the healthcare system. The Internet, social media, and societal norms are modifying the way Americans analyze information, make purchases, and relate to one other. At the same time, digital technology is providing consumers with more information on their own health than ever before. Disruptive market entrants and new models of care, such as retail clinics and accountable care organizations (ACOs), don't signal the end of the traditional healthcare market, but they do suggest that it will no longer be business as usual. It's no surprise that, in response to these trends, the role of the consumer is changing.

For providers, this means that healthcare is increasingly becoming a B2C marketplace, for which they are unprepared. Health insurance companies that traditionally sold commercial plans in group markets (e.g., Aetna, United Healthcare, and Humana) became very skilled at selling their plans to employers. Commercial employers bought health insurance for pools of employees—sometimes tens of thousands of them at a time. The decision-makers were often skilled human resource specialists who could estimate risk, compare prices, and optimize their insurance decisions appropriately. Now, many of those same companies have realized firsthand how selling directly to consumers on the public exchanges is an entirely different endeavor. To be sure, B2B marketing remains important (e.g., to improve insurer and provider contracting), and this is more familiar terrain. But healthcare provider organizations, apart from consumer-facing organizations like CVS and Walgreens that already have a significant B2C presence, are woefully underprepared to operate in consumer-driven markets. Traditionally, the B2C skillset has held much less value to them.

To meet these new challenges, doctors and other providers, health plans, insurers, and other companies must understand and respond to the needs and preferences of healthcare consumers. Although healthcare organizations have—for the most part—realized that new strategies are necessary, many have faltered when it comes to implementation. They will need to hone their understanding of each consumer's journey and individuals' decision-making processes. Consumers will have more options for places to receive care, better information at their fingertips, and different prices. Some of these consumers will utilize this information; some of them won't. Some will be willing to pay more for better service; others will not. Understanding consumers and their motives is critical to formulating business strategy.

The key tasks are to understand how individuals form opinions and make decisions, how segments of consumers differ, and importantly, how organizations should respond to that information. This process requires three main steps: (1) understanding consumer behavior and decision-making processes; (2) segmenting consumers and appreciating how consumer journeys differ among them; and (3) positioning and differentiating products and services to meet the needs of segments you elect to serve. The onus is not only on the supply side of care. For their part, consumers will need to give more attention to healthcare decision-making. System changes can support better decision-making, but individuals will need to become more engaged as well.

The availability of choice differs and will continue to vary across different segments of consumers. Those who live in urban areas have many hospitals to choose from, while those in more rural areas may only have one hospital that is hours away. Those with employer-sponsored health insurance may continue to have a greater number of choices and decision-making options, while those with Medicaid increasingly see narrow networks of physicians and limited decision-making capabilities.

Our aim in writing this book is to show that increased consumer choice can be beneficial, when applied appropriately. Though choice and autonomy are highly valued, particularly in our individualistic society, consumer choice has been limited in healthcare even as it has increased in other industries. This has left consumers frustrated by a system that's difficult to navigate and understand. We hope to improve the understanding of consumers within healthcare organizations—from doctors to hospitals, payers to insurers, from pharmacists to nurses. If healthcare organizations and the managers who run them better appreciate the range of factors that influence consumer healthcare decisions, we believe products and services will better meet consumer needs and, ultimately, health outcomes will improve.

Six Trends That Are Accelerating Consumer Choice

The timing of this book coincides with a changing role of the healthcare consumer. It is no accident that Americans want lower cost, higher quality, and more choices from their healthcare. The forces (Figure 1.1) that have fueled empowerment and higher expectations for their medical care are due to a combination of factors that

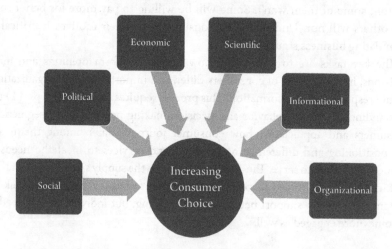

Figure 1.1 Six trends that are stimulating consumer choice.

have changed over the last few years: social, policy, economic, scientific, informational, technology, and organizational. We'll review each of these six areas in the following section.

Social

Increasingly, consumers have more options to consider and better ways of comparing their options across industries. *All* businesses are contending with questions about how to become more consumer-centric—creating a focus on how to design their products and services with the needs of their core consumers firmly in mind. Businesses realize that they are competing to make each consumer happy and to allow consumers to express their preferences about what they want, trading off costs, benefits, and services.

The Internet and social media have changed the way Americans access information, make purchases, and relate to one another. Consider the last time you tried a new restaurant in your neighborhood. Perhaps a friend posted a picture of a delectable dish on Instagram or Facebook. This prompted you to conduct a quick Google search, leading you to an online review praising the new restaurant. After a brief scan of the menu and recent reviews on your Yelp app, you made a reservation on your Open Table app for the following weekend. This all happened in a matter of a few minutes.

Consider how someone might have managed this process 20 years ago. Your friend might have called you (on a landline), suggesting you both try out a new restaurant that she heard about from a coworker. You had few tools for reviewing. If you were a particularly keen foodie, you might have called the restaurant to inquire about the menu. Or perhaps you asked friends in your neighborhood if they had dined there yet. Although consumer-to-consumer reviews have always been shared between family and friends, their reach was far less than today. This change is good news for organizations that deliver superior products and services and whose customers readily engage in positive dialogue about their offerings, but it sets the bar higher for other businesses.

Today, transparency has increased and, along with it, the speed with which consumers can make comparisons among alternatives. Opinions are easily shared on Yelp, Facebook, Twitter, and the like. That 68% of adults in the United States had a smartphone in 2015 means that the majority of consumer decision-makers carry a quick comparison tool in their pocket.[6] Consider the Twitter accounts of airlines and public transportation services. When frustrated customers experience a delay, they can easily tweet at the appropriate account not only to garner the attention of the organization but also to draw other peoples' attention to the issue. When the airline or train service responds, it acts not only to assuage the concerns of the frustrated consumer but also to improve broader public relations.

We are also in an age when expertise and training are less valued. In his 2017 book, *The Death of Expertise*, Tom Nichols discusses why this has happened.[7] With greater information parity between experts and nonexperts, expert recommendations are less trusted. Consumers can go online and search for a range of recommendations, making them more likely to question guidance from a professional. News has become more focused on entertainment, and nearly everyone demands to be taken seriously, even if their claims are unfounded or are based on impressions rather than evidence. Nichols argues that these trends have led to a rejection of expertise.

In the healthcare realm before the Internet age, a parent with a sick child had few options other than a visit to the physician. She might look up her child's symptoms in a medical textbook, but to do so took considerably more effort than the few clicks it now takes to search the Internet. When a physician makes a recommendation or diagnosis today, the parent can look up other possible diagnoses online and even connect with other parents. Consumers are more and more encouraged to be their own advocate, and whether for better or worse, they are armed with more information that gives them the confidence and ability to do so.

Political

Increased consumer involvement in healthcare is neither a left- or right-wing idea. Both Democrat and Republican policies have steadily created larger roles for consumers in the healthcare marketplace. Even while differing on specific policies, each has expanded health insurance choices in its own way. Democrats have led in the creation of Medicare, Medicaid, and the 2010 Patient Protection and Affordable Care Act (ACA). Under Republican President George W. Bush, Congress expanded drug choice in the Medicare Prescription Drug, Improvement, and Modernization Act. From both parties, there is an expectation of more involvement from consumers. Nevertheless, healthcare is unquestionably a deeply politicized topic in the United States today. Prior to the passage of the ACA, the last serious attempt at comprehensive health system reform occurred in the early 1990s when Hillary Clinton, then the First Lady of the United States, led an initiative to expand healthcare coverage. Those efforts were unsuccessful, and between then and 2010, most modifications were stop-gap measures that tweaked the existing system.

The enactment of the ACA, and the attempts at its repeal, have focused attention on healthcare and prompted a national conversation; consumers who had never paid attention to the issues before have been hearing about them daily. Whether you supported the new policies or opposed them, you could not escape the discussion. Most Americans were personally affected by legislative decisions. Most significantly, the ACA opened a mass market of health insurance coverage sold directly to individuals via state exchanges. Overnight, many more individual consumers were making important decisions about their health insurance. Many learned that they were eligible for Medicaid or used the public marketplace to find coverage from an insurance company.

The dramatic effort by President Trump and the Republicans to repeal and replace Obamacare has heightened Americans' attention to what they like and dislike about our current healthcare system. Although choice increased dramatically for those who lacked health insurance before, many found that the ACA was associated with rising premiums, shrinking benefits, higher deductibles, and diminishing insurance options. Meanwhile, premiums and deductibles were also rising for those already insured in the employer-sponsored market and Medicare, with the effect that affordability and declining benefits became an issue that concerned every American.

With the failure of the Republican majority in both Houses of Congress to "repeal and replace" the ACA, its future is unclear. The unpopular individual mandate, removed through legislation, has left uncertainty about the sustainability of affordable insurance offerings. What is not debatable, however, is the continued importance politically of health insurance. The problems and advantages of the ACA or its potential improvement or replacement are not going to go away. Whatever the ultimate outcome, the political process has not only raised awareness around the deficiencies of the ACA and the current system, but also made clear which policies the public feels overwhelming positive about (e.g., coverage of pre-existing conditions and extending family insurance to adult children up to age 26). Healthcare has moved to the forefront of public debate. On both the Left and the Right, politicians have made promises that choices available to consumers will increase. How this can be achieved for all Americans is not clear, but the appetite for increased choice has been whetted.

Economic

Healthcare in the United States has become very expensive, persistently outpacing inflation. Healthcare expenditures rose from 13% of the U.S. GDP in 1995 to nearly 18% in 2014. Much of this growth has been passed on to the consumer as additional costs and benefit restrictions. This change has hit almost all of those enrolled in employer-sponsored coverage, public programs such as Medicare and Medicaid, and those purchasing insurance in the ACA-sponsored individual, public marketplaces. While many solutions have been suggested, the truth is that no one is certain what combination of existing and new ideas is going to be necessary to change the cost curve.[8]

Before we discuss how this burden has impacted consumer choice, it's important to review, specifically, how these costs have increased. Health insurance premiums increased significantly throughout the 2000s, making health insurance one of the largest costs of hiring of a new employee. Between 2010 and 2015, average premiums

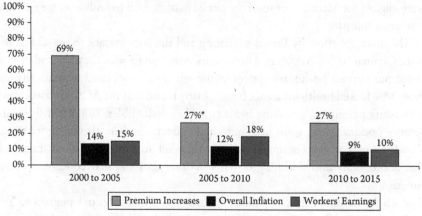

*Premium change is statistically different from previous period shown (p < .05)

Figure 1.2 Average premium increases for covered workers with family coverage (2000–2015). Source: The Kaiser Family Foundation and Health Research & Educational Trust, "Employer Health Benefits: 2015 Summary Findings," September 22, 2015. http://kff.org/health-costs/report/2015-employer-health-benefits-survey/, accessed October, 2015.

for covered workers with family coverage increased by about 27%, surpassing both overall inflation and workers' earnings, at 9% and 10% respectively. See Figure 1.2.

Premium costs are usually shared. A health insurance premium is the sum paid monthly to the insurance company to maintain coverage. In employer-sponsored plans, premiums are partially funded by the employer with the remainder paid by the employee. On the ACA individual market, if the consumer qualifies, premiums are partly paid by the individual consumer and partially covered by the government (about 85% of those insured in the individual market received financial assistance from the government to pay for their premiums).

When premiums rise in employer-sponsored plans, employees often feel good that employers are sharing the costs. However, in a 2015 paper, Katherine Baicker and Amitabh Chandra of Harvard noted that "increases in health insurance premiums do not get absorbed by an unlimited reservoir of profits or endowments—they are paid for by employees taking home smaller paychecks."[9] Ultimately, the burden of increased premiums falls on individuals and their families.

Insurers have long struggled to rein in healthcare expenditures. In the 1970s, the first wave of cost-saving options was introduced. The insurance offerings were split into either more expensive full coverage and open choice—the ability to use any doctor or hospital—or lower premiums for insurance covering closed networks of providers. Both HMOs and preferred provider organizations (PPOs,[§]) limited the

---

[§] Two types of health insurance plans that contract with medical providers, such as hospitals and doctors, to create a limited network of participating providers. You pay less if you use providers that belong to the plan's network. You can use doctors, hospitals, and providers outside of the network for an additional cost (HealthCare.gov).

freedom of their members to choose without restriction. By limiting their networks, PPOs and HMOs could better manage the costs of care and negotiate lower reimbursement rates in exchange for a guaranteed volume of patients.

As costs continued to escalate, insurers have found other ways to pass some of the increases on to consumers. So-called consumer-driven health plans were built on the use of financial disincentives to reduce expenditures. First introduced in 2001, this type of health plan tended to have lower monthly premiums than more traditional full financial coverage plans (e.g., such as comprehensive insurance, PPOs and HMOs). But the insurance came with significant charges to the individual consumer at the point of care. This method often created a significant personal financial hurdle to be overcome before the cost of care was covered.

The logic behind these high-deductible plans, in addition to reducing the cost burden of payers, was the potential to control demand for healthcare by exposing consumers to the actual costs of care.[10] The plans typically combine high-deductible health insurance with a tax-advantaged account like a health savings account (HSA, an employee-funded savings account) or a health reimbursement account (HRA, an employer-funded account), which can be used to help cover out-of-pocket costs.

In 2006, only 4% of workers were enrolled in high-deductible plans through their employers. In 2015, 24% of workers were.[11] In both high-deductible health plans and in more traditional plans, deductibles have increased markedly; see Figure 1.3. The Kaiser Family Foundation (KFF) found that premiums for employer-sponsored plans increased at a relatively modest average rate of 3% from 2015 to 2016. However, deductibles rose 12%.[12] The president of KFF, said, "We're seeing premiums rising at historically slow rates, which helps workers

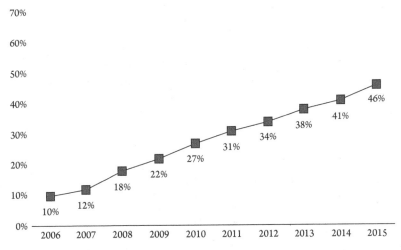

Figure 1.3 Percentage of covered workers enrolled in a plan with a general annual deductible of $1,000 of more (all firms). Source: Based upon data from the Kaiser Family Foundation (Percentage of Covered Workers Enrolled in a Plan with a General Annual Deductible of $1,000 of More for Single Coverage, By Firm Size, 2006–2015).

and employers alike, but it's made possible in part by the more rapid rise in the deductibles workers must pay."[13]

The growth in high-deductible plans reflects a broader trend of increasingly requiring individuals to contribute to their healthcare costs. See Table 1.1 for different types of cost-sharing mechanisms. The type and level of cost sharing vary by plan, as well as the type of healthcare service the patient utilizes.

As in employer-sponsored markets, many of the plans available on the health insurance exchanges also have high deductibles. Almost 90% of enrollees in ACA marketplace plans are in plans with high deductibles.[14,15] Consumers often select these plans because they have cheaper monthly premium costs and, on their face, look like good value for the money spent (though, of course, an unexpected medical need can be more costly in this scenario than under a traditional plan, where the consumer pays higher amounts in upfront premiums but less when they access care). As in the employer-sponsored market, costs on the exchange market are rising. In 2017, premium increases on exchange markets grew by more than 25%. Some consumers were insulated from this burden because government assistance grew as well, but for many, this increase drew attention to healthcare costs and stimulated nationwide discussion and calls for lower-cost options.

Rising premiums and soaring deductibles and copayments have stimulated choice—some are positive but others not so. On the positive side, having to pay ought to stimulate consumer demand for less expensive options that do not lower coverage or quality. Stuck in our current model of delivery and consumer demands, such options are not immediately obvious. However, the increasing gap between the insurance options that are available and what people want is a growing incentive for new products to emerge. The darker side of rising out-of-pocket costs is that they are a financial barrier that can force unwanted choices on patients. In some cases, lack of money may put a needed treatment out of reach. As consumers find themselves financially responsible for greater portions of the cost of their care, the role of the consumer in healthcare will increase. Consumers now have more incentive to weigh their needs and to shop around for the best deal.

Table 1.1 **Cost-Sharing Mechanisms**

Type of Cost Sharing	Definition
Deductibles	An amount that must be paid by the patient before most services are covered by the plan
Co-payments	Fixed dollar amount paid by the patient
Co-insurance	A percentage of the charge for services paid by the patient

Scientific

At the same time as consumers are assuming more of the cost burden, new, more personalized and expensive treatments such as biologics and precision medicine are becoming available. The increasing specificity of medication and other clinical interventions is creating a world in which consumers expect more customized treatment.

Throughout the 1900s, global pharmaceutical firms developed many blockbuster, life-saving drugs, from statins to broad-spectrum antibiotics. Many of these small-molecule medications significantly improved outcomes for common conditions, such as coronary heart disease and serious infections. The shareholders of pharmaceutical companies were amply and justifiably rewarded for the capital they risked in research and development.

Consider the recent Food and Drug Administration's (FDA) approval of Biogen's SPINRAZA, a biologic treatment for spinal muscular atrophy (SMA), a genetic, neurological disease found in children. The disease affects about 1 in 10,000 babies born each year, and it often results in death. For each child, the drug will cost $625,000–$750,000 in the first year and about $375,000 annually in the years after.[16] Innovative, more personalized treatments, such as this one, will undoubtedly improve outcomes and quality of life for those with serious medical conditions. However, they will come at a high cost to the overall system if insurers provide coverage for them. If they aren't covered, individual consumers may have to find other ways to cover the cost.

Miracle drugs such as these are celebrated by medical professionals and the public alike. Demand rises and the public expects that such life-saving treatments should be available. But the costs of development and use are prohibitively high, creating another gap between public expectations and the realities of what we can collectively afford. Whether science can respond to our new understanding of disease and create lower cost choices remains a question mark. Regardless, personalized and customized treatment has already changed expectations; consumers expect more individualized care, whatever the cost.

Informational

Information technology (IT) in healthcare has increased over the last 10 years. Electronic medical record (EMR) companies like Epic and Cerner have changed the way in which provider organizations collect and retain clinical and consumer information, giving them new tools for engaging and retaining customers. Within a health system, tracking patient information over time is increasingly feasible (despite the administrative headache it creates for clinical providers and other caretakers who must input it), and some organizations are beginning to use advanced analytics to prioritize projects and become more customer-centric.

More advanced IT has also enabled a host of new virtual options for care. These services give consumers convenient ways to access health providers from their couch—something that's probably particularly appreciated when one is bed-ridden with the flu. For example, NowClinic online care, a virtual clinic owned by OptumHealth, provides secure, real-time access to healthcare providers via the Internet or phone. Appointments are typically 10 minutes long and provide guidance and treatment for common issues like allergies or simple infections. Another online start-up, Maven, is a digital health clinic specifically for women. This online platform provides virtual appointments, as well as community discussion boards and articles on women's health issues. Maven combines the convenience of an online service with the targeted information necessary to add value to a specific demographic.

Technology-enabled solutions aren't reserved only for minor conditions; re-mote monitoring services make it possible to diagnose and monitor serious health conditions from afar. Philips has created a home telehealth business to ex-tend the continuum of care and monitor those with chronic conditions. This can be particularly helpful for patients living in rural areas, which often have fewer physicians. Using remote services can increase access, improve outcomes, and enable consumers and caregivers to manage conditions at home at lower costs with higher satisfaction. Remote monitoring can be used for services as simple as having people at home collect and report their own vital signs to more advanced care, such as the remote monitoring of intensive care units (ICUs) in areas without enough physicians.

Technological advances have also given patients the opportunity to access more health information than ever before. Online health communities, such as those created by PatientsLikeMe, permit consumer-led discussions of diseases and treatments. WebMD and other websites provide actionable information about even the rarest conditions. What's more, consumers have greater opportunities to collect information on themselves. Wearable devices track a person's heart rate, steps, and sleep, and access to personal health information has improved with innovations like patient portals. Products like 23andMe and Ancestry.com have made learning about one's genealogy and genetic profile a fun activity.

Nevertheless, the scope and use of IT has been much slower in healthcare than elsewhere. Seeing the remarkable advances in devices, services, and analytics in other fields, consumers want IT products and processes that serve them better in healthcare. This gap between supply and demand for useful, consumer-oriented IT represents a significant driver of innovation.

Organizational

Innovative models of care are changing the way healthcare is delivered and paid for, and some of these new models provide incentives for designing care around the consumer rather than the physician. Under the ACA, Congress created the Center for Medicare & Medicaid Innovation (CMMI), often referred to as the "Innovation Center," which is focused on developing and testing innovative healthcare payment and service delivery models. See Table 1.2 for the seven categories of innovative models of care, cited by CMMI.

Table 1.2 **Innovative Organizational Models**

Category	Description
Accountable Care	Accountable care organizations (ACOs) and similar care models are designed to incentivize healthcare providers to become accountable for a patient population and to invest in infrastructure and redesigned care processes that provide for coordinated care, high quality, and efficient service delivery.
Episode-Based Payment Initiatives	Under these models, healthcare providers are held accountable for the cost and quality of care beneficiaries receive during an episode of care, which usually begins with a triggering healthcare event (such as a hospitalization or chemotherapy administration) and extends for a limited period of time thereafter.
Primary Care Transformation	Primary care providers are a key point of contact for patients' healthcare needs. Strengthening and increasing access to primary care is critical to promoting health and reducing overall healthcare costs. Advanced primary care practices—also called "medical homes"—utilize a team-based approach, while emphasizing prevention, health information technology, care coordination, and shared decision-making among patients and their providers.
Initiatives Focused on the Medicaid and CHIP Population	Medicaid and the Children's Health Insurance Program (CHIP) are administered by the states but are jointly funded by the federal government and states. Initiatives in this category are administered by the participating states.
Initiatives Focused on the Medicare-Medicaid Enrolees	The Medicare and Medicaid programs were designed with distinct purposes. Individuals enrolled in both Medicare and Medicaid (the "dual eligible") account for a disproportionate share of the programs' expenditures. A fully integrated, person-centered system of care that ensures that all their needs are met could better serve this population in a high-quality, cost-effective manner.

(continued)

Table 1.2 **Continued**

Category	Description
Initiatives to Accelerate the Development and Testing of New Payment and Service Delivery Models	Many innovations necessary to improve the healthcare system will come from local communities and healthcare leaders from across the entire country. By partnering with these local and regional stakeholders, CMS can help accelerate the testing of models today that may be the next breakthrough tomorrow.
Initiatives to Speed the Adoption of Best Practices	Recent studies indicate that it takes nearly 17 years on average before best practices (backed by research) are incorporated into widespread clinical practice—and even then the application of the knowledge is very uneven. The Innovation Center is partnering with a broad range of healthcare providers, federal agencies, professional societies, and other experts and stakeholders to test new models for disseminating evidence-based best practices and significantly increasing the speed of adoption.

Source: Adapted from The Centers for Medicare & Medicaid Services.

CMMI and many private insurers are testing new payment models designed to motivate providers to improve quality and reduce costs. Although the results of cost-reducing efforts remain unproven, participating organizations have shown some modest improvement in consumer quality outcome measures.[17] Furthermore, some of these innovations require assessing consumer satisfaction, which should stimulate providers to listen to the consumer voice and respond accordingly.

The rationale behind such value-based models is that changing incentives will lead to changes in provider behavior. In the traditional, fee-for-service environment, provider organizations and physicians were rewarded for the quantity of services they provided. This motivated them to provide more care, some of it costly and some unnecessary. Though ACOs come in different forms, the basic premise is that healthcare providers accept financial risk and receive rewards based on the total cost of care delivered to a defined population. This risk should motivate them to change practices and develop protocols that improve value through the delivery of improved patient outcomes at lower cost.

However, reforms need not always hinge on using payment incentives to transform delivery. Consider patient-centered medical homes (PCMHs), for example. The National Center for Quality Assurance (NCQA), a nonprofit, defined the PCMH as "a model of care that emphasizes care coordination and communication to transform primary care into 'what patients want it to be.'"[18] As the name of the model suggests, it focuses on organizing services around the needs of the patient. It is claimed that such an organization can improve outcomes, reduce costs, and improve

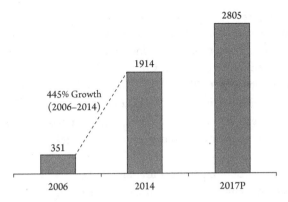

Figure 1.4 Number of retail clinics in the United States (2006–2017). Source: Adapted using data from Accenture, "US Retail Hail Clinics Expected to Surge by 2017 According to Accenture Analysis," 2014. Accenture, https://www.ahip.org/wp-content/uploads/2016/06/accenture-retail-health-clinics-pov.pdf

the experience of both the consumer and the physician. Again, there is little evidence yet that this model achieves those outcomes despite its theoretical appeal.

We have also seen a proliferation of organizational models that provide more convenient care. Retail clinics, often housed in pharmacies like CVS or Walgreens, provide efficient, convenient, and affordable care for consumers with common ailments. Figure 1.4 shows the growth in the number of retail clinics over the last 10 years.

Similarly, urgent care centers, which provide an emergency room alternative, grew in number from 6,003 in 2014 to 7,357 in 2016. By 2020, there are expected to be 11,454 urgent care centers with $19.6 billion in total annual revenue.[19]

The increasing variety of distribution channels in healthcare aims to meet the different needs of different consumer segments, just as convenience stores, supermarkets, and wholesale shopping clubs represent different channels reflecting different consumer priorities for food shopping. In many respects, healthcare is still catching up with other industries, gradually recognizing that consumers differ in where and what they want to buy. At the same time, although new distribution channels have given consumers more options, too many sources of information or places of care may overwhelm them if they aren't sure which to use.

Summarizing the Trends

In summary, healthcare has begun to change in response not only to growing expectations from consumers but also to competition among providers to increase or at least maintain market share. Consumers have more information at a time when policy is requiring their greater participation. They're selecting health insurance plans and engaging in national discussions about the future of our healthcare system. They're covering a greater portion of the costs associated with their care, giving them incentives to look for better value. Treatment options present more personalized solutions while improving IT infrastructures make it possible to track delivery of service, economic impact, and understand and guide consumers at the individual level over time. New models of care are increasingly prevalent, many of which are placing the consumer at the center. Different distribution channels, such as retail clinics and urgent care centers, show that differentiation in the market is already at work.

These trends are likely to continue. More consumer choice can be expected, and the supply side of healthcare will need to respond with better products, improved service, higher quality, lower cost, and innovative offerings to meet the public's existing demands.

Though people typically appreciate the ability to choose when given the chance, it can be particularly difficult to accommodate individuals' preferences in some healthcare decisions. There are times when the nature of the health situation, the physical condition of the individual, and the difference in knowledge between the patient and provider preclude the person from deciding on her own. Picture a man who has just had a heart attack coming into the emergency department on a gurney. The dichotomy between consumer and patient—between independence and dependence—can wax and wane over time for the same individual. There are other circumstances when the same person has enough time, knowledge, and support to make independent decisions on his own. This is true of many decisions around preventive services and chronic condition management. In these cases, people are able to collect information, compare options, and make more informed decisions. During unexpected, episodic, and emergency situations in inpatient, hospital settings, people more frequently defer to the clinical experts, especially if and when their conditions worsen. Figure 1.5 presents a continuum of choice. As the severity of an individual's condition worsens, he becomes less an independent consumer and more a dependent patient.

Importance

Creating a consumer-centric healthcare market is of utmost importance. Despite spending more than half as much *per capita* on healthcare as most other developed

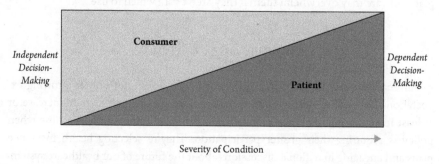

Figure 1.5 The continuum of choice.

countries, Americans are disappointed with the system. Consumer-driven change has the potential to enhance consumer satisfaction, value (improved outcomes and/or reduced costs), and business operations.

Consumer Satisfaction

Though choice and autonomy are highly valued in our individualistic society, consumer choice has been limited in healthcare even as it has increased in other industries. This has left consumers disenchanted with a system that is seemingly too difficult to understand. Finding and utilizing accurate quality and cost information remain elusive. Too often, consumers are asked to write down or input their personal information repeatedly because EMRs lack interoperability from one organization to another. They also find themselves at the mercy of contracting that occurs among delivery organizations, insurers, and employers, most of which happens without their knowledge. Simply put, healthcare consumers are highly frustrated by the red tape associated with accessing healthcare services.

Some have argued that individuals do not want to be decision-makers in healthcare.[20] Indeed, the word *patient* implies passivity. The word comes from the Latin *patior*, meaning to suffer or bear. The image most people conjure is someone deathly ill, lying in a bed, and waiting for the expert—the physician—to heal him or her.[21] The patient is dependent on the physician to make the best decision to solve his or her predicament.

However, research suggests that people value decision-making involvement. For example, a 2016 study showed how the presence of choice can improve the perceived side effects of medical treatments. In the study, researchers gave 60 participants information about two beta-blockers, including possible side effects, manufacturers, and minor differences between the two drugs. Participants were asked to indicate which drug they would prefer, and about half of the participants received their chosen medication. The rest were randomly assigned to one of the drugs (though both drugs were placebos). A day later, self-reported side effects averaged 3.9 in the group that had no choice, significantly above the 1.9 average in the choice group. The researchers concluded that giving individuals a choice may lead them to focus on information that supports their decision, whereas conversely, not having a choice may frustrate people and make them more sensitive to negative side effects.[22]

Furthermore, 2015 research by McKinsey & Company highlighted how consumers value the same qualities equally in healthcare and non–healthcare companies. See Figure 1.6. Consumers know what they are looking for in both.

Creating a system that is focused on the needs and wants of consumers will improve consumer satisfaction in several ways. Increased competition among healthcare organizations will drive innovations and improvements that make using healthcare products and services more personally satisfying, easier to use, more

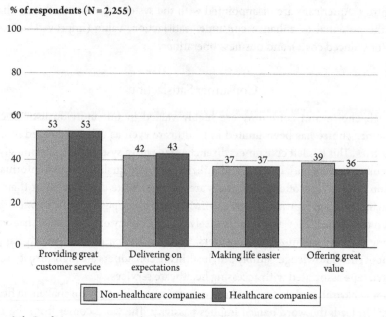

Figure 1.6 Qualities consumers value in healthcare and non–healthcare companies.
Source: Cordina, Jenny, Rohit Kumar, and Christa Moss. "Debunking common myths about healthcare consumerism." McKinsey & Company: Healthcare Systems & Services. December 2015. http://www.mckinsey.com/industries/healthcare-systems-and-services/our-insights/debunking-common-myths-about-healthcare-consumerism

convenient, and less expensive. In a consumer-driven health system, providers and insurers will need to find need gaps and opportunities to be successful in the market—or they will find their business position weakening with consumers.

Value (Reduced Costs, Improved Outcomes)

The healthcare system remains inefficient; we are routinely faced with the question of how to improve or maintain quality, usually defined in terms of healthcare outcomes, and simultaneously reduce costs, resulting in better value. Although there are other structural, technological, and political forces that will help to solve our national challenge, consumer-driven change is a powerful force that can contribute much to improved value in healthcare.

On the cost side, we are finally approaching the open-ended limits of what Americans can afford to spend on healthcare. For example, a 2016 consumer survey conducted in 11 developed countries found that the United States trailed other countries in making healthcare affordable and ranked poorly on providing timely access to medical care (except for specialist care).[23] When consumers have more options to choose from, businesses are more likely to realize that they are competing to make consumers happy—meeting their preferences by providing better services at a lower cost.

At the same time, improving healthcare quality outcomes remains challenging. As we mentioned at the outset, the United States routinely underperforms when compared to other developed countries on common indices of healthcare quality. According to the University of Wisconsin Population Health Institute, healthy behaviors determine 39% of a population's health, whereas 12% is attributable to medical services and 50% depends on social and economic factors.[24] Too many of the efforts from public policy stakeholders and insurers have focused on the smallest piece of the pie: medical services. Both have employed supply-side strategies to motivate health delivery organizations to provide better care, such as offering providers incentives to spur improved health behaviors changes in their patients. Many of these strategies have so far seen only modest success.[25] Incentives aimed directly at consumers and their personal life style choices might better activate and motivate people to choose healthy behaviors and may yield better outcomes in the long term. The success story of smoking reduction, as we discuss later, owed as much to strong social and financial incentives to influence consumer choices as to medical services.

Business Operations

For healthcare organizations, there is a clear payoff to investing time in these endeavors. With improved consumer knowledge, organizations can enhance the messaging and timing of their communications and health interventions. They will also find that they have an improved understanding of the best distribution channels to bring their products to the right customers, and that their services are delivered at times and in places where consumers can access them more easily. They can also develop newer, more targeted solutions that fill unmet needs. This has the potential not only to improve healthcare outcomes but also to reduce costs.

For example, a 2017 meta-analysis analyzed different programs aimed at reducing hospital readmissions by asking a simple question: "Are quality improvement interventions designed to reduce hospital readmissions associated with net savings to the health system?" The study showed that many types of interventions were successful at reducing readmissions, but not all were cost-effective for the hospital running the program. Interventions that engaged patients and family members were associated with larger net savings.[26] This suggests that hospitals may find it to their advantage to collaborate with consumers and families, involving them in their care.

In addition, as consumer satisfaction improves with an expansion of meaningful choices, employee satisfaction should improve as well, creating a virtuous circle in which both consumers and employers work in partnership to create mutually satisfying healthcare transactions and relationships.

Conclusion

The healthcare market is changing. We believe that instead of fighting the trend toward more empowered consumers, healthcare organizations should embrace the concept of using consumer choice where possible. Understanding and appealing to the consumer will be paramount in a system where individuals are financing a greater portion of healthcare costs and learning more about their conditions on their own. Ultimately, greater consumer involvement should improve consumer satisfaction with the healthcare system.

Increased consumer choice and consumer engagement in decision-making are evident across sectors from retailing to financial services. In response, these industries have developed more consumer-centric strategies to appeal to the heterogeneous preferences of their customers. Yet the healthcare sector has lagged in this regard. Perhaps healthcare is different, or perhaps it is simply just old-fashioned and behind the times.

As we have discussed, increasing choice does not mean ignoring the differences that make the healthcare marketplace unique. An entirely free market where consumers wield all decision-making power is dangerous; however, there are many areas of healthcare where increased choice can benefit the consumer and the system collectively. There are benefits and risks to expanding consumer choice and engagement in healthcare decision-making. Expansion will create greater competition among healthcare organizations. This may be threatening to providers at first, but ultimately competition should drive innovation and improved pricing. Insurers will need to reformulate their value propositions to attract customers. Doctors and hospitals must still maintain technical excellence, but not hide behind it; they will need to engage better with their patients and understand what is important to them in the experience

Further, while it will please those American consumers who traditionally value choice and empowerment, there are legitimate concerns regarding the expansion of consumer choice. Consumers may not take the time to make the most educated decisions, or they may make ill-advised choices, especially when facing life-changing medical diagnoses. Limited knowledge can be a dangerous thing. Choice overload may lead some consumers to avoid the decision-making process altogether.

However, broadly speaking, we believe the benefits of expanding consumer choice outweigh the risks. Organizations must empower patients to become better stewards of their own health decisions. If, as empowered consumers, they are more adherent to treatment, healthier, and more satisfied, employers and society as a whole will benefit.

For their part, consumers need to accept the responsibility that goes along with the right to be empowered. Every service encounter, whether it be at Starbucks or in a doctor's office, depends for its success on collaboration between buyer and seller.

Patients will need to pay more attention both to what is happening in order to be better consumers; they will need to be better prepared. An individual can prepare for a medical appointment by compiling a list of questions and rehearsing what to say when asked what's wrong and, later, making sure she understands and perhaps writing down specific doctor recommendations before or shortly after leaving. Consumers must learn to act on their own behalf and take responsibility for their healthcare decisions. If consumer and doctor do not see eye to eye or cannot trust each other, the outcome will be unsatisfactory—just as in the case of any other service encounter.

Consumer forces in healthcare are creating a wave of change that not only encourages consumer engagement in decision-making but requires it. We must understand both how consumers make decisions, as well as how healthcare system design can support increased and improved consumer choice. The time for harnessing consumer choice has come.

References

1. Fader, Peter. *Customer Centricity: Focus on the Right Customers for Strategic Advantage*. Second ed. Wharton Digital, 2012. Print.
2. Davis, Karen, Kristof Stremikis, David Squires, and Cathy Schoen. "Mirror, Mirror on the Wall, 2014 Update: How the U.S. Health Care System Compares Internationally." *How the U.S. Health Care System Compares Internationally*. The Commonwealth Fund, 16 June 2014. Web.
3. Tomes, Nancy. *Remaking the American Patient: How Madison Avenue and Modern Medicine Turned Patients into Consumers*. First ed. U of North Carolina Press, 2016. Print.
4. Ibid.
5. Council of Economic Advisers. "Methodological Appendix: Methods Used to Construct a Consistent Historical Time Series of Health Insurance Coverage." 18 December 2014. Web.
6. Anderson, Monica. "Technology Device Ownership: 2015." *Pew Research Center: Internet, Science & Tech*. 29 October 2015. Web.
7. Nichols, Tom. *The Death of Expertise: The Campaign against Established Knowledge and Why It Matters*. First ed. Oxford UP, 2017. Print.
8. "Health Expenditure, Total (% of GDP)." *World Health Organization Global Health Expenditure Database*. The World Bank, 2017. Web.
9. Baicker, Katherine, and Amitabh Chandra. "The Veiled Economics of Employee Cost Sharing." *JAMA Internal Medicine* 175, no. 7 (2015): 1081–1082. Web.
10. "Health Policy Brief: High-Deductible Health Plans." *Health Affairs* (2016). Web.
11. "2015 Employer Health Benefits Survey—Summary of Findings." *The Henry J. Kaiser Family Foundation*. 22 September 2015. Web.
12. "Average Annual Workplace Family Health Premiums Rise Modest 3% to $18,142 in 2016; More Workers Enroll in High-Deductible Plans With Savings Option Over Past Two Years." *The Henry J. Kaiser Family Foundation*. 14 September 2016. Web.
13. Ibid.
14. A high-deductible plan is defined as $1,300 for an individual and $2,600 for a family (not including cost-sharing reductions) in 2015 ("Health Policy Brief: High-Deductible Health Plans." *Health Affairs* 4 February 2016. Web).
15. Ibid.

16. Thomas, Katie. "Costly Drug for Fatal Muscular Disease Wins F.D.A. Approval." *The New York Times*. 30 December 2016. Web.

17. Zirui Song, Sherri Rose, Dana G. Safran, Bruce E. Landon, Matthew P. Day, and Michael E. Chernew. Changes in Health Care Spending and Quality 4 Years into Global Payment. *New England J of Medicine* 371;18 nejm.org october 30, 2014.

18. "Patient-Centered Medical Home PCMH." *NCQA Programs*. National Committee for Quality Assurance (NCQA). Web.

19. Japsen, Bruce. "Urgent Care Market Braces for CVS and Walgreens Entry." *Forbes* 3 February 2016. Web.

20. Meill, Augusta, and Gianna Ericson. "The Trouble With Treating Patients as Consumers." *Harvard Business Review*, 9 January 2012. Web.

21. Neuberger, Julia. "Do We Need a New Word for Patients?" *National Center for Biotechnology Information (NCBI)*. British Medical Journal Publishing Group, 26 June 1999. Web.

22. Lukits, Ann. "Giving Patients Some Choice May Boost Drugs' Effectiveness." *The Wall Street Journal*. Dow Jones & Company, 11 July 2016. Web.

23. Osborn, Robin, David Squires, Michelle M. Doty, Dana O. Sarnak, and Erik C. Schneider. "In New Survey of Eleven Countries, US Adults Still Struggle With Access to and Affordability of Health Care." *Health Affairs*. 1 November 2016. Web.

24. Booske, Bridget C., Jessica K. Athens, David A. Kindig, Hyojun Park, and Patrick L. Remington. "Country Health Rankings Working Paper: Different Perspectives for Assigning Weights to Determinants of Health." *University of Wisconsin Population Health Institute* (2010): 1–20. Web.

25. Berenson, Robert. "The AHCA Gets It Wrong: Health Care Is Different." *Health Affairs Blog*, 22 March 2017. Web.

26. Nuckols, Teryl K., Emmett Keeler, and Sally Morton. "Economic Evaluation of Quality Improvement Interventions to Prevent Hospital Readmission: A Systematic Review and Meta-Analysis." *JAMA Internal Medicine*. American Medical Association, July 2017. Web.

CONSUMER CHOICE IN THE HEALTHCARE SYSTEM

2

Is Healthcare Special?

We have described why pressures supporting greater consumer choice are rising. In Section 2, we will ask how the system itself has to change to provide a fertile ground for the expression of choice in healthcare. In this chapter, we will examine the balancing act of individual consumer choice and other national priorities.

In this endeavor, we will consider the following questions: Is healthcare different than other professions or industries? Are there special constraints to consumer choice that are unique to medical care? We see these differences not as evidence for or against a consumer-driven market-based system, but rather as a way to understand the special challenges that need to be addressed to enable choice to work better in healthcare.

Patients or Consumers: What's in a Name?

In this book, we often refer to those who use healthcare services as "consumers." This reflects our view that consumer choice and market forces are not only appropriate in healthcare but are underutilized in stimulating improvements for those who receive services.

Many disagree, however, that a consumer-oriented viewpoint is appropriate for healthcare. They argue that market-based forces in healthcare often reveal how different healthcare is from other market-driven industries. For example, they point out that healthcare delivery often lacks the ideal economic conditions needed for an effective market to work; that the impact of consumer choice on the patient–doctor relationship presents unique challenges; and that there are many decisions in which the patient is not a competent decision-maker.

The issues in branding the patient a "consumer" are part of a broader, long-standing debate regarding whether market forces should be used in healthcare at all. In a free market system, the prices of goods and services are determined by the open market without government intervention. Demand from buyers for a product or service creates competition among sellers, which leads to choices for consumers.

Consumers exert influence through their buying decisions. Most buyers have a maximum price they are willing to pay, and sellers have a minimum price they are willing to accept for their offerings. The point at which the supply and demand curves meet is the equilibrium price for the service given the quantity demanded. For a variety of reasons, it is difficult to determine how close or how far from this ideal healthcare is, or rather, if healthcare is more of a mixed picture where choice is sometimes helpful and other times not.

The classic, and most cited, article warning about the reliance upon market forces in medical care was written by Nobel economist Kenneth Arrow in 1963. In this seminal work, he describes some of the characteristics of medical care that make it fundamentally different than the typical commodity and inconsistent with the competitive model.[1]

Arrow first discusses the nature of demand in the medical care market. Apart from preventive and chronic services, for which the consumer can plan and shop around, the need for medical services is irregular and unpredictable. Falling ill is generally never planned. Furthermore, he argues, in more instances than not, the quality and immediacy of care are of paramount importance for a patient; the immediate need for care may be associated with high risk of death or impairment.

Arrow also highlighted the asymmetry in information between buyer and seller. The patient often has far less knowledge than the clinical provider, who trains professionally for years. Moreover, performance is difficult to assess because of the uncertainty in determining the quality of the product. Bad outcomes from an illness can happen even with the best expert support. Arrow also argues that the expected behavior of a clinical provider is different than other professions, in that they have an ethical code of behavior that favors patient primacy. In this context, he describes the mutual benefits of a trusting relationship. It is expected that physicians will make decisions with the patient's best interest in mind.

For some, Arrow's arguments are no longer persuasive. Most recently, a vigorous defense of consumer choice and market forces has come from Avik Roy in *National Affairs*, and *The National Review Blog* in which he counters Arrow's main points.[2] His argument is based on the claim that for each of Arrow's concerns, there are industry examples of the same type of problem, and that there are ways to get around Arrow's concerns. Berenson, in the context of a spirited attack on the Republican-dominated House proposal to replace Obamacare, counters Roy by citing recent evidence that consumers do not appear capable of making good health choices.[3] By and large, however, arguments on both sides of this long-standing disagreement are theoretical and not supported by strong evidence.

Feelings clearly run strong about whether a market system is appropriate in medical care. In fact, it has often been considered inappropriate to even describe patients as consumers. For example, in 2011, Paul Krugman wrote in *The New York Times*:

Here's my question: How did it become normal, or for that matter even acceptable, to refer to medical patients as "consumers"? The relationship between patient and doctor used to be considered something special, almost sacred. Now politicians and supposed reformers talk about the act of receiving care as if it were no different from a commercial transaction, like buying a car—and their only complaint is that it isn't commercial enough. . . . The idea that all this can be reduced to money—that doctors are just "providers" selling services to health care "consumers"—is, well, sickening. And the prevalence of this kind of language is a sign that something has gone very wrong not just with this discussion, but with our society's values.[4]

Krugman's aversion to acknowledging patients as consumers comes from several questionable notions. First, he objects to admitting that healthcare, like other products or services, has economic costs for each person who plans or does use it. The second, to which we return later, is his concern about adverse effects on the relationship between doctor and patient.

What Krugman fails to understand is that money has always been a factor in medical care. As a result, modern healthcare in the United States has *long* been a commercial transaction. Let's remember that the dictionary definition of a consumer is "one that utilizes economic goods."[5] In the era of comprehensive insurance—that is, until recent times when high deductibles were introduced—medical costs did not involve the consumer to the same extent that they do now. But even then, patients were paying for health insurance and making market decisions about what type of policy to buy. Prior to the 1960s, when comprehensive insurance emerged, doctors were paid directly by patients. Today, all doctors' incomes, including those working for nonprofit organizations, are benchmarked against those earned by similar specialty doctors in the fee-for-service world. Krugman's wish that money not enter medical care seems romantic and naïve.

Black, White, and Gray

We believe that the general economic argument about consumer choice and market forces is interesting but not very relevant. As we have pointed out in detail, market forces have long been active in some areas of medical care. With more financially influenced consumer choice, healthcare is shifting further toward consumer empowerment. Consumer expectations of choice are growing.

A far more useful position, in our view, is to accept that healthcare in the United States is now a mixed economic model. Rather than debate consumer choice in black or white terms, we prefer to look at the shades of gray. In reality, most industries operate in a mixed model. There are benefits and drawbacks to both free markets and those that are more regulated or managed. Collectively, consumers have substantial influence over pricing and product development. In many industries, competitive marketplaces have helped consumers. Personal computers were prohibitively expensive when they first became available to consumers 40 years ago; today quality has improved and prices have plunged. Conversely, in industries where competition is scarce and choice constrained, consumer interests can suffer. Consider wireless Internet providers. In many areas, consumers have few options to choose from; unsurprisingly, these providers charge high prices and routinely receive poor customer service ratings.

Few industries operate today in entirely free or completely efficient consumer markets; nor would healthcare. The government regulates markets to protect both businesses and consumers, as well as to ensure a stable economy and collective priorities. This is, in many instances, good for society. For example, government patents and copyright laws protect businesses that innovate and create new ideas. If businesses knew that their inventions might be copied, few would invest heavily in expensive scientific research that collectively benefits development of new medicines. Or, consider how governments regulate food processing to protect consumers against foodborne diseases. Further, there are societal issues to be addressed, such as environmental pollution that markets ignore if left unchecked. It is collectively in everyone's best interest to live in pollution-free neighborhoods. Without government-mandated targets for automobile emission levels, car manufacturers might not invest in environmentally friendly models.

If the healthcare system is to become a better functioning market and patients good consumers, the system must select those transactions where choice works and those where it does not. The medical economy would also need to function better in a supply and demand model. For example, consumers already have much control over which primary care providers they patronize. If the market functioned better, their choices would improve the overall system. Informed consumers would choose doctors who provide the best care at the lowest prices, and to win over consumers, providers would lower prices and improve the overall value of their offerings. Competition among providers would spur innovation and, over time, the market would better meet the needs of all consumers. Those who promote these free market principles in healthcare believe that market forces—if used appropriately—have the potential to improve service, drive down overall system costs, and improve clinical quality.[6] Protecting patients from bad choices and assuring that doctors do not take advantage of patients are important cautions as consumers exercise choice. Other industries have dealt successfully with similar problems. By carefully defining the areas where choice is appropriate and assuring that choice is structured to protect consumers, we believe potential negative consequences can be minimized.

The initial question in this section asked if we are patients or consumers when we are dealing with healthcare. Depending on the nature of the decision to be made, we are both, but in differing proportions at different times.

We prefer to examine what can be done to make choice work better to benefit patient/consumers and improve the healthcare system. As patients make choices more often, and as they pay closer attention to the costs associated with healthcare, how can they become better at exercising choice? When entertaining the aforementioned question, Arrow's thoughtful analysis serves not to reject consumer choice, but rather to draw attention to the special concerns he raises regarding choice in order to try and mitigate them.

In this chapter, we will examine four areas that deserve to be recognized as significant special problems with consumer choice in healthcare. From there, we will put forth ways in which they may be approached. These areas are as follows:

1. *The special relationship between doctor and patient*: Is there a special relationship between doctor and patient that could be threatened by enhanced consumer choice?
2. *Ethics and morality*: Is it our national responsibility to provide healthcare for all, and what effect does this have on consumer choice?
3. *Individual choice versus collective benefit*: How do we handle the tension between stewarding the collective resource of an insurance pool and enhancing the choices of individual consumers?
4. *The health consequences of consumer choice*: What areas of medical care are most problematic to consumer choice, and where do we need to think twice about whether consumer choice can work?

The Special Relationship Between Doctor and Patient

A central point in Arrow's analysis, and reinforced in Krugman's passionate concern, is the issue of the doctor–patient relationship. Krugman's "sickening" feeling seems to stem from his conclusion that when patients buy and doctors sell medical care, the transaction taints and diminishes a "sacred trust" between consumers and doctors; a concept that stipulates that doctors will act only in each patient's best interests, uninfluenced by money, personal feelings, or other factors. This concept, in which the doctor understands the patient, is empathic, and takes on the responsibility for applying his or her scientific learning and skills to deliver what the patient needs, is deeply ingrained in our collective attitude about doctors. We agree with it. It is essential that patients trust their clinician's competence and motives and that the clinician deserves the trust.

In purely practical terms, a trusting relationship serves many purposes. It enables patients to feel reassured that they are in good hands, and it is generally accompanied by a reduction in anxiety as well as an increase in hopefulness. Because consumers cannot easily assess the quality of their medical care, they must trust that the doctor who delivers it knows what he or she is doing. We would all be worse off as patients and consumers if we did not trust medical care or the medical professionals delivering that care. Moreover, without a trusting relationship between patient and doctor, medical care would be reduced to an impersonal interaction in which patients would receive only competent technical care. In the absence of a "sacred trust" between patient and doctor, the resultant care would not be sufficient to help patients through life-stage transitions, the deep psychological and moral challenges of serious illness, and end-of-life issues.

Doctors have long recognized the importance and special nature of their relationship with their patients. The idea of swearing to uphold their special responsibility to their patient is central to medical socialization. Doctors reinforce their commitment to service in their oaths and ethics—they affirm that their work is a calling as well as a way of making a living. Medical ethics reflects this special concern for the needs of the patient by emphasizing three attributes to which doctors commit: patient autonomy—in which the patient has the right to choose and her choice will be honored by the doctor; beneficence—that the doctor should honor her commitment to promote the well-being and best interests of the patient above all other considerations; and nonmaleficence—the idea that the doctor will do no avoidable harm (*primum non nocere*). The patient thus expects and hopes that doctors and nurses will fulfill their promises. It is this commitment to the calling of medicine that contributes to the high esteem and trust with which patients view doctors. The profession has sought to maintain this image in part because those who are a part of it recognize how important patient trust is to their autonomy, success, and influence. It is of interest that money itself is not mentioned in the oaths taken by doctors; they seem to have gotten the message that the issue of financial self-interest should not be raised.

Healthcare is not unique in regard to the importance of trust. In the consumer world, companies work very hard to increase consumer trust in their product through its performance and messaging, and to reinforce and enhance trust through their branding. Trust attracts customers. From an early age, we are taught to be skeptical when we are being sold something, but we instinctively want to trust the seller. In turn, all companies seek to reinforce and tap into our desire to trust.

What is different in medical care is that the product is itself, in part, the trusting relationship. Healthcare is unique in that trust is associated with better outcomes; many studies have demonstrated better results and higher satisfaction when the patient–doctor relationship is strong. The fact that doctors take an oath that they will be patient centered and trustworthy contributes to societal norms that accept the idea that medicine is unique and that the advice and actions offered by medical providers can and should be trusted.

Can patients trust doctors in a consumer choice environment? The primary concern about trust raised by Arrow is that monetary self-interest among doctors is a threat to the patient–doctor relationship. In discussing why, he points out that "One consequence of such trust relations is that the physician cannot act, or at least appear to act, as if he is maximizing his income at every moment of time. As a signal to the buyer of his intentions to act as thoroughly in the buyer's behalf as possible, the physician avoids the obvious stigmata of profit-maximizing."[7]

Is the special patient–doctor relationship in medical care undermined by increased consumer choice? Critics of consumer choice argue that it is. Healthcare differs from many other industries in that individual consumer choice in healthcare is limited by the nature of medicine, a discipline built upon facts based in science. In a free market, consumers must be able to discern the differences among options and make choices based on that information. In healthcare, this is often more difficult, as most providers have years of training that consumers cannot match. Therefore, trust in the doctor is absolutely necessary.

Are there special constraints on consumer choice that ought to be addressed to protect trust? Because none of us really wants to deal with doctors or hospitals we don't trust, both consumers and the providers need to pay attention to and enhance the factors that support trust. The most important among these is to assure patients that their doctors are not making decisions based on their own financial self-interest at their expense. Currently, the data suggest that patient trust in doctors and nurses is high, but this is not without several potential threats. For example, the patient–doctor relationship was undermined in the era of primary care "gatekeeping" in the 1990s, when primary care doctors who referred less made money if their actual expenditures on specialist and hospital care were lower than their predicted budget. The fear that doctors were withholding care contributed to the collapse of this cost-saving initiative. In the current era of the accountable care organizations (ACOs), the patient–doctor relationship is again being challenged, as organizations and the doctors that belong to them are rewarded if they reduce expenditures for the populations they serve. A market force—financial incentives to reduce costs—is being used. Nevertheless, most doctors probably still put patient needs first. Definitive proof is not available, but few of the ACOs have saved much money, while improved quality measures suggest that they are not scrimping. Nevertheless, the potential threat is worrisome; financial conflict of interest on the part of doctors should be avoided.

Many doctors also have reacted negatively to increased consumer involvement for other reasons. Unsurprisingly, many physicians are against consumer choice solutions in healthcare on the grounds that they do not believe patients are capable of participating or judging the value of clinical care. In her 2016 book, Nany Tomes, a historian who spent years researching consumerism in U.S. healthcare, noted this pushback from the medical establishment:

> This historical perspective helps to clarify why American physicians have found the tenets of medical consumerism so off-putting even as they have endorsed the ideals of patient-centered medicine. While agreeing that patients need to be treated with respect and care, doctors do not necessarily see consumerism, with its emphasis on comparison shopping and

second guessing of medical advice, as the best way to reach that goal. . . .
Having devoted decades learning how to practice medicine, physicians understandably have balked at the idea of being "shopped for" by laypeople
who may have spent an hour or two reading up on their symptoms.[8]

It would be a loss to all if consumer choice undermined the patient–doctor trust
relationship. To protect against that, government, insurers, and providers need to
be aware of the dangers associated with consumer choice and be selective to protect against potential damage to the patient–doctor relationship. Regardless, there
are other aspects of enhanced consumer choice that can strengthen trust. Helping
patients to participate in their own choices and feel in control can enhance trust.
Shared decision-making is a method widely employed by professionals in medical care; the best doctors have always done it. Encouraging and responding to the
patient's preferences is good practice and enhances the relationship. Developing
better measurements of the care that is delivered should bolster trust, even though
it may initially be threatening to doctors. Simply being available when needed will
enhance trust. These methods to augment trust between patient and doctor merit
consideration and should be utilized.

We contend that strengthening the ability of consumers to choose their doctor
can actually strengthen the bond between patient and doctor. If a doctor consistently fails to establish a trusting relationship (or some other attribute of importance
to the patient), many, if not most patients, will choose to switch to some other care
provider who does. This is consumer choice working to preserve the sacred trust for
those patients who value this in their medical care. So long as the patient trusts that
the doctor puts his patient's interests ahead of what's best for him financially, all is
well. For many patients, monetary interests are secondary; a healthy patient–doctor
relationship relies upon a doctor's ability to listen to patients at a time of worry and
to make them feel that they are in good hands. If the patient trusts the doctor and
the doctor takes on this responsibility seriously and effectively, this sacred trust relationship will be preserved and work to the patient's benefit.

Ethics and Morality

All advanced countries consider it a matter of national obligation to protect selected
basic personal needs of its citizens. Among these are public safety, shelter, food, and
education. It is hard, for example, to imagine a policy that left Americans on the
street to freeze or to starve to death.

The vast majority of Americans believe in access to good healthcare, including
providing insurance to those who cannot afford it. The World Health Organization
has stipulated that healthcare is a right. It is clear by our national behavior that
Americans also expect some level of basic medical care to be part of our nation's
social contract with our fellow citizens. In an editorial in the *Journal of the American*

Medical Association in early 2017, Howard Bauchner spoke for most doctors by asserting that all Americans should have access to medical care as a right.[9]

This moral position is supported by national surveys. The Pew Research Center reported in June 2017 that 60% of surveyed Americans believe that the government should provide insurance for everyone.[10] They report that "Even among those who say the federal government is not responsible for ensuring Americans have health care coverage, there is little public appetite for government withdrawing entirely from involvement in health care coverage. Among the public, 33% say that health care coverage is not the government's responsibility, but then add that programs like Medicare and Medicaid should be continued; just 5% of Americans say the government should not be involved at all in providing health insurance."

More anecdotally, the strength of feeling about the right to care is revealed in the vehemence with which people complain about threats to take away insured services such as Medicaid, Medicare, or the insurance offered in the state exchanges under the Affordable Care Act. At an individual level, the medical profession and our society already acknowledge care for certain medical conditions as a moral requirement. We reject turning away a person at the emergency department in need of treatment for which the person cannot pay. Most people agree that, in a civilized and economically developed society, a basic level of primary and emergency care should be available to all. If someone in a car had a bad accident, it would be morally reprehensible for a medic to respond, only to leave the injured person on the side of the road because he or she didn't have a health plan that covered emergency care. Denying access to emergency services is viewed as unacceptable.

Moreover, a considerable body of research supports the value of access to care for all. In a 2017 review of the evidence that insurance for medical care makes a difference in health, Sommers, Gawande, and Baicker thoroughly review the research literature and conclude that "insurance coverage increases access to care and improves a wide range of health outcomes."[11]

In other markets, money determines what you receive. There is an implicit understanding that if you cannot pay for a product or service, you may not be able to access it. Limiting access to healthcare services based only on ability to pay raises thorny ethical and political questions that differentiate it from other markets. Healthcare differs from other industries in that its pricing structures and resource allocation are influenced by the aforementioned importance of morality and ethical constraints.

Some of these concerns can be attributed to the fact that healthcare, the treatment of the ill, is a mission-based endeavor. People seek services often when they are at their most vulnerable, creating dramatic stories that elicit sympathy and undermine tough allocation decisions. Moreover, its service providers take the Hippocratic or other Oath, swearing to uphold ethical standards that prioritize the rights of patients.

But reason leads us to the conclusion that there must be limits to benefits. Too often, we think of healthcare as a general category, without being specific about details. Yet it is clear that in a system in which access to care is a right and where government or business subsidizes those who cannot afford it, costs, unless constrained in some way, will continue inexorably to rise out of control. Ageing of the population and the continued increase in very expensive diagnostic and treatment methods virtually guarantee that we cannot sustain an open-ended system; we cannot cover everybody for everything medically available today, and certainly not in the future. We will discuss this further when we later discuss the issue of rationing.

Accepting constraints to what a public service covers is generally accepted. There are few areas of life where we have unfettered access to services. In an analogy, we can accept that housing is also a human right. Basic services should be available to all; no one should be on the street without shelter. However, that doesn't mean that we all have the rights to the same kind of housing. Where we live and what we own are determined by what we can afford.

We believe that there is only one reasonable option for healthcare, and its implementation is inevitable. That is to create a basic healthcare system for every American with funding mandated privately or provided by the government, but with specified limitations in the benefits, as decided in a process viewed as fair. Such a system should be complemented with an open private medical market. If we are correct about the need for a basic healthcare system that covers all Americans, then a supplemental private system must enable consumers to spend as much as they want on services that cannot be included in a system designed to provide effective care for all at an affordable cost.

Determining what will be covered in the basic system is not simple. We have to debate what level of benefits is basic. Some would limit the basics to what clearly works, with proven outcomes: prevention, first-contact generalist care, and those tests and treatments that indisputably work and whose benefits achieve a defined set level of quality-adjusted life years (QALYs), a standard measure used in cost-effectiveness analyses. Others argue that basic services should be much more comprehensive.

What is important is to find a process to make these allocation decisions that is seen as fair by most Americans. Daniels and Sabin, in their book *Setting Limits Fairly*, explore this issue and conclude that stewardship of the common resource is important and inevitable; their answer is that accountability, legitimacy, and fairness need to be built into the decision processes.[12] This is how single-payer, government-funded systems often operate: with fairness in mind. They treat everyone the same, meaning both that people are treated equally when they need it most, but also that certain services are not covered. If a treatment isn't worth paying $10 million for one person, it isn't worth it for another. In fact, in other countries, differences in access and extent of care vary considerably, most by quiet management of waiting times or referral barriers in countries like England or Canada. In the

Daniels and Sabin model, benefits can differ explicitly, but the process for deciding needs to be transparent and deemed fair and equitable by the public and, hopefully, the consumer.

This goal, and the challenge, of trading off affordability and accessibility against comprehensiveness of benefits and freedom of choice are not new. Rawlsian philosophical theory offers a view about how to do it and is interesting to consider in a healthcare context. In the 1970s, philosopher John Rawls attempted to deal with difficult questions around distributive justice. How should governments and political leaders make decisions? Rawls contended that such decisions should be made behind a "veil of ignorance." This "veil" blinds people to facts and biases about themselves, so that their decision is not tailored specifically to their own personal situation. What would you choose in society if you did not know where in the social strata you might fall? Rawls believed that decisions made this way would be fairer. Rawls positioned his theory as hypothetical, because in practice it is nearly impossible for individuals to leave behind their own lived experiences and biases.

We Americans have already had experience in attempting to build a system that rations fairly. In the early 1990s, Oregon went through an extensive allocation exercise regarding how to spend its limited Medicaid budget.[13] Led by their physician-governor, Gov. Kitzhaber, they used expert and lay input and an open process to create a ranked list of what would be covered as priorities. But defining the limits of what is fair, right, or necessary turned out to be more than a technical cost-effectiveness exercise. The Oregon approach was later modified based on a more subjective assessment—that priority should be given to the sickest.

It's also argued that consumers perceive fairness differently in the realm of medical care. In his book *Misbehaving*, Richard Thaler, a noted behavioral economist, examined what makes an economic transaction seem "fair" to consumers.[14] Two of the specific situations he analyzed are helpful in understanding the extent to which healthcare is held to a higher moral standard than other industries. In one situation, he presented the following situation to study participants: "A store has been sold out of the popular Cabbage Patch dolls for a month. A week before Christmas a single doll is discovered in a storeroom. The managers know that many customers would like to buy the doll. They announce over the store's public address system that the doll will be sold by auction to the customer who offers to pay the most."[14] More than 70% of the study participants found this situation unfair. However, when the situation was modified slightly, and Thaler noted that the proceeds of the auction would benefit a charity, nearly 80% of people then found the situation acceptable.

In a second exercise, the scenario was changed to a medical context. A flu epidemic was occurring in a small town and there was only one package of medicine remaining. In this situation, participants felt it was unfair to auction the medication off, even when the proceeds of the auction went to charity. Thaler explained as follows:

> Most European countries (as well as Canada) provide health care to their citizens as a basic right, and even in America, where this view is resisted in certain quarters, we do not turn uninsured accident victims away at the emergency room. Similarly, no country permits a free market in organs, although Iran does have a market for kidneys. For most of the world, the idea that a rich person who needs a kidney should be allowed to pay a poor person to donate one is considered "repugnant," to use a word favored by economist Alvin Roth to describe such market transactions.[15]

The big issue for America is how much care is a right and, if defined, how much should be spent on it. Should the allocation be made by ability to pay, or do we have an ethical responsibility to provide at least a basic system determined by need and putative benefits for the individual and society? Free-market economic solutions are often resisted in healthcare due to these concerns.

In the countries where healthcare is viewed as right, the decision is usually made in the political process with representative government setting priorities for allocating the nation's collective government resources. Medical care competes with infrastructure, education, social security, and defense, to name a few; politics determine the outcome. If a country determines that it has a national interest and obligation to cover some level of a system of healthcare, it needs to define what it means and how much it will allocate of its money to cover its costs. Government also must be responsible for assuring that there are trusted regulatory bodies that determine the details of what is on offer and what an individual can and cannot receive.

Even if the decision-making process is open, fair, and trusted, however, these conversations become more difficult as the services become more complex. Where do we, as a society, draw the line of necessity? Which procedures or drugs should be deemed "critical," and which are "elective"? What should society be responsible for and what should we require of the individual? Most insurers deem purely aesthetic plastic surgery procedures, such as a facelift, elective. The person undergoing the surgery is doing so in an effort to maintain a more youthful appearance and should pay for the procedure.

But the answer is not always so straightforward. Consider the costs of gender reassignment surgery for transgender individuals in prison, an issue that became contentious after several lawsuits were filed around the country. Transgender inmates alleged that gender dysphoria, the condition of not identifying as the sex indicated by bodily organs, was a medical condition, and gender reassignment surgery was necessary, given the discrimination they faced behind bars.[16] In 2015, a California court ruled that the state should cover the sex reassignment surgery for one inmate; it was the first time public funding would be used to support such a procedure.[17] Prisons in California already provided hormone therapy to transgender inmates, but gender reassignment surgery is far more expensive. The surgeries can cost anywhere from $50,000 to $100,000, compared with $500 to $3,000 for hormone therapy alone.[18]

Or consider healthcare services for infertility, such as in vitro fertilization (IVF). On average, each cycle of IVF costs over $8,000 plus $3,000–$5,000 for medications.[19] For many people who struggle with infertility, this is unaffordable. Fierce debate exists about whether insurance plans should cover these costs. Although some states, like California, have required insurers to cover IVF, others have not.[20]

What these examples point out is that the decision-makers need to deal with myriad issues regarding what constitutes a good and fair national system. For example, many conditions are the result of self-inflicted choices that people make—failing to use seatbelts, smoking, substance abuse, and lifestyle choices such as obesity and lack of exercise. Should patients like these be covered and to what degree—completely or with some financial penalties? On the other hand, for many medical conditions the individual is not responsible. Consider multiple sclerosis (MS), an uncommon disease that causes damage to the myelin sheath, often resulting in disability at a fairly young age. The exact cause of the disease remains unknown, though experts believe that it is likely due to a combination of environmental, genetic, and immunologic factors. The average cost of treating MS can reach up to $100,000 a year.[21] Further, as a chronic condition, lifetime costs per person are estimated to be more than $4 million (in 2010 dollars).[22] How much financial responsibility should the individual bear for a condition outside of her control?

Any market-based solution in healthcare must acknowledge the characteristics that make it fundamentally different than other markets. We know that a purely capitalist market that ignores these differences will not work; monetized consumer choice must be balanced with national ethical and moral priorities. For this reason, there should be significant government protections set up for consumers, especially for those who lack the financial resources to participate fully in the market.

The consequence of this argument is that America should, and ultimately will, have a system of basic care that is fair, equitable, and accessible to all regardless of ability to pay. However, as a collective enterprise for all citizens, we know from experience in other countries that such a system usually will have limitation in its funding and thus its coverage. Most such systems restrict consumer choice in order to protect the common resource as they strive to achieve the most benefit for the most people.

There is no theoretical reason why significant consumer choice cannot, however, be retained within a basic system. For example, if a standard *per capita* cost for treating a particular condition were distributed as a voucher and a patient was able to spend it on one of several competing treatment options or providers, choice could be maintained and market forces might, in fact, improve the system.

However, maintaining choice would not be free; excess capacity is typically needed to enable choice, and there are added costs, such as marketing, when providers must compete for market share. The cost of choice would need to be measured against its benefits in better satisfying consumers and increasing innovation.

Individual Choice Versus Collective Benefit

Once consumers buy, or are given, insurance to pay for medical care, they enter a special economic arrangement. Their care is paid for from collective funding, generated by those who share in the risk pool. That makes medical care different than most businesses, even those that prepay and pool risk such as life insurance. The healthcare system, like other insurance, has a built-in tension between what individuals claim for and the security of the collective resource. However, in life insurance, actuaries can predict most of the claims expense and self-interest is minimized. Most people want to live, so claiming is both a clear endpoint and also not one that most people want.

Our health insurance by contrast, pays out for individual services that are difficult to categorize and easy to manipulate. This makes our piecemeal payment system particularly vulnerable to misuse and overuse. It is difficult to define and confirm services, exposing medical insurance to pay for conditions that are not necessarily medical and treatments that may not be appropriate. The user has little financial incentive to be prudent, since much of his or her cost is covered by insurance. And current practice leads patients and families to believe that they have the right to decide what they deserve to get. Finally, the very definition of what is considered eligible for payment lies mostly in the hands of the providers of care, who benefit financially from their decisions under fee-for-service reimbursement. For these reasons, as well as other factors such as high input costs and the progressive influx of expensive new tests and treatments, costs have been difficult to control in our system of insurance.

Full-coverage collective insurance structurally encourages consumers to overuse the common resource. In 1968 ecologist Garrett Hardin described a general phenomenon where rational self-interest acts to drive overuse and spoil a common, shared resource. He called this the Tragedy of the Commons, using the name coined by William Forster Lloyd, who first discovered the economic principles in the mid-19th century. They both describe a circumstance in which a collectively supported Commons was open to all for grazing. A herdsman had an incentive to overuse the resource because the benefit to him and his herd exceeded his cost, since the cost was shared by all. Soon all herdsmen overgrazed the grass, and the resource itself was destroyed.[23] Howard Hiatt described this phenomenon as it affected medical care. When medical care is paid for collectively and risk is pooled, it is a common resource for all those who have signed up, and the individual incentive is purposely tilted toward using it if you are sick. But because the individual is sheltered from the cost, a portion of the use can be inappropriate or unnecessary.[24]

In healthcare, our choices can affect the collective healthcare insurance pool in several ways—for better and for worse. As a positive example, if you are young and healthy, your choice to purchase insurance helps reduce average risk and expenditures in the insurance pool, and it lowers premiums for everyone. If you eat well, exercise, drive safely, and avoid smoking, you not only improve your own health but also reduce healthcare costs. Finally, if you are a thoughtful, careful, and well-informed consumer in your decisions, your choices stimulate innovation and improvement by favoring the best producers among competing service offerings.

Conversely, unconstrained choice has downsides. First, overusing the resource can ultimately lead to financial losses and threaten the financial health of the risk pool. Doctors, drug companies, hospitals, others on the supply side that make money by selling their services, are believed to waste resources on unneeded tests and treatments.[25]

Second, choosing unhealthy habits is dangerous not just to oneself but to the collective resource as well. If you smoke or drink heavily or adopt unhealthy behaviors such as eating poorly and rarely exercising, you are more likely to experience a wide range of medical conditions, including cancer, diabetes, and heart disease. When you receive a diagnosis of heart disease after years of these habits, your medical expenses contribute to the rising cost of care. In effect, this drives premium growth the next year, ultimately affecting everyone in your insurance pool. Those costs are borne by the collective, even though you, in this case, suffer too. If you decide to drive recklessly, for example, your decision may adversely affect you, but it also has the potential to negatively affect others in your community. If you crash your car after a few drinks, you might injure other drivers or hit a pedestrian. Health insurance costs go up as others subsidize your bad behavior. Or if a citizen chooses, against all evidence and advice, to smoke every day and contracts lung cancer, he imposes multiple costs on society including loss of productivity because he can no longer work, the expenses of treatment, and even the externality of secondhand smoke that may adversely affect family and friends.

Choosing to forego medical care can also lead to harm and extra costs. For example, avoiding vaccinations can diminish herd immunity and expose others to preventable illness. Prevention, screening, and behavior modification of unhealthy behaviors can prevent disease, detect disease early, and avert complications caused by delay.

Third, choosing not to participate and pay into the collective is another threat to its economic model and survival. For the common resource to be adequate to provide care for those who need it, those who are relatively healthy, with lower risk, must be part of the pool. The moral hazard created by allowing healthy, low-need people to opt out is a threat to all. For this reason, we do not believe that consumers should have the choice of having no insurance. For a basic care system to work, everyone must participate, whether through universal health insurance or through the use of incentives and regulations that assure that everyone has insurance.

In these ways, consumers affect the collective by their choices. This is not new. In his famous treatise "On Liberty," philosopher John Stuart Mill noted that a problem arises when a citizen, in expressing his freedom, causes harm to others. In other words, you are entitled to make your own choices, so long as they don't negatively impact other individuals or the larger community. When choice is a personal matter and does not adversely affect the collective resource, there is no need to intervene. However, when choice hurts the collective, interventions are necessary.

Governments often impose regulations and limitations on healthcare systems to promote collective interests. Having a healthcare system that works well for most people is in the best interest of the country. For the most part, governments have four options to influence consumer healthcare choices in ways that maximize benefit for both individuals and society. First is messaging, communicating advice about healthy lifestyles and behaviors or sharing data that enable consumers to make intelligent comparisons among hospitals and doctors. Second are financial incentives to modify consumer choices, including taxes that raise the price of consuming harmful substances. A third option is regulation that prescribes behavior such as requiring the purchase of health insurance and banning or severely limiting access to products deemed harmful. Finally, and most important, governments determine, or at least can modify, the basic structures of healthcare delivery and financing to achieve a balance between competing interests of individuals and the collective. Structural decisions such as hospital and doctor reimbursement, benefit coverage requirements, and the use of subsidies to assist those who cannot afford to buy into insurance are clearly powerful and important decisions to be made. Such structures can be very difficult to change in the American political system of balanced legislative and executive authority, as we have discovered recently.

These four approaches are not mutually exclusive. The largely successful fight against tobacco, for example, has included public service advertising and product label messaging, steadily escalating increases in federal and state taxes on tobacco products, bans on sale to minors and media advertising of tobacco products, and other restrictions and regulations. The importance of personal freedom has, however, been emphasized by the tobacco lobby to preclude an outright ban on tobacco products.

Consumer choice can also be structured to mitigate the Tragedy of the Commons and to reduce inappropriate care. In most industries where the benefits and costs favor the individual user, regulation and/or market forces are used to protect the common resource. Carbon trading is a good example of this approach. In healthcare, financial barriers to use, such as copayments, coinsurance, and deductibles, have been widely used. At high levels, however, these financial barriers prevent consumers from getting services they need, leaving the system little different than what we have now, where ability to pay determines what services you receive.[26] We need other ways to control costs and drive up quality.

The payers also have the incentive to "manage care." Given a fixed financial resource, the more that insurers can do to improve health, lower hospitalization rates, reduce waste, and "right-size" the use of medical care, the better. In the United States, managed care, which gives providers both authority and responsibility for allocating resources, has been a favored tool to balance choice and the collective. The Nixon administration coined the term "health maintenance organization" (HMO) to describe organizations that insured populations of patients and were managed with the objective of keeping within the overall available funds. Over the past two decades, physician-led control of populations and their pooled resources has grown. Many view this as giving too much authority to doctors and not enough to patients, but managed care is probably here to stay within any basic care system that is developed.

There is clearly a strong attachment to personal freedom in U.S. society. Not everyone agrees that freedom of individual choice should always trump government or provider organization intervention, but, perhaps more so than in other developed countries, this sentiment enjoys widespread support in the United States. The view is pervasive that government should not be able to require citizens to buy health insurance and impose a financial penalty if they do not comply.

At the same time, there is recognition that good health is collectively beneficial for society. For that reason, the healthcare marketplace involves a greater amount of government regulation than many others. Initiatives delivered through doctors might be easier for patients to accept, but ultimately such control diminishes choice. It is not clear yet if consumers will accept these restrictions.

Should we be able to choose which healthcare services we can access? Or should the government either dictate or delegate to providers the authority to determine what everyone can receive? The reality is a mixed picture in which choice and collective interests trade off. The question then is when and how should the government, business funders of health insurance, insurers, and physicians themselves intervene in healthcare choice?

Whether the government creates a single-payer model for all or patches together universal but basic insurance coverage for all, individual choice is, to some degree, going to be modified to ensure that the common resource is protected. Collective payment, by whatever form is around to stay. The effort to protect the integrity of insurance will surely modify choice. The auto insurance industry faces some similar problems and offers some instructive lessons. First, insurance coverage is a requirement, to protect others and to get a good mix of those with good as well as bad driving records; in medical care, we likewise believe it should be a requirement to have insurance because without inclusion of all consumers, costs will rise, pricing out many who need it. In auto insurance, claiming for minor damages is limited by the use of deductibles; the lower the threshold for insurance to kick in, the higher the premium. The same mechanism is now being used in medical care, where high deductibles reduce the rate of claims. In medicine, however, this financial barrier often prevents someone who needs and should get care from getting it, and the consequences can be dire. In minor auto body damage, one can decide to drive a damaged car, and the effects are cosmetic but not serious. Finally, auto insurers seek to reduce bad behavior that leads to accidents. Traffic tickets are a surrogate for bad behavior; those with infractions reduce their good driver bonus points and pay a higher premium because of their personal behavior. In medical care, this approach has not proven popular but certainly could be used. An example that has been tried is to reduce premiums to reward those who do not smoke.

In conclusion, we argue that consumer choice can be active and utilized both for personal satisfaction and for the collective good. Making transactions clear and letting patients make their own choices across benefits, risks, and financial costs of medical interventions is desirable. When choice threatens the collective resource, however, it needs to be determined if the benefits warrant the expense. By careful selection of financial rewards and barriers as well as other nonmonetary incentives, consumer choice can be "nudged" toward maximizing health outcomes and individual satisfaction while still protecting the collective.

Special considerations in medical care mean that choice must be managed, especially because there is a collective interest and a limited resource. The trick is to shape the system to maximize individual health, the health of the insured population, and the fiscal integrity of the collective. We should have as much choice as is possible when it benefits the collective, and the least choice when choice hurts both the individual and the collective. When consumer choice only benefits the individual or when consumer choice only benefits the collective, priorities must be set.

The "R" Word: Rationing

No discussion of freedom of choice and protecting the commons would be complete without discussing rationing. Whichever side you take about financing and controlling costs (government-run single-payer vs. capitalist free market) or in-between, it's important to recognize that use of healthcare has *always* been limited in some fashion regardless whether this is called "rationing" or not. However, in the United States this is rarely acknowledged; there is a perception that limitations on care are a bad thing.

Many Americans equate our market approach as the evil force that limits access to care. Consider the scathing responses Jeff Jacoby received in reaction to his opinion piece in the *Boston Globe* in March 2017 when he argued for a more market-based healthcare system to reduce costs and improve quality. One response read:

> Markets are the land of supply and demand. When there is blight on the coffee crop, the price goes up and people buy less. Medical care does not conform to the rules of supply and demand, since much of it is governed

by what is called inelastic demand, meaning that the percentage change in demand is less than a percentage change in price. My 96-year-old father-in-law had his pacemaker replaced, not because the hospital was running a special, but because not doing so meant the end of his life. It is time to take the delivery and funding of health care out of the market.[27]

The issue with this statement is that resource allocation will remain a challenge even if you remove market forces (i.e., supply and demand) as the method for doing so. Like it or not, America and other nations must, and will, continue to limit medical care for the common good. Many on the Left associate government-funded, single-payer systems with open access to care, yet these systems often do just the opposite. To lower costs and combat the expected tendency of individuals to overutilize care, single-payer systems find ways to limit access and prioritize care to make it available to those who can most benefit. Methods include constraining capacity (such as limiting hospital beds in England and CAT scanners in Canada), asking primary care to be gatekeepers, regulating, or imposing financial incentives.

The recognition that health care delivery and financing must be managed is not new. In 1974, John Krizay, the director of the Office of Monetary Affairs, and Andrew Wilson, a labor economist, wrote a book entitled *The Patient as Consumer*. Written about 10 years after the creation of Medicare and Medicaid, many at the time were questioning whether a national health insurance plan was imminent. Analyzing from this perspective, the authors put forth two main points: (1) medical care is not free, and the public ends up paying for the expansion of government-subsidized health; and (2) the potential demand for healthcare is unlimited. In regard to the second point, the authors noted: "the demand for medical services seems to increase as their availability increases. People are reluctant to consider the formulation of policy that involves the rationing of medical services. And yet, freed of all economic restraints, consumer demand for medical services might well prove impossible to satisfy."[28]

Many, including the authors, believe that it is inevitable that open-ended insurance benefits will end except for those who are willing to pay a lot for unlimited care. As yet, however, we have chosen to use the dirty word "Ration" to describe this in U.S. health policy discussions. In reaction to the proposed Republican replacement bill in March 2017, Ezekial Emanuel, Arron Glickman, and Emily Gudbranson published an op-ed in the *New York Times* criticizing the bill. The attention-grabbing title read, "How Republicans Plan to Ration Health Care." They wrote, "This [plan] would be even worse than going back to the days before the Affordable Care Act. It would force states to ration care and deny some Americans lifesaving treatments or nursing home care."[29]

Although Emanuel and his coauthors aptly pointed out some of the most glaring issues with the bill (namely its damaging effects on Medicaid), they failed to discuss that rationing, or restricting care, is exactly how other healthcare systems have begun to deal with the unlimited demand for healthcare services and the threat to collective resources dedicated to paying for medical care. (However, we should note that Emanuel has written extensively on the overuse of medical care, and others have actually referred to him in the past as a proponent of rationing.)[30]

Regardless of what we call it, this discussion points again to an important point: patient choices are always limited in some way. Many different mechanisms are used—some visible, others hidden. There may be restrictions on the availability of high-priced drugs and new, expensive surgical procedures for older patients. Expensive treatments are often excluded by imposing restrictive cost benefit thresholds on their use. Queues are allowed to develop, such as rising waiting times for elective procedures.

For an illustration that reveals how public opinion forms, consider the following passage from an article in the *New York Times Magazine* written by Princeton bio-ethicist Peter Singer:

> You have advanced kidney cancer. It will kill you, probably in the next year or two. A drug called Sutent slows the spread of the cancer and may give you an extra six months, but at a cost of $54,000. Is a few more months' worth that much?
>
> If you can afford it, you probably would pay that much, or more, to live longer, even if your quality of life wasn't going to be good. But suppose it's not you with the cancer but a stranger covered by your health-insurance fund. If the insurer provides this man—and everyone else like him—with Sutent, your premiums will increase. Do you still think the drug is a good value? Suppose the treatment cost a million dollars. Would it be worth it then? Ten million? Is there any limit to how much you would want your insurer to pay for a drug that adds six months to someone's life? If there is any point at which you say, "No, an extra six months isn't worth that much," then you think that health care should be rationed.[31]

The Health Consequences of Consumer Choice

Protecting the consumer from harm has special importance in healthcare. To be sure, government often protects consumers; regulation of drugs and devices, litigation for damages, consumer reviews, and product safety are intended to reduce potential harm. But for most products, the lion's share of responsibility of using the product rests with the user. In medical care, the responsibility for protecting against harm shifts to providers and government.

Healthcare is different in two ways. First, medical decisions, either by the provider or patient, often have life-threatening consequences. If your car is repaired badly, you may not be able to drive, but it is unlikely to expose you to dangers of life and limb. Second, doctors call attention to the special risks of bad decisions by emphasizing *primum non nocere*—do no harm—as one of their three ethical obligations of their caregiving profession.

Healthcare calls for heightened attention to ensure that consumer choice does not expose patients to harm. For this reason, policy makers, insurers, suppliers, and providers of care need to understand where and when to increase the use of consumer choice and when not to use it. In this section, we discuss how policy makers and managers can determine when and where consumer choice should be considered and not.

We have argued that societal forces will increase demand for consumer choice in healthcare. Making a blanket decision about when choice is possible or even preferable is impossible. But looking systematically at the circumstances offers a way for both providers and patients to determine where increased choice is appropriate or not. The ability of the system to respond to demands for choice varies by the type of medical action being considered. The serious consequences of bad decisions in medical care make it important to assess the specific details of where choice works well and where choice is not feasible. Increasing the opportunity for consumer choice is an important goal. Selecting where this is safe is a first step.

Is There a Way to Determine When Choice Is Feasible in Clinical Care?

Healthcare is a dauntingly diverse and complicated enterprise. It comprises services and consumer decisions as different as selecting from the multiple types of health insurance and choosing end-of-life care, from whether to take over-the-counter drugs to vetting a referral to a specialist to deciding about a nursing home. Although increasing the opportunities for consumer choice is a goal of this book, we know that some choices in medical care are off limits or even dangerous. Though it's clear that people appreciate being given choice, there are times when the nature of the health situation, the physical condition of the individual, and the difference in knowledge between the patient and provider preclude the person from deciding on his or her own.

There are, of course, many different medical situations in which consumer choice is an option. In this section, we will suggest a consumer choice framework for sorting through the things we put patients through in medicine—things like considering insurance, assessing symptoms, making a diagnosis, deciding about an expensive referral, implementing treatments, and providing physical and emotional support.

Figure 2.1 repeats an earlier illustration representing a way to characterize the patient's capacity to choose wisely when they are sick. At one extreme, patients have complete capacity to make an informed decision that suits their preferences. Think of the symptomatic treatment of a cold. The patient has considerable personal

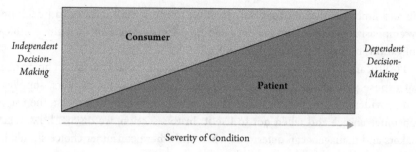

Figure 2.1 The continuum of consumer choice and medical condition.

experience and is reasonably knowledgeable in dealing with this. The medications are clearly labeled with dosage levels, have low risk, and the cost is clear. The patient can predict the risks and benefits with some confidence. At the other extreme, picture a person who's just had a serious car accident and injuries, coming into the emergency department on a gurney. In this condition, urgency, complexity, and infrequency of encountering such a problem as well as anxiety, disorientation, and acute suffering make it very difficult to expect a patient to be making sound choices.

The balance between consumer and patient can wax and wane over time for the same individual. There are times when people have enough time, knowledge, and support to make decisions on their own. This is true of many decisions around preventive services and chronic condition management. At these times, people have the ability to collect information, compare options, and make informed decisions. In unexpected, episodic, and emergency situations in inpatient, hospital settings, people more frequently defer to the clinical experts as their conditions worsen. Even individual patients can show variation in their orientation to making their own decisions as their health status and circumstances vary.

Moreover, individual choice in healthcare is, and always will be, limited by difference in knowledge between provider and consumer. Most providers have years of training; to expect consumers to acquire the level of sophisticated knowledge needed to engage in a debate among equals is neither feasible nor desirable. Furthermore, one can think of many examples where giving patients all of the decision-making power—even with extensive education—might be dangerous.

Therefore, patients can't be consumers in all transactions. There are several major factors that work against good consumer choice. These are the urgency of the healthcare intervention, its medical complexity, and the frequency with which it occurs. In general, the less urgent the transaction, the less complex and more understandable the problem is, and the more times it happens (enabling a patient to learn), the more prepared the patient is to be a consumer and the more likely it is that consumer choice can be offered with the expectation of a successful outcome.

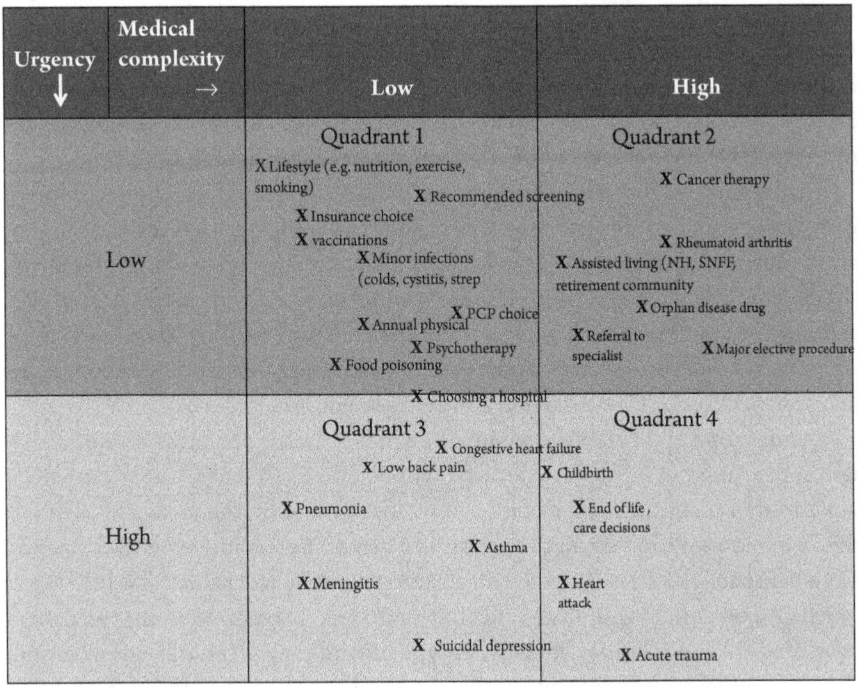

Urgency ↓	Medical complexity →	Low	High
Low		**Quadrant 1** X Lifestyle (e.g. nutrition, exercise, smoking) X Recommended screening X Insurance choice X vaccinations X Minor infections (colds, cystitis, strep X PCP choice X Annual physical X Psychotherapy X Food poisoning X Choosing a hospital	**Quadrant 2** X Cancer therapy X Rheumatoid arthritis X Assisted living (NH, SNFF, retirement community X Orphan disease drug X Referral to specialist X Major elective procedure
High		**Quadrant 3** X Congestive heart failure X Low back pain X Pneumonia X Asthma X Meningitis X Suicidal depression	**Quadrant 4** X Childbirth X End of life, care decisions X Heart attack X Acute trauma

Figure 2.2 Types of healthcare decisions.

Figure 2.2 plots a number of healthcare transactions according to urgency and complexity. Each transaction also comes with a high or low frequency of occurrence, which we will discuss as we examine each quadrant. Our purpose is to make it possible for the system designers to assess where consumer choice can best be offered and to enable the providers of care to make the choice experience better in these cases.

Figure 2.2 illustrates that not all healthcare choices are the same. Quadrant 1 shows nonacute and medically straightforward situations. In these circumstances, the consumer is not rushed in making the decision and does so on a routine basis. Of all healthcare choices, these are most likely to resemble common processes of buying in other consumer-driven markets, such as retailing. This quadrant includes the daily lifestyle decisions we all make that affect our health. We already make lifestyle choices: selecting what we eat, how frequently we exercise, and whether we choose to smoke or drink alcohol. And the vast majority of us manage common health conditions that are not medically serious, such as colds, minor infections, cuts, and bruises. Note that the more frequently these problems occur, the greater the opportunity for the patient to learn about them from experience. With more skill and knowledge, the ability of the consumer to choose increases and her autonomy grows. Remember Sheila in Chapter 1, who had learned a lot about strep throat and was able to consider a broader array of choices than someone suffering from this problem for the first time. Some choices are already made by consumers before they experience a clinical event that brings them into contact with the medical care system. This includes buying the right insurance for our needs and in light of our risk tolerance and deciding who our primary care doctor will be.

Buying medical insurance, deciding on whether one needs or wants a primary care clinician and who that will be, determining what prescription coverage to buy, and choosing what hospital to go to already are mostly consumers' choice. However, these decisions are often, if not most of the time, made with inadequate understanding of what you are "buying" and of the risks and benefits of the alternative options. We will return later to interventions that might improve these decisions and enhance consumer satisfaction and engagement.

Quadrant 4 highlights the decisions in which a person requires the most assistance; the patient is facing a medically unfamiliar decision that requires immediate attention. In such cases, the patient is often dependent on the medical system, or family members, to make decisions on her behalf. For example, when someone has a heart attack and is taken to the emergency room, the patient has little time, practical experience, or ability to affect the outcome. Though decisions consumers have made in the past may affect what type of care they receive in this situation, they have little decision-making ability in real time. Nevertheless, a family could prepare for unanticipated emergencies by selecting the ER of choice in their area— before anyone needs to use it. People can also prepare for these kinds of situations by creating advance directives, which include both living wills and designating power of attorney. Living wills are legal documents that stipulate what kinds of medical interventions the patient does and doesn't want once he or she is incapacitated. Power of attorney allows someone else to make healthcare decisions if the person is temporarily or permanently unable to make such decisions. Although there are ways for people to prepare for unanticipated medical decisions, they rarely do. In a 2014 study, only 26.3% of the more than 7,000 Americans surveyed had advance directives.[32] Other studies have found that this percentage remains low even among the chronically ill.[33] This leaves a lot of opportunity for making better choices.

Quadrant 2 includes nonacute decisions that are medically and, at some times, socially complex. As we amplify the increasingly consumer-driven nature of healthcare, this quadrant is likely to change the most. However, unlike those in Quadrant 3 and 4, individuals have time to process alternatives. As methods for comparing options improve, consumer control of choices in this arena has the most potential to increase, shifting the individual from passive patient to informed consumer.

Rheumatoid arthritis is an example of a chronic, nonurgent but complex medical condition where choice can increase. In the past, patients handed over many of these decisions to the experts. Because the decisions occur frequently and patients are capable of learning about their disease, they often end up knowing as much about their personal illness as the experts do. Individuals can gain the know-how needed to exercise a lot of personal discretion in choices about short- and long-term management, their costs, and expected personal benefit.

Even socially complex issues present an opportunity for increasing choice. In a discussion about the need for a nursing home, a patient, especially with assistance from family and friends, can be supported to fully engage in the decision. The issue usually is as much about costs, social supports, risk tolerance, and personal values as it is medical.

Finally, medical referral to a specialist is increasingly an area where choice is affected by financial factors. As higher deductibles become barriers to access, the choice becomes one of finding the balance point between personal benefits, which vary by individual, and costs in financial outlay as well as clinical risks. In this category, which is growing in importance, we believe that most patients need an expert at their side—one who is trusted and can interpret the medical issues and advise them about the decision. We call this the trusted advisor role. It can be assumed by primary care doctors or nurses and even, in narrow areas of medical conditions, by lay advisors (this already exists, for example, in alcohol counseling about choices to be made for those who seek help through Alcoholics Anonymous). No matter who the expert, consumer choice can be improved by expert personal consultation in medically complicated situations.

Quadrant 3, by contrast, depicts decisions that are acute and require immediate attention. They are frequently but not always medically difficult to understand. Some of these conditions, especially when the symptoms are dramatic and unfamiliar, are best handled by seeking the help of doctors and letting them figure it out. Many of these issues, however, such as a cold, urinary tract infection, or food poisoning, are acute but occur often enough that the consumer becomes practiced in dealing with them. Once we have reached adulthood, most of us know how to care for ourselves when we fall ill with a common ailment. Someone with an acute gastroenteritis, for example, might take the day off work, stop eating but maintain fluids, take over-the-counter medicine, and rest.

When the condition is chronic but associated with frequent, severe, and even potentially dangerous exacerbations (asthma, congestive heart failure, low back pain, and type 1 diabetes are examples), patients can learn their disease and treatments and actually begin to exercise medical control. In these cases, putting patients in charge can make a significant difference in satisfaction and outcomes. Although good doctors have encouraged this for years, they need good industry support in education and methods to encourage responsible autonomy that reduces the need for medical intervention and transfers control to patients.

Further, we can modify some circumstances to make choice possible in urgent situations where it may not initially appear feasible. Moving the decision point earlier, to before the event happens, creates enough time, expert and family help, and emotional detachment for patients to make up their minds about what they want. When the decision is medically complex but not rushed, expert advice and formal decision support can bring such decisions closer to the patient.

Even when later circumstances arise in which a patient is in no condition to choose, we can still plan ahead so that individual preferences are incorporated in decision-making. By discussing end-of-life preferences and choices coupled with formal methods such as advanced directives, power of attorney, and living wills, patients can choose what is important for them. End-of-life decisions represent a special opportunity for consumer choice to be enhanced. In his book *Being Mortal*, Atul Gawande points out how important it is to ascertain what older people want in their last period of life, and how rarely this is asked about and implemented.[34] Advanced directives show us that it is both feasible and better for the opportunity to choose to come early, while the patient is still capable of expressing his or her wishes.

Conclusion

If healthcare were in no way different than other industries, the framework for consumer choice would be familiar. You would get what you could afford to buy. Prices would rise and fall based on demand. Consumers would need to be protected. Market forces would be monitored for restraint of trade, and mergers and market domination would be assessed by government agencies. Suppliers would be watched for fraudulent practices. Unfair or inordinately risky practices would be regulated.

But we have described some unique conditions in healthcare that call for constraints on and adjustments to consumer choice. We believe these special conditions can be addressed and that the benefits of consumer choice can be sensibly unleashed with a low level of risk.

First, we discussed the general issue of whether consumer choice and market forces are appropriate in medicine in the first place. Strong arguments have been made that medical care does not have the characteristics that lend it to consumer choice. On the other hand, costs are now being transferred to patients who are being pushed to make choices that are, in fact, similar to other decisions that they make as consumers. These forces are increasing, so, in our view, we have no alternative but to try to construct a system that not only enables patient-consumers to make better choices but also to protect them from harm. And we can structure the injection of consumer forces so that they enable market forces to improve the system overall.

Second, we have argued that the United States has an ethical responsibility to deliver necessary medical care to those who need it. Having a system based on consumer choice and market forces is unacceptable if we violate our ethical responsibility by allowing insurance premium payments or out-of-pocket costs to rise beyond the reach of all but the wealthiest. There is no actual choice in such a circumstance.

We must extend health insurance to all Americans at a price they can afford. Experience in other countries suggests that a two-tiered model appears to work the best—insurance to cover very good but basic healthcare for all combined with a voluntary private system for those who wish to pay more. By and large, this model satisfies the ethical and moral responsibilities of a nation while still meeting the criteria of fairness and affordability. The basic system must reduce overall expense of medical care and also selectively subsidize its costs to bring it within the reach of those who need it but cannot pay for it. For this insurance to be affordable, the publicly supported care system will need to restrict some benefits. It cannot offer everything that the wealthy will be able to buy privately.

The third constraint is that any basic universal system must balance individual gain with protecting the collective resource. There is no basic model that can operate without insurance (public or private) that collectivizes risk and spreads it among defined populations. In insured populations, we must determine how consumer choice applies when one is attempting to balance providing and paying for services with protecting the integrity of the common financial resource.

In this case, we must find the right balance between individual choice and collective good. The guiding principle here is to maximize choice when it does not adversely affect the common resource, but also to use financial incentives and controls to nudge choices that improve the individual's health (and benefit the collective) and, at the same time, to penalize dangerous behaviors. For example, recommended preventive screening like mammograms should have no financial barriers to use, or even rewards. On the other hand, if individuals' dangerous choices worsen health status, we favor using incentives, including rebates to those doing the right thing, or surcharges for those with bad personal health habits like smoking or obesity. In this, we draw on the automobile industry as an example of how to discourage bad behaviors by reducing good driver points in response to traffic violations.

Finally, we present a systematic way to think about where choice works and where it should be restricted because of potential harm to the patient. Although there are limitations to the application of choice, our current system clearly underutilizes choice where it could help and is not creative about how its reach could be expanded.

Consumer choice is not a panacea for our healthcare problems. Its use must navigate through concerns and constraints unique to medical care. Nevertheless, there is considerable unutilized potential for consumers to exercise more choice to make their own experience of care better and, through active consumer input, to find and encourage improvements that will make our healthcare system better.

References

1. Arrow, Kenneth J. "Uncertainty and the Welfare Economics of Medical Care." *The American Economic Review* 53, no. 5 (1963): 941–973. The American Economic Association. Web.

2. Roy, Avik. "Health Care and the Profit Motive." *National Affairs* 33 (2010): n. p. *National Affairs*. Fall 2017. Web. See also Roy, Avik. "The Gospel According to Ken Arrow." *National Review*. N.p., 30 August 2010. Web.

3. Berenson, Robert. "The AHCA Gets It Wrong: Health Care Is Different." *Health Affairs Blog*. N.p., 22 March 2017. Web.

4. Krugman, Paul. "Patients Are Not Consumers." *The New York Times: Opinion*, 21 April 2011. Web.

5. "Consumer." *Merriam-Webster*, n.d. Web.

6. Herzlinger, Regina E. "Why Innovation in Health Care Is So Hard." *Harvard Business Review* May 2006: n. p. 31 July 2014. Web.

7. Arrow, Kenneth J. "Uncertainty and the Welfare Economics of Medical Care." *The American Economic Review* 53, no. 5 (1963): 941–973. The American Economic Association. Web.

8. Tomes, Nancy. *Remaking the American Patient: How Madison Avenue and Modern Medicine Turned Patients Into Consumers*. First ed. N.p.: U of North Carolina, 2016. Print.

9. Bauchner, Howard, MD. "Health Care in the United States: A Right or a Privilege." *JAMA*. American Medical Association, 03 January 2017. Web.

10. Kiley, Jocelyn. "Public Support for 'Single Payer' Health Coverage Grows, Driven by Democrats." *Pew Research Center*. N.p., 23 June 2017. Web.

11. Summers, Benjamin D., Atul A. Gawande, and Katherine Baicker. "Health Insurance Coverage and Health—What the Recent Evidence Tells Us." *New England Journal of Medicine* 377, no. 6 (2017): 586–593. Web.

12. Daniels, Norman, and James E. Sabin. *Setting Limits Fairly: Learning to Share Resources for Health*. N.p.: Oxford UP, 2008. Print.

13. Kitzhaber, J. A. "Prioritizing Health Services in an Era of Limits: The Oregon Experience." *British Medical Journal* 307, no. 6900 (1993): 373–377. Web.

14. Thaler, Richard H. *Misbehaving: The Making of Behavioral Economics*. W. W. Norton, 2016. Print. p. 129.

15. Ibid., 130.

16. Perez-Pena, Richard. "California Is First State to Adopt Sex Reassignment Surgery Policy for Prisoners." *The New York Times*, 21 October 2015. Web.

17. Ibid.

18. Ibid.

19. "State Laws Related to Insurance Coverage for Infertility Treatment." National Conference of State Legislatures (NCSL), 1 June 2014. Web.

20. Ibid.

21. Owens, Gary M., "Economic Burden of Multiple Sclerosis and the Role of Managed Care Organizations in Multiple Sclerosis Management." *AJMC*, 31 May 2016. Web.

22. Owens, Gary M., Eleanor L. Olvey, Grant H. Skrepnek, and Michael W. Pill. "Perspectives for Managed Care Organizations on the Burden of Multiple Sclerosis and the Cost-Benefits of Disease-Modifying Therapies." *Journal of Managed Care Pharmacy* 19, no. 1 Supp A (2013). Web.

23. Hardin, Garrett. "The Tragedy of the Commons." *Science* 162, no. 3859 (1968): 1243–1248. Print.

24. Hiatt, Howard H. "Protecting the Medical Commons: Who Is Responsible?" *New England Journal of Medicine* 293, no. 5 (1975): 235–241. Web.

25. Brownlee, Shannon, Vikas Saini, and Christine Cassel. "When Less Is More: Issues of Overuse in Health Care." *Health Affairs Blog*. 25 April 2014.

26. Wharam, J. Frank, Dennis Ross-Degnan, and Meredith B. Rosenthal. "The ACA and High-Deductible Insurance—Strategies for Sharpening a Blunt Instrument." *New England Journal of Medicine* 369, no. 16 (2013): 1481–1484. Web.

27. "Free Market Is No Prescription for Our Health Care Woes." *Boston Globe: Opinion Letters*. BostonGlobe.com, 25 March 2017. Web.

28. Krizay, John, and Andrew Wilson. *The Patient as Consumer*. Lexington, 1974. Print, p. xxii.

29. Emanuel, Ezekiel. "How Republicans Plan to Ration Health Care." *The New York Times*, 7 March 2017. Web.

30. McCaughey, Betsy, "Obama's Health Rationer-in-Chief." *The Wall Street Journal*, 27 August 2009. Web.

31. Singer, Peter. "Why We Must Ration Health Care." *The New York Times*, 15 July 2009. Web.

32. Rao, Jaya K., Lynda A. Anderson, Feng-Chang Lin, and Jeffery P. Laux. "Completion of Advance Directives Among U.S. Consumers." *American Journal of Preventive Medicine* 46, no. 1 (2013): 65–70. *AJPMonline.org*. Web.

33. Novotney, Amy. "The Living Will Needs Resuscitation." *Monitor on Psychology*. American Psychological Association, 10 October 2010. Web.

34. Gawande, Atul. *Being Mortal: Medicine and What Matters in the End*. Metropolitan Books/ Henry Holt & Company, 2014.

3

Creating a Consumer Marketplace

In Chapter 1, we focused on the reasons why healthcare has lagged behind other industries when it comes to consumer involvement and choice. We also discussed why those conditions are changing today. Gone are the days when employers who sponsor health insurance plans absorb ever-increasing medical costs. The consumer has increasingly borne the brunt of these increases in medical costs, and it is changing the *status quo*. At the same time, new models of care and more precise treatments are pushing the system to treat individuals as just that—individuals. As deductibles rise and policy places a greater onus on the individual to make decisions, the consumer will not only expect more autonomy and choices but will demand them. Some of these decisions will result in difficult choices and tradeoffs for consumers; they will need help to assess their own benefits, costs, and risks and decide whether and how they will spend their money on medical services.

In Chapter 2, we acknowledged the ways in which the healthcare market differs from other markets. As a result, there are indeed some choices we cannot have, and there must be safeguards in place to protect patient-consumers, particularly when they are most vulnerable. Furthermore, we must always remember that the healthcare system is a collective resource, and individual choice must be balanced against collective priorities. Debates about whether a market should exist or not in healthcare are likely to continue, but we believe these disputes are short-sighted. A healthcare market has always existed; however, we, as consumers, were not always aware of it. As we shape our burgeoning consumer market, we should focus our energy on creating a marketplace that serves as many people as well as possible.

Merely making consumers pay for care does not constitute a market system. Issues such as affordability, differentiation of options, parity of knowledge of buyer and seller, and consumer competency are all factors that enter the equation. Nevertheless, without some financial skin in the game, consumers have had weak incentives to engage in the choice process. Moreover, the hodgepodge design of our healthcare system has a number of features that have severely inhibited the effectiveness of consumers in making healthcare work for them. Now that consumers are again paying for portions of healthcare, how can we make consumer choice work better?

In this chapter, we will focus on the enabling conditions necessary to enhance consumer choice. We believe that all consumer marketplaces—including those in healthcare—are enabled by the following six conditions to optimize consumer choice. These conditions facilitate choice from both the consumers' and the suppliers' perspective. If these conditions are met, consumers will be more educated, see better products and services come to market, and be protected from bad actors and potentially poor decisions. If these conditions are met, insurers and providers will be activated to produce what patients and payers want.

1. *Consumer-centric orientation*: Organizations operating in a consumer-centric marketplace will focus on satisfying what their customer wants and needs; in a product-centric organization, suppliers design products and processes to meet their own needs.
2. *Meaningful differentiation*: Choice is not only a function of quantity of options but also of the differentiation among them; consumers must be able to perceive meaningful differences among the available options.
3. *Relevant metrics*: For consumers to understand what a successful product or service looks like, the market must develop appropriate performance measures that are accepted by both suppliers and consumers.
4. *Information transparency*: Consumers must find it easy to access objective, comparable information regarding the different choices available in the market. Critically, a supplier's success or failure must be quickly accessible and easily understood by consumers and producers.
5. *Consumer protections*: A well-functioning consumer market assures safety, accessibility, and quality to its users. In addition, it protects consumers from fraudulent actors who might persuade them to select poor choices.
6. *Balanced incentives*: Any well-functioning consumer market appropriately recognizes and rewards both consumers for participating in the system and making good choices, and suppliers for offering superior products and performance.

These conditions follow a logical flow. First, the producers should be consumer-centric in understanding and responding to their customers' needs. Then there must be differentiation among the options available for a choice to be relevant at all. Next, there should be ways to measure the performance of different alternatives using reliable metrics, and it then follows that both buyers and sellers must be able to access complete information that is clear and comprehensible. Protections should ensure consumer safety. Incentives should stimulate consumers to act on that information and to motivate successful producers to do more.

Next, we review each of these areas in greater depth, describing why each condition is critical for creating a consumer market. For some of the conditions, we will refer to examples outside of healthcare to demonstrate their general relevance. We will also discuss why many of these conditions are not currently met in healthcare today.

Consumer-Centric Orientation

Organizations operating in a consumer-centric marketplace will focus on satisfying customer needs; in a product-centric organization, suppliers design products and processes to meet their own needs.

As we discussed in Chapter 1, medical care has historically been a product-centric industry. Medicine has focused on producing and deploying new and profitable methods and technologies, rather than creating value by reducing costs, making the experience of users better and competing for their customers. When most organizations in a market are product-oriented, investment dollars are earmarked for product research and development, and one-size-fits-all production efficiency. For a market to support consumer choice, a majority of organizations within that market must operate with a consumer-centric mindset. Many markets, such as online retail and personal finance, have shifted toward a consumer-centric approach over the last decade. If patients, as we have argued, want more and better choices and will use their market power to reward those who provide them, then consumer-centric organizations within healthcare will grow. The growth of these consumer-centric organizations will, in turn, attract consumers away from product-centric competitors.

Many in healthcare are reluctant to look outside the industry for examples of successful consumer-centric models. However, by examining a successful nonmedical consumer-centric organization, one can draw helpful parallels. Amazon, for example, uses marketing analyses and a customer-centric strategy to provide multiple benefits to its various consumer segments. Its strategies have changed the *status quo* in online retail, and many organizations have followed Amazon's customer-centric approach in the years since the company began as an online book retailer in the 1990s.

Throughout the company's history, CEO Jeff Bezos has prioritized Amazon's customers in almost every decision he has made. The company works hard to learn each customer's needs, and it is accessible, customer-service-oriented, and accountable for its actions. This requires Amazon to communicate openly and establish trust with its customers.

At times, this strategy has been misunderstood. When Amazon introduced customer reviews onto its website, Bezos received backlash for encouraging potentially negative discussion of products. He recounted, "One [person] wrote to me and said, 'You don't understand your business. You make money when you sell things. Why do you allow these negative customer reviews?' And when I read that letter, I thought, we don't make money when we sell things. We make money when we help customers make purchase decisions."[1]

The company has created a win-win mentality with its customers and, interestingly, with its fellow suppliers. To enhance the search possibilities, Amazon even publicizes products they may not sell themselves. This has enabled them to become what is known as a dominant exchange—a place everyone goes to find what they want. They also select ads and make recommendations to their customers based on their past purchases. This has improved customer loyalty to services like Amazon Prime, which offers free two-day shipping to customers who pay a yearly $99 fee. Though Amazon remains tight-lipped about specific costs, some analysts have estimated that Amazon loses $1 billion annually on Prime-related shipping expenses.[2] However, it has been credited with creating a loyal customer base. In 2016, reports estimated that Amazon Prime had over 60 million members, around half of the company's total customers.[3]

Amazon's strategy stems from Bezos's belief that, in the long term, consumer and shareholder interests are aligned.[4] Though Amazon has had some tough years, this strategy has largely paid off. Unlike many companies founded about the same time, Amazon survived the dotcom bust in the early 2000s. At the beginning of 2016, it announced operating profits of $2.2 billion on $107 billion of sales.[5] Perhaps as equally impressive as these financial metrics, a public opinion survey in 2015 ranked Amazon as the number-one company for customer satisfaction.[6]

Amazon is a remarkable example of a customer-focused company that started that way. Can industries that have not traditionally been consumer-centric make the shift? Experience suggests so. Consider the modern supermarket, which provides nearly all day-to-day food needs. Eighty years ago, people had to visit multiple counters in a grocery store or even separate stores to buy their food. They went to a baker for their bread and a butcher for their meat; the grocery store only provided nonperishable goods. In the early 1900s, innovators announced the concept of the supermarket, which had both refrigerated and nonrefrigerated sections. This was much more convenient for the individual shopper, who could browse the store at her leisure and discover new products. The shopper often ended up buying more than she planned. The larger size of supermarkets generated economies of scale and lowered prices for consumers.

Also consider the example of the financial services industry. If a consumer wanted to buy 100 shares of a stock in 1980, she had to go through a broker. Brokers charged commissions, which varied according to the size of the order. This made investing time-consuming and expensive.

Today, the investor can easily use Vanguard, Robinhood, or a similar service to make her own investments at much lower cost without the middleman. Robinhood, a start-up launched in 2015, states that its mission "is to democratize access to the financial markets."[7] Everything is done through an app on the user's smartphone or tablet, and once a user has linked the app to his bank account, he can start trading within minutes. Popular with millennials, the app boasts style and simplicity, attracting beginner investors to try the platform. Most significantly, the company neither requires a minimum deposit nor charges a broker fee when a user buys or sells stock. The co-founders, who were roommates at Stanford, formulated the idea for the company after working in the financial services industry. They realized that electronic trading firms were charging investors up to $10 per trade, though it cost the firms "next to nothing" to place the trade.[8] The company earns money by collecting interest on the cash and securities in Robinhood accounts. With more than a million users, the company has saved its investors collectively over $200 million in fees since 2015.[9] Robinhood recognized that consumers wanted cheaper, easier ways to invest their money and developed a new service in response to that demand.

As we have discussed in our introduction, healthcare has traditionally operated with a product-centric approach. Investment dollars have been heavily focused on product research and development, with consumer research typically coming into play at the tail end to help companies formulate their go-to-market strategies. Although this has accelerated the development of advanced technology, it has resulted in a lack of understanding of consumer needs.

For too long, the healthcare industry has retained a model structured upon an "if I offer it, they will come" mentality. Many of its accepted policies and practices have been focused on the convenience of doctors, not patients. Availability is often limited to select hours and days of operation, predominantly concentrated in urban locations. The burden of travel falls on the patient to go to the office to receive care. An undressed patient waiting and shivering in a paper gown is made uncomfortable for the efficiency of the doctor. Some of these inconveniences are necessary to make medical care better, but many are designed to help doctors run their practice.

Shifting from this mindset toward activating consumer choice is a big challenge. The first step is for the industry to shift from feeling that patients will come no matter what, to realizing that many are facing rising financial barriers and are being offered less expensive alternatives in drugstores and on the Internet, for example. Ultimately, heightened competition for patients will spur doctors to change. If physicians and hospitals need to become more consumer-oriented to attract paying patients, they will do so.

Meaningful Differentiation

Choice is not only a function of quantity of options but also of the differentiation among them; consumers must be able to perceive meaningful differences among the available options.

It is not enough simply to have a variety of choices without meaningful differentiation between the available options. As we think about the relationship between differentiation and consumer choice, there are three issues of importance. First is the number of alternatives available in a market. If consumers have only one or two options to choose between, they are restricted in their decision-making. This not only limits the level of consumer choice, but, over time, a monopoly or duopoly can drive up prices and harm consumers. The second area of importance is the variety among potential options; how different are the choices from one another? If there are many different options but they are all so similar that they are essentially the same, there is really no use in offering consumers a choice at all. And lastly, there is the presentation of choice, which affects how consumers can compare apples to apples. If alternatives are not presented in a way that highlights the differences among them, consumers may struggle to make the right decisions for themselves.

Consider, for example, the last time you went to the drugstore to purchase toothpaste. Though the toothpaste market is largely dominated by two or three major companies, there are many different brands and varieties available to choose from. You can buy toothpaste with whitening effects or one with extra anticavity protection. You can select different flavors or tube sizes. There is no one-size-fits-all solution that will satisfy all consumers. The manufacturers and the distributors (i.e., retail pharmacies and grocery stores) help consumers understand the differences among the products through their branding and advertising and by packaging and displaying them according to their differences.

In healthcare, it is often difficult to perceive the differences among products and services. Though we know that differentiation exists in the market, we struggle to understand which differences are significant and which options are uniquely well suited to us as individuals. Among delivery providers, there is vast differentiation, but these differences are often very difficult for the consumer to perceive without using a service and, even then, information on which to make a decision is sparse. Furthermore, for an emergency service, there is little time to make a decision based on a comparison of alternatives. Consider a heart attack. We know from the literature, for example, that measures of quality of cardiac care differ widely from hospital to hospital, even within the same geographic area. However, this is not something you, as a consumer, are likely to be aware of.

Another issue regarding meaningful differentiation in healthcare is that of clinical significance. At times, differences between available options are irrelevant clinically. For example, consider pharmaceutical products and their product advertising. Ads claim specific benefits that differentiate them from their competitors. These distinctions often represent statistically significant findings in research studies; however, these findings are typically not ones that are important clinically. A good example is the many of oral medications for Type 2 diabetics. The differences between many in a class of drugs, despite manufacturers' claims, are so minimal that expert guidelines consider them equivalent choices.

Relevant Metrics

For consumers to understand what a successful product or service looks like, the market must develop appropriate performance measures that are accepted by both suppliers and consumers.

Measurements of product characteristics and performance are essential for consumer choice and markets to work. A requirement for good purchasing decisions in any industry is that the individual buyer be able to assess the value of what he or she is buying and predict the product's expected benefits, its cost, and its service/satisfaction characteristics. For this to happen, metrics must be developed that are relevant to consumer choice.

Healthcare performance metrics are important for both patients and providers—the users and suppliers of healthcare services. For patients, consumer choice is optimized when they have reliable measures to judge what they have received or offered and compare it to alternatives. Reliable measurements enable them to assess value, or the relationship between expected benefits and projected costs. If consumers are not given the right data and do not understand a product's personal benefits and its costs, they are likely to make mistakes. They may choose an inferior alternative when another might have provided a better outcome; or they may proceed with a flawed understanding of the benefits of the choice they have made. If their expectations are not met, the consumer may feel cheated, disappointed, and even angry.

Likewise, for insurers and clinicians, metrics measuring their performance are essential. Increasingly, payments are related to performance. Whether the reward mechanism is through pay-for-performance or through growth in market share, organizations and individual physicians need to be able to prove what they contribute by measuring what they do. Metrics make it possible to reward exemplary behavior and to identify inferior performance. For example, a new Centers for Medicare and Medicaid Services (CMS) program called Medicare Access and CHIP Reauthorization Act (MACRA)[10] will use performance metrics across a number of dimensions as a factor in reimbursement levels.

Performance is a key differentiator in marketing when it is validly measured rather than merely claimed. Based on the measured performance of their different features (service, clinical excellence, low cost, etc.), providers can responsibly justify their assertions that they are better as they compete for patients' business. If a provider can prove that it is better than its competitors, it can attract customers and thrive.

Good measurement serves other important functions for providers. It is a requirement for accreditation. Reimbursement is increasingly linked to performance through value-based payments and other methods. Metrics are essential to improvement; scorecards enable doctors and hospitals to know what they need to deliver as well as to show what has or hasn't worked, and whether they have been successful. If you cannot measure what you do, you have no basis to make it better.

Measuring Clinical Performance

Consumers and payers want to know if they are getting value for money and will increasingly demand that medical care providers provide that information. Consumers generally trust that their doctors are really good. They don't need to evaluate clinical performance personally, but they certainly want to know that someone else is.

Clinical metrics are not well developed. In 1997, McGlynn summarized the state of clinical performance measurement. She glumly concluded that "the definition of quality illustrates the complexity of the concept and its evaluation." Her conclusion was that much still needed to be done.[11] Although McGlynn's article is 20 years old, performance metrics still have a long way to go. Considerable work has been done in clinical care performance measurement research and development since the 1990s, but even now there is considerable debate about what metrics are relevant. Even with the marked growth of information technology (IT), its medical applications, and the electronic medical record (EMR), we are still struggling to define the metrics to measure comparative performance of providers of services.

If outcome measures were readily available, then performance could be assessed and, by correlating them with related costs, the results of both individual and collective medical care could be determined. However, clinical outcomes, beyond a handful, have been notoriously difficult to measure and their use has been limited. Outcome metrics required by payers (government and private insurance) today focus on only a half dozen that lend themselves to measurement, and the same limited set, such as hemoglobin A1C to measure blood sugar control in diabetics, are used by virtually all insurers. Further, many doctors do not perceive these metrics now in use to be valid indicators of their performance; rather, they feel that most of these measures miss the point of how doctors really add value. Almost universally, primary care physicians (PCPs) say that the important work that they do is not being measured. However, these limitations in outcome metrics do not indicate that they are not useful as part of an overall package of performance measurement; they are, but many more valid and reliable metrics are needed.

Because outcomes are hard to measure, medical care evaluation has turned to a three-element model first developed some 40 years ago by Avedis Donabedian. In his model,[12] Donabedian measured structure, process, and outcome. In many, if not most medical actions, outcome is difficult to assess and to ascribe to the doctor. Surrogate measures for outcomes—structure and process—are used instead. If all the right enabling indicators are in place (cleanliness, safe equipment, staff training) and clinicians are following best practices as represented by scientifically derived evidence-based guidelines and expert standards of practice, these process measures can serve as surrogates for outcomes. This is an imperfect solution, but it may be the best way to measure performance, given the uncertainty around any individual's course of disease.

Process measures are frequently derived from clinical expert guidelines to assist doctors and reassure patients. Between research evidence and customary standards of care, there are many condition-specific guidelines for diagnosis and treatment. These are procedural manifestations of the best evidence supporting medical decision-making. Examining how well doctors follow such guidelines could potentially constitute an important metric for patients who are deciding who will deliver their care. The proportion of cases in which doctors adhere to guidelines, combined with an analysis of their reasons for choosing differently, is a potentially useful measure of clinical competence.

Ultimately, doctors themselves will need to solve the metrics challenge. Accreditation and certification are uniformly used as surrogates for professional competence today. However, these measures are often only indirectly related to actual clinical performance and are too often not reflective of the care actually delivered. There are good reasons for clinicians to want to do better. The top doctors today have much to gain by measuring their performance. Today, they remain indistinguishable from other medical professionals who are lacking in skill or training. In fact, if they can document that they are better, they should benefit through greater patient volume and preferential reimbursement. Moreover, since they are already "better," they have little to lose in measuring their own performance. At some point, we believe that doctors will recognize these benefits, and the better doctors will lead the system in developing, applying, promulgating, and publishing professional assessment measures.

In sum, it is important for the industry or outside regulators to set a standard of clinical practice, help doctors develop the means to measure it, and guarantee that assessment of doctors is in place to assure that they meet or exceed these standards.

Metrics for Insurers

Attempts to measure the performance of insurers have a long history. As HMO-type health plans began to grow nationally in the 1980s, they realized that consumers and government regulators would want to accredit them, assess their performance, and perhaps regulate them. In 1990, the industry formed a not-for-profit assessment group, which eventually became the National Committee for Quality Assurance (NCQA). Since that time, NCQA has become the primary evaluation and measurement organization for health plans. Their primary approach to measurement has been the development of an annual assessment of performance called the Healthcare Effectiveness Data and Information Set (HEDIS). Their website today describes HEDIS as: a tool used by more than 90 percent of America's health plans to measure performance on important dimensions of care and service. Altogether, HEDIS consists of 81 measures across 5 domains of care. The NCQA assessment leads to an organizational rating on its criteria. Because so many plans collect HEDIS data and because the measures are so specifically defined, NCQA claims that HEDIS makes it possible to compare the performance of health plans on an "apples-to-apples" basis.[13]

Many measures important to consumers are already available. For example, costs and benefits are already universally detailed in insurance contracts. Expenditures are available in claims databases. Out-of-pocket costs to the patient are already known to each insurer and could also be reported by consumers.

Consider an example: the choice of health insurance policies on the exchanges set up by the Affordable Care Act. AccessHealth CT was established in Connecticut in 2012 to run the insurance exchange. Its chief executive, Kevin Counihan, later became chief executive of the federal site, healthcare.gov. Counihan set out to give consumers choices in a manner that facilitated easy and intelligent comparisons. First, he secured support from two of Connecticut's largest health insurers, both well-known brand names. They agreed to offer standard plans at three price/service levels to facilitate apples-to-apples comparison shopping by consumers. They were also permitted to offer nonstandard plans if they wished. Importantly, Counihan invested in developing an online savings calculator that enabled visitors to the AccessHealth CT website to plug in some basic financial and demographic information and figure out which policy was right for them. In this way, the consumer was enabled to make an educated choice rather than guess which policy to buy or, worse, leave the exchange website confused and frustrated without making a purchase. Simply put, to achieve a positive outcome, health insurers or possibly a third-party company must be able and willing to present the information in a consumer-friendly way.

Other measurements could be collected by consumers after their actual experience. The specific questions should reflect those issues of concern to prospective customers and that can also be influenced by the insurer. A brief question at the time a bill is submitted can determine if a patient is surprised; the resulting percentage can reflect how well informed the patients, and their doctors, are about their coverage.

Measuring Consumer Service and Satisfaction

By the beginning of the millennium, experts were promoting more patient-centered approaches to care. This led to the use of many types of patient surveys, probing their experience. The CMS has begun to incorporate standardized patient experience metrics into its reimbursement rating schemes. For example, the CMS introduced the Value Based Purchasing (VBP) program, which was created under the ACA to encourage hospitals to provide more efficient, high-quality care.[14] This initiative required hospitals to use the Hospital Consumer Assessment of Healthcare Providers and Systems (HCAHPS) survey.[15] This standardized survey, started in 2006, is sent to a random sample of discharged patients; it asks them about their experience in the hospital over nine areas important to the consumer experience, ranging from communication with staff to the physical environment. The HCAHPS survey enables comparisons between hospitals on factors important to consumers.[16] Prior to the development of the survey, many hospitals collected information on patient satisfaction, but there was no national standard for reporting it.[17]

More recently, an exciting movement to use patient reported outcomes (PROs) has begun to emerge.[18] This approach surveys patients to determine the degree to which the desired outcomes of their intervention have been achieved. Metrics are chosen from a variety of specific domains corresponding with patients' functional outcomes, such as pain, mobility, depression, and quality of life. PROs have been shown in specific cases to be of value, and their applicability today is steadily moving from research to operational use.[19]

Developing Metrics

Insurers should take the lead in metrics development and consumer information. The industry could undertake the work to standardize and codify these processes and agree to create consumer-friendly performance scorecards. It is in their interest to do so; if they do not, governments at the state and federal levels will determine what is to be measured and will take over a role best suited to insurers, for whom performance measurement of their clinical suppliers is essential to their mission.

Clinical providers should be part of the measurement solution. Externally imposed measures have produced little useful improvement in outcomes measurement, added workload, and have prompted much pushback from doctors. Supported by payers, insurers should ask doctors themselves to help figure out what to measure. Insurers should encourage, or even require, them to participate and reward those who do so.

Meanwhile, we should be grateful that most patients trust their doctors and the medical care system.[20] This gives us time to develop the best ways to measure important elements of consumer value. Secular trends in improving interoperability of EMRs, experience with user feedback from other industries, increasing consumer choice that stimulates research, sophisticated analytic tools, and an increasing body of research results now make the environment a better one in which to learn what to measure.

It is good news for consumer-oriented performance measurement that PCPs are increasingly joining organized practice groups (80% of PCPs now practice in groups of more than four).[21] These can be free-standing, part of an integrated care delivery network like Kaiser-Permanente, vertically integrated hospitals, or accountable care organizations (ACOs). First, such organizations can be held responsible for assessing how their doctors, individually and collectively, are doing. The capacity for direct performance measurement is greater in organized groups than for individual doctors or small practices. Local measurement with peer involvement has the advantage of being formative (it helps mitigate problems and leads to learning and improvement) rather than being merely summative or judgmental (as in pay for performance done on data alone). Furthermore, doctors often complain that what is measured is neither what they spend most of their time doing nor what is most important to their effectiveness. Peer assessment remains the best way to assess the knowledge, skills, and attitudes of individual doctors. Finally, by working together, larger groups can aggregate data so that random variation has less effect, so trends and important differences can attain statistical significance. These more reliable data measurements make it easier for such groups to report their performance; consumers can feel reassured that the basics of medical performance are being measured and managed when they obtain care from an "accountable," integrated, group.

For metrics to help consumers make good choices, both consumers and the doctors must trust the data. Yet the past performance of healthcare measurement has left the public doubting its value. Consumers often encounter claims of comparative performance that are not based on trustworthy evidence.[22] The public seems to expect that insurers, with the help of provider groups, are in the best position to measure how they are doing and to vouchsafe that their providers have met threshold standards of clinical care.

Information Transparency

Consumers must find it easy to access objective, comparable information regarding the different choices available in the market. Critically, a supplier's success or failure must be quickly accessible and easily understood by consumers and producers.

Consumers facing a choice need information if they are to make good decisions. That information must be user-friendly and, even then, consumers may need education and help. They need measures of insurer and provider performance, as we have described, and they should be able to access their own medical records. A market that does not educate and inform the consumer will struggle to promote consumer choice. To optimize consumer decisions, this information, including data down to individual clinicians, should be collected, measured, and made transparent. Enhancing access to data that are specific to the individual consumer is particularly important.

This requirement goes one step beyond that of relevant metrics. It is not enough to simply measure performance; the system must make good use of the data and make it available to and usable by consumers when they are making choices. Though information transparency has increased in healthcare, two notable challenges remain. First, consumers lack an aggregated source of comparative information for decision-making. And, second, it is hard to access their own records.

Aggregated Information

Healthcare lacks an aggregated resource where consumers can find information on the wide range of variables important to their decisions (e.g., price, quality, experience, physician bedside manner). Such comparative services do exist in other markets. Consider TripAdvisor, which demonstrates the reach and power of recommendation services for consumers. It has become the world's largest travel site with 340 million unique monthly visitors and 350 million online reviews covering 6.5 million hotels, restaurants, and attractions.

There is no widespread informational service hub comparable to TripAdvisor in the medical world. This is primarily because medical care presents daunting challenges not faced when assessing travel services. For illustration, we will consider the challenges around comparator sites for physicians, although many of these same challenges exist in the health insurance market and for other healthcare businesses. Beyond checking public records for malpractice judgments and fines against doctors, consumers can visit sites like Health Grades, ZocDoc, and RateMDs; however, some of these sites are struggling to develop critical mass.

Although many studies measure components of the healthcare system, few have developed how to aggregate these into a meaningful, consumer-oriented comparative scorecard nor measured the psychometrics of the measures (validity, reliability, predictive capacity, etc.). One such proposal defined the problem and organized a framework based on the Institute of Medicine's (IOM) six domains of quality. In this proposal, the authors argued that "consumers care about the quality of medical care but do not pay attention to currently available quality information or use it to make more informed health care choices." In their view, we need to "help consumers understand the overall concept of quality and the different elements that make up quality of care."[23] Using the six IOM domains, the authors constructed a framework for "understanding, measuring, and evaluating the quality of medical care." Through focus groups, they determined the performance information that consumers considered to be most useful when selecting a doctor.[24] Their findings suggested that the broader framework helped patients to determine the quality of information that would be useful in assessing their options.

Others argue that an aggregate scorecard is not helpful. Instead, they propose organizing metrics around individual patient profiles to make them more useful to consumers, who want to know "who and what is best for my own health conditions."[25]

Direct Consumer Feedback

What is holding back the growth of TripAdvisor-style review sites for the likes of PCPs, pediatricians, heart surgeons, psychiatrists and other clinicians involved in healthcare delivery? We propose seven key impediments to their use in health-care. While some of these barriers can be overcome by better designed survey methodologies, others are structural and intractable.

Inertia

Patients are accustomed to, and accepting of, being told what to do by providers of care and payers. Therefore, consumer empowerment in healthcare is not as advanced as in other industries such as travel and financial services. Furthermore, doctors are doing well. They are dubious about the value of patient feedback and not much interested in hearing about their success and failure rates. They regard gathering such data as a poor use of their time. There is also concern that doctors might avoid difficult patients to boost their ratings.

Privacy Concerns

Rating a doctor is more personal than rating a hotel, where the efforts of many staff combine to determine overall consumer satisfaction. Hotels can perhaps be evaluated more dispassionately. In addition, rating doctors may require the reviewers to refer to details of their own conditions and/or treatments, which could make them readily identifiable.

Compromised Objectivity

TripAdvisor feedback is spontaneous rather than systematic. In many cases, they develop relationships with their caregivers that render their reviews idiosyncratic. Comments thus reflect the selection bias of those with strong feelings, thus compromising the objectivity of the aggregate measurements and limiting their credibility and usefulness to doctors or patients to what can be learned primarily from anecdotal comments.

Small Samples

The efficiency and validity of consumers' hotel comments are enhanced by multiple reviews aggregated from the wisdom of global crowds. Evaluations of a single large hotel are generated from a base of hundreds of transactions with new customers every day. Most individual healthcare providers generate far fewer transactions. Health plans with multiple providers have a larger base of transactions and may generate more valid information.

Few Comparables

Many business travelers stay in more than 20 hotels each year. They develop a smart shopping expertise that enables them to write insightful reviews. Each stay is a separate transaction. Patients do not have contact with many doctors in the same specialty and therefore cannot easily compare their experiences.

Fear of Reprisal

Hotel reviews are reasonably anonymous. Hotel customers need never return to the same hotel again. In the case of doctors, however, patients may need to see them repeatedly. If reviews are sufficiently detailed to be useful, the patient may be identifiable. They may fear that negative reviews may damage their relationship with their doctor.

Physician Resistance

Doctors are at best ambivalent about the value of physician-rating web sites. Many question the validity of this approach for many of the methodologic reasons noted above. Without doctors trusting the feedback and knowing how to interpret and use it, they will find ways to discourage its use or ignore what might be useful information that could help them improve. Sabin,[26] a psychiatrist and medical ethicist, argues the pros and cons of internet rating sites and concludes that "Online rating systems can be a thorn in our sides, but they are not going away, and we physicians will have to learn to live with them." His recommendation encourages doctors and their professional organizations to strengthen the methodologies, study how best to utilize the available information, and disseminate best practices.

Potential Opportunities

Do some clinical specialties lend themselves more than others to online review sites? The early experience with patient reported outcomes suggests that the more standardized the work, the more that reviews can be of value. For example, providers doing repetitive surgery such as cataracts, hernia repairs, and joint replacement are good candidates for generating useful reviews. When healthcare services are more personalized and variable, as with primary care, it is harder to standardize and reduce bias.

Nevertheless, as consumers become more empowered, we are likely to see increased efforts to express their opinions about physicians, surgeons, psychiatrists, and other healthcare professionals. Methodologic problems will continue to limit the validity of individual doctor feedback. It is prudent, at this early stage, to hope that reviews will be of use primarily in pointing out strengths, weaknesses, and opportunities for change. They may be helpful in formative assessment, in which feedback is used for teaching and improvement. The use of nonsystematic reviews for summative assessment—final judgments about hiring, firing, rewarding, or accrediting individuals—are currently more problematic.

But getting to scale with enough reviews to earn consumer trust is the key challenge for such feedback. In any geography or medical specialty, there must be enough doctors being reviewed by consumers for the overall ratings to carry credibility as "the wisdom of crowds." The number of hotel night stayovers far exceeds the number of visits to an individual doctor. The same chicken-and-egg issue faces all website developers: you need consumers to submit reviews, but you need reviews from which they benefit to persuade them to reciprocate by adding reviews themselves.

Transparency and Patient Records

The Health Information Technology for Economic and Clinical Health (HITECH) Act of 2009 promoted the adoption and meaningful use of EMRs. By 2015, 83% of U.S. hospitals had at least a basic EHR, a marked increase compared to 2008, when only 9% had one.[27] These figures demonstrate the fast growth and adoption of EMR technology among health delivery providers.

Although electronic record systems were adopted quickly, methods of communicating across systems and data bases have been slower to develop. Interoperability issues make it difficult for provider organizations and insurers to interact and share data with one another and, even more so, to provide integrated medical data to individual patients. Most EMRs have been closed systems, which is reassuring to those with privacy concerns, but also hinders efforts to share data across sites of care. This means that despite filling out a medical history form the last five times you have visited a physician, you will be asked to fill out another for each new physician you visit unless your care is in an electronically integrated plan. Each organization typically has its own patient portal, which doesn't communicate with other organizations. To be sure, regulators are forcing EMRs to develop inter-operability capabilities for a set of limited, but basic data; progress is being made, albeit slowly.

Most doctors are not satisfied with electronic records either. The available EMRs are hard to use, expensive, and inefficient; using them steals time from di-rect patient care. Surveys indicate that most physicians believe EMRs have the potential to improve the quality of care; however, today, their EMR is a leading source of physician dissatisfaction because of "poor usability, time-consuming data entry, interference with face-to-face patient care, inefficient and less fulfilling work content, inability to exchange health information, and degradation of clinical documentation."[28,29]

Moreover, increasing consumers' access to their own medical records remains a major challenge. According to the Office of the National Coordinator for Health Information Technology, 63% of office-based physicians had an EMR system ca-pable of enabling patients to view their medical records electronically. Yet only 41% of office-based physicians had an EMR that allowed patients to download their medical records, and a meager 19% had a system that enabled patients to send their medical record electronically to a third party. Most notably, only 16% of all physicians had EMRs that provided all three functionalities to patients—viewing, downloading, and transmitting their records.[30]

EMRs have fallen far short of making data available to individual patients. Theoretically, an electronic record of health and the use of medical services should enhance transparency. A primary care doctor's EMR holds much but certainly not all of the data on a consumer's health experience. Other sources include data from outside hospital and doctor visits, insurance transactions, pharmacy records, glucometers, and Fitbits.

Many problems block the EMR from functioning as an adequate patient record. These include the following: multiple electronic databases for a patient are not interoperable; medical information, other than tests and treatment choices, is recorded with minimal standardization and codification; and they are a record mostly for doctors, so the concepts and terms are difficult for consumers to understand.

To underscore the potential importance of consumer-focused records, consider the functionality of online and mobile banking services. Many of us regularly use electronic banking to monitor our accounts, make deposits or withdrawals, and easily transfer funds. Imagine how this experience might change if it were like your digital medical record. In this hypothetical scenario, the bank would keep track of your account information in a closed electronic system that does not communicate with other banks. If you wanted access to your personal banking record, you must request a paper copy of it. In addition, once you receive your record, the information is largely organized in a way that only makes sense to bankers; to the average person with a bit of personal banking knowledge, it is difficult to decipher. Despite the absurdity of this situation, this is the status quo in healthcare. Consumers do not have an easy way to access their records. When they are able to obtain them, consumers often find them difficult to comprehend.

This process is slowly beginning to change. We know that many clinical providers have implemented patient portals to give consumers access to their medical records. Some have even gone a step further—giving patients access to their physicians' notes online once they are back in the comfort of their home. This may not only jog a consumer's memory but also gives him or her access to the insights and thoughts behind the physician's prescriptions.

A comprehensive medical record that travels with the patient could solve a lot of current problems. Medical errors and clinical confusion could be reduced. Because of interoperability problems, new providers (if you move to another city, for example) cannot automatically access your medical records when you seek care. Say that you are highly allergic to the antibiotic penicillin. You have known this since you were 6 years old and have had to repeat it to every healthcare provider you have ever encountered. You have listed it on doctor's office forms, as well as the countless health forms you have filled out for other organizations, such as your school or employer. Your doctor at home would never give you penicillin because it is flagged that you are allergic. Unfortunately, you develop a high fever while traveling and finally drag yourself into an urgent care center, toxic and tired. The doctors there decide to start you on broad-spectrum antibiotics. In this confusion, you forget to mention that you are allergic to penicillin. The center does not have access to your medical records. Serious problems are bound to follow.

If consolidated medical records were accessible and their use under the control of the consumer, coordination of care would improve. Our current, disparate way of organizing records hinders the ability of individuals to navigate outside the system, make outside medical appointments, transfer records from one organization to another, or sign up for new health insurance plans. Having a copy, or control over your own records, would make it easier to go to a new physician and seek a second opinion. Moreover, having access to your billing records would enable you to check for accuracy and dispute charges.

Supported by RWJF in 2010, researchers undertook a year-long trial of the OpenNotes program, in which 105 doctors shared their records with more than 19,000 patients at three separate health systems across the country.[31] They found that when patients had access to their physicians' notes, they not only felt more in control but also achieved a better understanding of their health condition. They were more likely to adhere to their medications. Although patient support for the program prior to its rollout was high, many physicians had significant concerns; however, none of the physicians in the study stopped sharing visit notes with their patients once the study ended. With the positive response, the movement to share notes has grown beyond the three centers originally studied. Dr. Alistair Erskine, chief informatics officer with Geisinger Health System—one of the systems to start sharing notes as part of the pilot study—discussed how the technical aspects of sharing notes is easy, but "far and away the bulk of the work was around convincing people and holding the provider's hand that the sky wasn't going to fall, and letting them know this is actually a good thing in terms of helping the patient understand what they had said in the clinic."[32]

Despite such efforts and ever-increasing data on healthcare consumers, there is no way of organizing it into a manageable data set for each person. For example, you might wear a Fitbit or Apple Watch, collecting information on your daily fitness level. This information largely stays with you, unless you choose to share it with your social network. The consumer world of technology and data in healthcare is often separate from that of providers or insurers. Complete medical and billing records primarily reside with the organizations that deliver and pay for healthcare services. Each delivery provider you go to maintains your clinical records, while insurers track billing. Your physician or hospital network might have your EMR, but this is not necessarily available to you without your requesting it. The patient portal that you have access to may not include the same information as the EMR, since most do not include physicians' notes.

For years, many in healthcare have articulated the importance of a consumer-facing digital health record. Why is this important? At the most fundamental level, if consumers owned a consolidated medical record of all their care, it could be shared. The personal record would enable providers, families, and the consumers themselves to coordinate, integrate, and manage their care and transitions across different providers and episodes of illness. Errors could be prevented or mitigated. Furthermore, if there were a consumer-oriented record that they could understand (not the technically complicated but necessary doctor-oriented medical record), consumers would be better educated, informed, and more empowered.

Another possible advantage of a consumer-facing digital record would be the empowerment of consumers, and the reduction of consumers' lock-in and dependence on their existing providers and health insurers. One could argue that lack of interoperability is a fundamental barrier to consumer choice and inhibits market forces. Markets work when consumers have readily available alternatives. If the costs of switching to another supplier are high, a consumer's probability of choosing to change suppliers diminishes substantially. When consumers cannot take their records with them, they are obliged to continue visiting the same provider or groups (which is good for health system business).

Finally, if each consumer "owned" a copy of his comprehensive medical record in a distributed system, risks from cyberattacks could be reduced. Trusting an organization with your medical records may be unwise. In May 2017, the National Health Service (NHS) in England was hacked, creating a situation in which millions of medical records were rendered inaccessible.[33]

Each consumer deserves the chance to understand his or her own medical history. For this to happen, the consumer-centered record should include an easily readable, narrative summary of the consumer's health and illness in lay language. The more consumers understand about their health and healthcare, the more confident and effective they will be in making choices.

Electronic medical records are currently neither consumer nor patient-centered. Rather, they are primarily designed to serve doctors and insurers, even though doubts persist about how well today's EMRs do so. We should focus more of our attention on creating a medical record that a patient owns, can access easily, and controls. Consider how outcomes might be different if each patient had a thumb drive dangling around her neck with patient medical information, including major medical conditions, primary care provider, and allergies. Medical errors might be reduced. In reality, thumb drives are being replaced by cloud storage, but this example points out that a basic consumer-facing record need not be complicated or high-tech.

Creating a consumer-facing digital record involves some notable challenges—among them, trustworthiness, accuracy, reliability, and accessibility. Again, consider how you use online or mobile banking services. You are not necessarily using them every day, but you trust that when you want to access them, your information will be accurate, up-to-date, and presented in an organized format. The same logic applies in healthcare. Most of the time, you probably do not want to think about, or spend time organizing, your medical records. However, when you are suddenly ill, being able to access your medical records easily in an organized format can be invaluable.

How do we go about creating this consumer-facing digital health record? First, provider organizations must overcome their reluctance to establish an open digital relationship with patients. Doctors have many concerns ranging from fear of malpractice, to risks of patient misinterpretation, to threats of privacy. Privacy protection is an important standard to uphold, but it should not be an excuse for withholding a patient's record. Second, there must be an organization to aggregate the records. This might be a healthcare delivery organization or an insurer, or it might be a third party, like Google or another technology company. One of the largest challenges will be pulling together islands of data from different types of software systems and databases. Developing new technologies to share useful information among key stakeholders—including consumers—will enhance the power of potential partnerships.

Some efforts already point toward solutions. Consider how TeamPatient, a digital health startup, is taking on this complex challenge. Unlike many other coordination programs that focus solely on connecting providers to one another, TeamPatient is centered on the patient. Its platform not only engages the patient using straightforward, easy-to-understand communication methods but also gives the patient control over who can access his or her medical records. Initially, the company has focused on geriatric patients with chronic, lifelong conditions who need a great deal of home-based care. These patients are often difficult for health plans to manage. They are in contact with many different care providers, which ultimately makes it more difficult to consolidate their information.

TeamPatient has begun implementation with one large health system client in New Jersey. As a regional hospital that pulls patients from a large surrounding area, the health system has 27,000 ER visits yearly from geriatric patients. This entire group of patients is managed by about 25 care coordinators—physicians who focus solely on managing transitions of care. When a geriatric patient ends up in the ER, he spends an average of 18 hours in observation before he is either released or admitted into the hospital. During observation, the patient decides whether to join the TeamPatient program, at which time the cloud-based platform begins aggregating his data. The patient, or designated caregiver, gives others on the "patient team" (the patient's circle of family, friends, and healthcare providers) access to view and edit the data.

The platform also organizes tasks, disseminates information, and provides notifications for both medical and nonmedical needs. Geriatric patients often have multiple conditions managed by different specialists, many of whom are involved in follow-up care. This challenge is compounded because many patients have difficulty remembering physicians' instructions or the medications they are supposed to take. Most reporting systems give patients a written discharge report with follow-up instructions. These are often complex and not patient-friendly. Instead of relying only on written communication, the TeamPatient platform enables physicians and caregivers to record conversations and follow-up instructions. Patients and their caregivers can listen to these recordings through their phones once they are at home or in a post-acute setting. A healthcare provider who is given access can schedule tasks for the patient and issue reminders that prompt the patient to complete them. For example, a patient with a joint replacement might be reminded during the day to elevate her knee.

This digital support system addresses several well-known barriers to continuity in geriatric care management today, while still allowing the patient to choose whether to follow the instructions. As the geriatric population grows, many more institutions will need to develop digital services that integrate multifaceted medical and nonmedical care needs. By placing the patient in the center—and in the driver's seat—and connecting the patient with her team, providers can substantially simplify the disjointed process that currently exists. Finally, because patient information is entirely in one place online, TeamPatient may be able to understand care processes better over time and across sites of care for patients with chronic diseases.

Consolidating an individual's medical information into one document has proved challenging. Almost a decade ago, Google ventured to fill this need by offering Google Health, a platform for consumers to consolidate and organize their disparate health information. Google, a company known for disrupting, changing, and improving the way things are done, shut its health business down after 3 years because of low consumer use.[34] Why did it fail? First, Google Health was too early to the game. Consumers were not yet ready to take a leadership role in organizing their records; they were still acclimatizing to the introduction of digital technology in healthcare, which was far behind other industries. Second, Google Health did a poor job of digitally connecting consumers to physicians' offices. Third, Google Health did not adequately show consumers what they could do with their stored information.[35]

Which healthcare stakeholder is best suited to aggregate and organize consumer medical records? In 2017, our team conducted a representative survey in Massachusetts with MassInsight and Opinion Dynamics. We asked 450 consumers: Which organizations would you most trust to organize and hold a complete set of your medical records—records that would be available to you as well? Their responses are given in Figure 3.1.

Health insurers came out on top, with 61% of the consumers stating that they would trust them to organize their medical records. Local hospitals came in a close second, with 47% of consumers. There may also be a place for a third-party aggregator to work with health insurers or hospitals to provide data storage and organization solutions. Google Health's experience taught us that this third-party aggregator will need to interface seamlessly with providers and insurers.

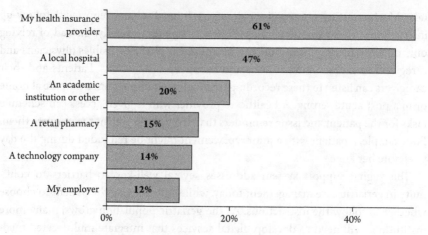

Figure 3.1 Which organizations would consumers trust with their medical records? Source: Data from MassInsight / Opinion Dynamics Survey, Spring 2017.

Insurers are in the best position to organize healthcare information. They already own financial and clinical information that is consolidated around each individual. The industry could standardize and codify these inputs, create methods to consolidate the information, and help consumers use it to exercise the choice available to them. This process would also facilitate the development of meaningful metrics and consumer-friendly performance scorecards.

A range of data solutions will likely be necessary to address the variation in consumer needs in the marketplace. We may see solutions come from traditional healthcare stakeholders, as well as from newcomers. Some consumers will need significant support aggregating and organizing their records, while others will be capable of compiling records on their own. Some consumers simply have a greater number of health needs and will want to integrate the information and access it frequently. Additional consumer research is necessary to understand the range of consumer needs in this arena.

Consumer Protections

A well-functioning consumer market assures safety, accessibility, and quality to its users. In addition, it protects consumers from fraudulent actors who might persuade them to select poor choices.

Government Regulation

Government has an important role to play in facilitating consumer choice. Healthcare policies regarding delivery and financing, regulation and taxation, are the most important determinants of our healthcare system and are central to the architecture of key participants such as Medicaid, Medicare, and commercial insurance.

Government regulation should serve four important roles in a consumer choice healthcare market: (1) consumer protection; (2) consumer access; (3) assuring fair competition; and (4) protecting the financial integrity of collective insurance. Speaking to the first role of government regulation, when patients are enabled to make choices, they are exposed to the risk of being hurt or hurting themselves. Government regulation can reduce this risk; not all businesses or individuals can be trusted. The government must continue to watch for market abuses or dangerous medical care that take advantage of unsuspecting consumers. For example, the Food and Drug Administration (FDA) exists to protect consumers from medications that might harm them. Someone who has an untreatable cancer might try an unsubstantiated treatment he may have found online. Regulations exist to protect this person against a treatment that might do more harm than good. Government supports caregiver standards by requiring certification of technical competence through such mechanisms as licensing, testing, and accreditation. Government should protect against the misuse of dangerous substances, which it does for narcotics by requiring that prescriptions can only be written by federally authorized doctors. As consumer empowerment grows in healthcare and other sectors, it will increase the pressure for consumer protection.

Second, accessibility to care, as we argued in Chapter 2, is a key responsibility of government. If care is neither affordable nor otherwise accessible, an individual has no choice as a practical matter; government must subsidize access. One of the most important characteristics of our system is how it treats citizens who cannot afford to pay for insurance. Our current ambivalence about access to care exists because our political leadership is split. The good news is that policies can change through our political process, ultimately through the politicians that our public sends to Washington. When we develop a national viewpoint about the structure, function, and accessibility for all, change is more likely.

Third, we have assigned to government the responsibility of assuring fair competition. Choice thrives when competition is robust. In healthcare, the restraint of trade issue is of growing importance. Health systems, for example, are vertically integrating, as well as enlarging their market shares locally through mergers and acquisitions. Several delivery systems have grown to be so dominant that insurers cannot drop them, thus enabling them to demand higher reimbursements in rate negotiations. Any single or dominant provider undermines competition and causes cost increases. Monitoring and regulatory interventions remain an important government function.

Finally, governments need to assure the fiscal integrity of insurance pools. Regulation defining adequate financial reserves is one avenue to provide this protection. For those advocating more active approaches, government can promote healthy behaviors and protect against bad ones, as they do with seatbelt use laws.

For the government to deliver any of these four or other goals, it must legislate more effectively. Collaboration among factions of policy makers in Washington must increase. A polarizing political climate has meant that tensions in health-care often fall along partisan lines. New ideas are opposed simply because of who presents them and which party they come from. This even extends to individuals; for example, we know that while overall consumer opinions on the Affordable Care Act often parallel political party preferences, even while many of its individual provisions receive bipartisan support.[36,37]

Expert Protection: The Trusted Advisor Role

When consumers lack clinical knowledge, those who must make important medical choices may need the help of experts. Decisions such as these are difficult for consumers to make alone. Fortunately, many of these choices occur when there is sufficient time to get help to make an informed choice. There are ways to support consumers across the care continuum to ensure that they are adequately informed and advised about decisions they face. Traditionally, this has been a role filled by physicians. More recently web sites can provide some good information to those sophisticated enough to understand and to know if their sources are trustworthy.

Doctors are familiar with this advising process. For years, surgeons have been required to ask for informed consent, wherein benefits and risks are explained prior to a surgical procedure. Although it is often challenging to predict and explain personal benefits and risks of recommended care, primary care doctors already do a good bit of this counseling. The idea of shared decision-making has gained prominence in recent years, although this is often more a goal than an established process. A good example is the way that a PCP presents the option of the prostatic screening antigen (PSA) test to a male patient. The decision about whether to do the test or not depends on personal preferences, and it is the responsibility of the PCP to explain and predict benefits and risks to the patient so that he can make a good personal choice.

This decision-making challenge is becoming more complex today. In this era of high deductibles, patients face a new twist. Now many patients need to pay a lot out-of-pocket to access the care, so the discussion today has broadened to include their cost and ability to pay. Rising deductibles are a financial barrier to care forcing patients to choose whether to pay for a referral to a specialist, use an expensive drug, go to the hospital, or undergo an expensive procedure. They, or someone else, are forced to make decisions about whether the benefit to them is worth the personal cost in money as well as medical risks and benefits.

Like most consumers, patients now face a typical buying decision where their financial costs must be weighed against the putative benefits and risks based on the underlying condition and circumstances of the individual. Patients cannot easily make these medical judgments on their own, especially now that money is a factor. This advice is still best given by a personal physician. We believe that PCPs are especially well positioned and prepared to serve as the "trusted advisor" with regard to decisions consumers must make about costs and benefits of care. They understand the technical issues, know the patient well, and have earned the trust of patients to interpret and explain the risks and benefits to them. Efficiency concerns might suggest that advising be delegated to others; perhaps this role could be filled, for simple decisions, by nurses, lay advisors, or even, sometime soon, predictive algorithms. But as care choices become more complicated, the expertise of a doctor is usually needed more than ever.

Patients should feel that the advice is trustworthy. For that reason, we believe that a financially unbiased doctor or nurse should be prepared to serve as a trusted advisor to his or her patient, especially when the proposed services will be performed by a specialist or hospital that has a financial interest in pushing the patient to "buy" their recommendations. The trusted advisor role has risen in importance now that patients become consumers who face a financial hurdle to access care. Now more than ever patients need a trusted expert guide by their side who knows them and helps them understand their choices.

Balanced Incentives

Any well-functioning consumer market appropriately recognizes and rewards both consumers for participating in the system and making good choices, and suppliers for offering superior products and performance.

In giving consumers more choice, there is the risk that they will make poor decisions. This is a problem—both for individuals and for the collective healthcare system. And while aggregating information and giving people access to their own records are critical for creating a consumer marketplace, having access to accurate information often is not enough to motivate consumer or supplier behavior change. This is where incentives come in. Using incentives in a consumer marketplace can encourage consumers and providers of services to make good decisions for themselves and make their healthcare system work better. In their book *Nudge*, Richard Thaler and Cass Sunstein suggest using the term "libertarian paternalism," which they define as the following:

> Libertarian paternalism is a relatively weak, soft, and nonintrusive type of paternalism because choices are not blocked, fenced off, or significantly burdened. . . . Rather [private and public choice architects] are self-consciously attempting to move people in directions that will make their lives better. They nudge.[38]

Incentives are inducements that motivate behaviors or actions. Although money is usually the first thing that comes to mind, there are many other types of inducements ranging from social pressures, such as recognition and stigmatization, all the way up to intrinsic satisfaction. Incentives in a consumer marketplace can encourage consumers to be active and productive decision-makers themselves. We can use these nudges and incentives to motivate consumers to make decisions that improve their own health and the function of the insurance collective.

We can also use system-wide incentives on the supply side to reward suppliers for delivering higher value products. Reducing supply-side incentives that dampen consumer choice can also mobilize consumers. Today, in healthcare, incentives on both the supply and demand side are broken. However, there is a good reason to believe that with additional experimentation and research, this could change for the better. We will take a closer look at the role of both consumer and supplier incentives in healthcare.

Consumer Incentives

Consumers of healthcare are not optimally incentivized today. This is not surprising, since most policy efforts have focused on changing supply-side incentives. In the consumer realm, we must address several key questions: Does consumer behavior respond to incentives? Which incentives work best for consumers? What types of behavior should the system "nudge?"

Today, rising costs are being passed on to the consumer in the form of co-payments and deductibles. As out-of-pocket costs have risen, consumers are forced to examine their options and to determine what they get for what they can afford to pay. This model, judiciously applied, gives consumers personal financial incentives and can enhance the care and attention they give to healthcare decisions. At too high levels, however, choice disappears. Keeping deductibles in a delimited zone is an important step in using cost to stimulate consumer choice. However, consumers need to be protected from hurting themselves by rejecting services they need because they cannot afford it. Although no one knows exactly the right "financial risk" levels to balance choice and safety, many variations are emerging and experience will help us find the proper tradeoffs.

There is ample evidence that incentives can change consumer behavior. In a 2016 study, researchers implemented an incentive program at elementary schools in which children received a special token each day as a reward for consuming at least one serving of fruits or vegetables. The tokens were worth 25 cents, and the children could spend them at the school store, school carnival, or a book fair. The researchers found that these short-run incentives created healthier eating behavior changes that persisted for months after the incentives were removed, perhaps reflecting habits that had formed, tastes that had changed, or new peer influence that fruits and vegetables were now more "popular" among the children.[39]

The success of the decades-long campaign to reduce smoking is another demonstration of the behavior-modifying power of incentives. The number of adults currently smoking declined from nearly 21 of every 100 adults (20.9%) in 2005 to about 15 of every 100 adults (15.1%) in 2015.[40] Moreover, since the landmark tobacco settlement of 1998, the rates of smoking in middle and high school students have halved. This was achieved through a combination of selective incentive "nudges."[41] Taxation raised the cost of cigarettes; cigarette advertising was banned; public advertising and federally mandated package labeling warned of the risks associated with smoking; employers provided services to help smokers quit because it would reduce their costs and increase productivity; doctors were financially rewarded for actions to facilitate quitting; and activists managed to change laws so smoking was banned in restaurants and public places. Smokers were effectively stigmatized.

Yet there is much evidence and experience that changing consumer behavior is not easy. Simply having information on what is healthier is not always enough to create behavior change. Let us consider something as simple as healthy eating habits. Even when people have access to information about what is healthier, they do not necessarily choose the healthier option. For example, when restaurants began to post caloric information along with recommended calorie intake on restaurant menus, there was no evidence that consumers changed their ordering decisions to healthier options; in fact, researchers documented a slight increase in caloric intake.[42]

Although a 25-cent token likely will not create lasting behavior change among adults, as it did among children in the aforementioned study, financial incentives are often used by employers to motivate employees to adopt healthy behaviors. In 2015, more than 80% of U.S. employers offered an employee wellness program as a benefit to help employees lose weight, improve chronic health conditions, stop smoking, or make other healthy lifestyle modifications.[43] Employers often use incentives to encourage eligible employees to take part in workplace wellness programs. In 2014, one study found that the employee participation rate for employers that did not use incentives was around 20%, while employers who used rewards had a 40% participation rate, and employers who used penalties and/or rewards had a 73% participation rate.[44] In 2015, The Institute for Health and Productivity Studies at the Johns Hopkins Bloomberg School of Public Health collaborated with the Transamerica Center for Health Studies to explore, among other things, which incentives were most likely to change employees' behaviors in a cost-effective way. Although many programs provide some type of incentive, the Institute's findings indicated that it was important to provide positive, visible rewards related to health.[45]

Employers are not the only ones focused on using financial incentives to change consumer behavior. Health insurers use financial incentives to alter demand for some medical services. As we have mentioned repeatedly, health insurers are increasingly using high-deductible health plans and other cost-sharing mechanisms to give consumers reasons to be prudent about utilization. These changes are largely motivated by the desire of both employers and insurers to reduce their burden of the bills and to encourage consumers to take more active roles in their care (and, ultimately, to shop for less expensive services). However, we have since learned that consumers can make poor decisions when it comes to price shopping for medical care by incorrectly understanding the financial risks they were choosing.

Moreover, when care costs money, some consumers may not be able to pay for the treatment they need. Over 30 years ago, a seminal study conducted by the Rand Corporation[46] concluded that low co-payments indeed led to decreases in utilization, but that some patients who were less well-off reduced care that they should have accessed. In the current era in which deductibles have become much higher, researchers have yet to conduct studies to determine how the financial barrier affects care-seeking behavior. Clearly, self-pay is likely to reduce utilization and insurance costs, but will it do so at the cost of a less healthy population?

Careful design of deductibles and co-payments can mitigate some of these risks. Desirable activities like prevention (immunizations) and early detection (such as mammography) can, and are already, covered with minimal co-payments or deductibles. Full coverage of expenses for primary care and generic drugs could facilitate the use of both.

Rising out-of-pocket costs are thus both good news and bad news in this regard. Making patients pay a portion of costs forces them to pay attention. If they bear no costs of care, patients have no reason to act as consumers. Their choice decisions are limited to personal risks and benefits. If costs are too high, consumers may not be able to participate; they lack the means to purchase care, regardless of whether it is necessary. For consumer choice to work to increase value, we will need to find the right level of monetary incentive for each person; like Goldilocks, the incentive must be not too much, not too little, but just right.

By introducing cost-sharing plans, insurers hoped that consumers would become more savvy and cost conscious and shop around for the highest value care. In theory, someone with a high-deductible health plan might take the time to research additional sites of care and find one that delivers the highest quality level at the lowest cost. However, a 2015 study found that when employees were required to switch from an insurance plan that provided free healthcare to a high-deductible health plan, total healthcare spending went down—due entirely to reductions in the *quantity* of care delivered.[47] But these reductions were of both potentially valuable care (e.g., preventive services) and potentially wasteful care (e.g., imaging services). These plans may reduce the overuse of medical care and moderate further premium increases, but they also have the potential to dissuade consumers from accessing necessary care. The researchers also found no evidence that employees were price shopping for care within 2 years of switching to a plan with high-deductible coverage. To date, the little research available suggests that a moderate financial hurdle does not lead to negative impact on health in the specific circumstances that were studied.[48] But it seems that high-deductible plans are a blunt force mechanism for motivating consumers to reduce their medical costs. We have much to learn about which incentives work best.

While financial incentives can be powerful motivators, incentives need not always be monetary. There are other ways in which health insurers, delivery providers, employers, and government actors can motivate consumers to make good choices. Messaging can speak to the emotional biases of consumer decision-making. Consider how this might work in flu vaccinations. We know that many young people skip their yearly flu shots for a variety of reasons. They run out of time to receive the shot, or they feel invincible; maybe they simply fear the pain and annoyance of receiving the shot. Vaccination protects populations through herd immunity; when a large portion of a community is immunized, most members are protected against the disease because there is little opportunity for an outbreak to occur.[49] For younger people with less risk of serious disease, the rationale for vaccination is mostly to protect the elderly or other vulnerable members of the population. Psychologists have demonstrated that there are circumstances under which some altruistic young people will choose to get vaccinated to prevent morbidity and mortality among others.[50] The researchers suggested that incentives for young people could include social responsibility. Healthcare organizations could use incentives such as these to catalyze public health campaigns.

We also know that consumer behavior can be influenced by comparison to peers. Energy companies take advantage of this when they send you a bill comparing your energy use for the month to others on your street. If you used less energy, you probably feel motivated to keep it up. If you used more, you may be moved to cut back, not wanting to underperform in comparison to those around you. In one study, researchers assessed participants' walking behavior via pedometer; participants walked 1,120 more steps per day when they received feedback on how they compared to others than when they received only individual feedback.[51]

The influence of others is not always a positive force. One study showed that when people receive information on the activity levels of others, they tend to converge over time to the lowest-performing members of a group.[52] The discrepancy between these findings and the pedometer study may be explained by how the information was presented or by the timing of the information. Additional research on the effects of comparative information is necessary to determine how it can be most appropriately used to improve public health.

It is important to remember that, for all of these interventions, individual consumers will react differently. In one study on smoking relapses among those trying to quit the habit, researchers showed that certain personality traits made one more likely to restart smoking sooner.[53] These included a lower distress tolerance and greater behavioral disinhibition. Segmenting consumers and offering different incentives for different groups will be likely to lead to more positive outcomes.

For example, we could design various incentive systems aimed at encouraging healthy behaviors, which would help both the individual and the collective insurance pool. In the form of bonuses or reduced charges for good behavior, financial incentives can influence people to eat well and maintain an optimal weight, exercise, take their prescribed medications, and avoid dangerous actions like failing to wear seatbelts.

The use of incentives to positively influence healthy behaviors has been slow to catch on. However, the use of surcharges because of accidents in automobile insurance is widespread and believed to reduce risky behaviors; there is no reason why such incentives would not work in healthcare. We could also allow consumers to share in cost savings generated by their changes in behavior. This approach can be tailored to a specific segment's needs and its willingness or ability to pay. Such innovative types of incentive systems are necessary on the consumer side of the equation, where they are currently lacking. Payers, providers, employers, and government stakeholders must work to understand how to motivate and reward consumers to do what is in their own, as well as in the system's, best interests.

The use of monetary incentives like deductibles has other consequences. First, financial barriers to care inevitably lead to a two-tiered system. Even when basic care is provided to all through subsidies, most countries enable supplemental care to be purchased privately. This is almost unavoidable in countries with market economies and consumer freedom. Many people will want to purchase extra care if they can afford it. Such care, in a properly designed national system, will be of lower benefit/cost than the basic system for all, but it may indeed provide additional benefits. The basic system can cover a lot but, ultimately, it will never be able to keep up with all that research and entrepreneurship will make available in the future to those able to pay.

What behaviors should be targets for change in a consumer choice system of care? Clearly, incentives should first activate consumers to become involved in their care and to start exercising their preferences where they can. Second, incentives should encourage health-enhancing behaviors; this is not only good for the individual but for the collective population in the insurance pool. Third, incentives should stimulate consumer feedback on the services they receive. Finally, perverse incentives that reduce consumer choice and hamper market forces, such as high switching costs and the reluctance of providers to measure performance and improve care should be removed, changed, or mitigated.

Supplier Incentives

Any consumer-oriented market should not only target incentives to consumers but also reward suppliers for delivering higher-value products and services. In 2006, Michael Porter and Elizabeth Teisberg defined "value" in healthcare as the health outcomes achieved per dollar spent.[54] Under this definition, value creation is not a function of either cost-cutting or quality improvement, but where both of these concepts are jointly considered. In a later paper, Porter further described this definition of value and its relationship to the healthcare consumer:

Value should always be defined around the customer, and in a well-functioning health care system, the creation of value for patients should determine the rewards for all other actors in the system. Since value depends on results, not inputs, value in health care is measured by the outcomes achieved, not the volume of services delivered, and shifting focus from volume to value is a central challenge. Nor is value measured by the process of care used; process measurement and improvement are important tactics but are no substitutes for measuring outcomes and costs.[55]

Since this was written, much thought and energy have been spent to find innovative ways to create a system that delivers higher value care. We know that physicians, like consumers, do not always change their behavior simply in response to performance information. For example, a 2017 study of prescribing behavior found that when doctors were shown the Medicare allowable fees in the EMR at the time they placed an order for a test or procedure, they did not significantly change their behavior. The authors of the study concluded that "price transparency alone may not lead to significant changes in clinician behavior, and future price transparency interventions may need to be better targeted, framed, or combined with other approaches."[56] In other words, stronger incentives on the supplier side are necessary to motivate higher value care.

Both government, through the ACA, and private insurers have been using financial incentives to motivate providers to improve value. Public and private payers have engaged in a range of new reimbursement contracts with health delivery providers; these include ACOs, global payment with quality measures, and bundled payment models.[57] These approaches create a fixed target of payment for a specified population under care or for a procedure, such as a knee replacement. If the providers can keep costs below that target, they share in the savings. Prior to the advent of these models, medical payment operated predominantly with fee-for-service (FFS) for visits or procedure-based reimbursement. In the FFS model, physicians and other providers are incentivized to increase the volume of care they deliver. Research has shown that financial incentives motivate physicians to increase healthcare services delivered.[58] As reimbursement rates increase, there are increases in the quantity of care provided. Most of the new contracts seek instead to reward providers for the quality of the care they deliver and their conservatism in expenditures, rather than the quantity of care.

Implementing such contracting is difficult. Some experts have noted that it is important not only to change how medical practices or hospitals are paid but also to change how individual physicians are paid. If practices are paid using value-based contracts, but these practices continue to pay their physicians based on visit volume, large-scale change will be more difficult to foster.[59] Another challenge today is that some delivery providers are operating under FFS for some patients, while simultaneously implementing value-based contracts for others. This is not that surprising, since providers of care typically work with many different payers, and their compensation negotiations with each differ. Further, some service lines are better suited for innovative, value-based payment models. However, this is an important operations issue. Dr. Rushika Fernandopulle, the CEO of Iora Health, a primary care provider network, described this challenge in a blog post, writing, "As long as you do any [fee-for-service], you still need the old coding and administrative systems, and it is very difficult to truly change the processes, technology, and culture."[60]

Reducing disincentives is an important step for providers. Reimbursement barriers are major impediments to consumer choice. An example is visit-based FFS reimbursement for primary care providers, which forces them to increase office visits. Satisfying their patients' needs can often be better done by phone or email, neither of which is now reimbursable. By reducing FFS visit payment incentives, many clinicians and their organizations could restructure to satisfy their patients better by providing more access and quicker resolution of problems, and they could use the freed-up time in the office for clinical and patient journey processes that are truly important.

We believe that there are five major provider impediments that create barriers to a consumer choice marketplace: (1) FFS payment that creates provider barriers to flexible, patient-centered responses to care seeking; (2) malpractice, which heightens defensive medicine and causes overtreatment, subsequently raising costs and potentially hurting patients; (3) constraint of trade that reduces competition and thus innovation (4) fear of and resistance to activated consumers among doctors; and (5) public advertising that encourages overuse of expensive, marginally effective tests and treatments.

These barriers could and should be mitigated or removed. Initial efforts to reduce the first three of these barriers have already begun. FFS is often being replaced in organized provider groups by salary or salary plus small bonuses related to visit volume. Concierge medicine and some ACOs are supplementing FFS with monthly payments for managing care. Bundled payments are a method being experimentally used by the CMS in Medicare. Malpractice reform has been on the table in healthcare reform discussions in 2017. Attorneys General are also worried about acquisitions and mergers that can diminish competition; they are beginning to challenge this threat in the delivery system when there is a concern that market forces will be weakened.

Doctor resistance to consumer choice is not surprising, but it is susceptible to change. The profession has long enjoyed its autonomy and control. However, there is no more powerful incentive than attracting enough business to make a living. If consumer choice is growing and influencing where, when, and from whom patients receive care, then the provider side will likely respond by supplying them with what they want. The stronger the financial incentives, the more doctors will shift toward supporting choice. Money goes with the patients as they exercise their choice; this is a strong incentive for providers to become more responsive in order to attract patients. Even in a system in which provider groups and clinicians are paid a capitation (a monthly sum for each patient who has chosen to be in their practice) rather than FFS, the providers have strong reason to satisfy patients so that they will choose to stay in their practice at the next annual re-enrollment.

Direct incentives could further nudge doctors and reduce resistance. Incentives function best when they make it easiest for a system to do the right things. They should operate in the background, giving a nudge instead of a restrictive regulation or rule.[61] More targeted stimulatory incentives could reward providers for delivering a superior patient journey; these incentives could be measured by systematic or voluntary feedback, which would compare actual patient experience to their expectations about important benefits.

Drug advertising is hurting our system of care by influencing the public towards new and more expensive medicines whose benefits, in many cases are small or even unproven. For example, new cancer drugs are being advertised even though most have not demonstrated significant survival benefits. Banning cigarette advertising has contributed to reductions in smoking; if we want to reduce the steep upward slope of drug costs, we should either ban or tightly regulate their public advertising.

It is clear that our system is just beginning to make the changes necessary to incentivize higher value on the supplier side. Beyond simply defining what success— or higher value—looks like in the healthcare market, we must rigorously measure it and hold suppliers accountable to meeting objectives. If suppliers do not provide higher value services, there must be real consequences in the market. Only then will provider organizations and individual physicians feel the push to provide higher quality and lower cost care.

Aligning Consumer and Supplier Incentives

Some strategies, such as reference pricing, seek to align incentives for consumers and suppliers. Under a reference pricing arrangement, the payer limits what it will contribute financially for a given procedure. The payment limit typically falls around the midpoint price in the local market, so that consumers can still access that service. If the consumer chooses a provider charging above the limit, he must pay the entire difference himself. This approach steers consumers to choose higher value providers.

There are both consumer and supplier incentives at play here. Consumers are incentivized to choose a provider whose charges fall under the given limit, while providers must reduce their cost of care to be viable competitors in the market. In practice, this strategy has reduced cost variation in certain markets while maintaining quality standards. In a 2015 blog, Boynton and Robinson highlighted how reference pricing worked to address wide cost variations in their California market:

Prior to the implementation of reference pricing, for example, the prices CalPERS faced ranged from $12,000 to $75,000 for joint replacement surgery, from $1,000 to $6,500 for cataract removal, and from $1,250 to $15,500 for arthroscopy of the knee.... Well-constructed reference pricing offers meaningful choices to consumers and savings to purchasers, with no sacrifice of quality. It helps move health care from a provider-dominated to a consumer-engaged system.[62]

Experts caution that reference pricing only works in healthcare markets where the procedures are shoppable beforehand, as consumers must be able to assess the various options.[63] Further, it doesn't work for emergency situations or conditions where the severity varies substantially and costs are difficult to predict. However, it does highlight that changing both consumer and supplier incentives can maintain quality of care while improving overall value in the system.

We still have much to learn about when incentives work and how to use them in healthcare. However, there is good reason to believe that with additional experimentation, incentives could result in meaningful and lasting change. Removing ineffective or perverse incentives and implementing good ones is a critical step toward making a consumer choice system work.

Conclusion

We believe that if these six enabling conditions are addressed, the environment will become more consumer-oriented. However, achieving system-wide change will require action from stakeholders working together across the healthcare industry—and beyond. This includes traditional healthcare players, such as health delivery organizations, clinicians, payers, retail pharmacies, drug and device manufacturers, and government. But it will also require significant efforts from employers and consumers themselves. Too often, we look at each of these stakeholders individually. We can no longer accept that each of these parties acts independently. Most healthcare solutions will involve multiple stakeholders.

In fairness, integration in healthcare has improved over the last few years. Our healthcare system has become more collaborative and the gulfs between doctor, health system, and health insurance plan have lessened. Vertical integration is occurring; health systems have bought up physician practices in large numbers, and hospital networks are growing. More physicians are employed by healthcare systems today than a decade ago. New payment programs, such as ACOs, are encouraging provider organizations and insurers to work together to develop care management strategies across the care continuum—ultimately improving transitions of care and reducing overall system costs. At the same time, some delivery systems are vertically integrating to become health plans, taking on the risk of insuring their populations from both a provider and payer perspective. In these situations, insurers and providers become one and the same. New sites of care, such as retail clinics in drugstores and urgent care centers, are contracting with health systems in innovative ways to integrate care across the continuum.

Despite these new ties across organizations, individual consumers too often remain unaware and uninvolved. Do you know if your physician group is participating in an ACO or how much of its revenue stream falls under value-based care models? Even as collaborative efforts between provider organizations have increased, the consumer is too often left out of these discussions. It is becoming increasingly clear that we must incorporate the consumer in these system-wide changes. To do so, healthcare stakeholders must embrace a better understanding of the consumer and take the time to understand the consumer decision-making process and what attributes consumers value. In the chapters that follow, we will address these concepts.

References

1. "Jeff Bezos on Leading for the Long-Term at Amazon." *Harvard Business Review*, 30 March 2015. Web.
2. Mangalindan, JP. "Inside Amazon Prime." *Fortune.com. Fortune*, 3 February 2015. Web.
3. Shi, Audrey. "Amazon Prime Members Now Outnumber Non-Prime Customers." *Fortune. com. Fortune*, 11 July 2016. Web.
4. See "Jeff Bezos on Leading for the Long-Term at Amazon." *Harvard Business Review*, 30 March 2015. Web.
5. Wells, John R., Galen Danskin, and Gabriel Ellsworth. *Case Study: Amazon.com, 2016.* Harvard Business Review, 2015. Print.
6. Smith, Aaron. "Amazon Is America's Best Company. Says Who? You!" *CNNMoney*. Cable News Network, 15 June 2015. Web.
7. "Robinhood." *Robinhood—Free Stock Trading*. Web. https://careers.robinhood.com/
8. Ibid.
9. "Robinhood's Best of 2016." *Under the Hood*. Robinhood Blog, 12 January 2017. Web.
10. "CMS Quality Measure Development Plan: Supporting the Transition to the Quality Payment Program." 2017 Annual Report. *Center for Clinical Standards and Quality Centers for Medicare & Medicaid Services (CMS)*. Web.
11. Mcglynn, Elizabeth. A. "Six Challenges in Measuring the Quality of Health Care." *Health Affairs* 16, no. 3 (1997): 7–21. Web.
12. Donabedian, Avedis. "The Quality of Care: How Can It Be Assessed?" *JAMA* 260, no. 12 (1988): 1743–1748. Web.
13. "HEDIS & Performance Measurement." NCQA website. 2017. Web.
14. Department of Health and Human Services: Centers for Medicare and Medicaid Services. "Hospital Value-Based Purchasing." *CMS website*. 2015. Web.
15. Ibid.
16. "HCAHPS Fact Sheet." 2009. Downloaded from hcahpsonline.org. *Hospital Consumer Assessment of Healthcare Providers and Systems*. Web.
17. Ibid.
18. Baumhauer, Judith F. "Patient-Reported Outcomes—Are They Living Up to Their Potential?" *New England Journal of Medicine* 377, no. 1 (2017): 6–9. Web.

19. Rotenstein Lisa, Robert Huckman, and Neil Wagle. "Making Patients and Doctors Happier—The Potential of Patient-Reported Outcomes." *The New England Journal of Medicine* 377, no. 14. (2017): 1309–1312. Web.

20. Harris Poll. in Health Care Sector, Pharma/Biotechnology and Insurance Show Considerable Reputational Risk. January 17, 2017. Web.

21. "2016 Survey of America's Physicians: Practice Patterns & Perspectives." *The Physicians Foundation.* 2016. Web.

22. "Finding Quality Doctors: How Americans Evaluate Provider Quality in the United States: Research Highlights." *APNORC.org.* The University of Chicago, 2014. Web.

23. Hibbard, Judith, and L. Gregory Pawlson. "Why Not Give Consumers a Framework for Understanding Quality?" *The Joint Commission Journal on Quality Improvement* 30, no. 6 (2004): 347–351. Web.

24. Pillittere, Donna, Mary Beth Bigley, Judith Hibbard, and Gregg Pawlson. "Exploring Consumer Perspectives on Good Physician Care: A Summary of Focus Group Results." *The Commonwealth Fund.* January 2003. Web.

25. Mcglynn, Elizabeth A., Eric C. Schneider, and Eve A. Kerr. "Reimagining Quality Measurement." *New England Journal of Medicine* 371, no. 23 (2014): 2150–2153. Web.

26. Sabin, JE. "Physician-Rating Websites." *Virtual Mentor* 15, no. 11 (2013):932–936. http://virtualmentor.ama-assn.org/2013/11/pdf/vm-1311.pdf

27. Henry, JaWanna, Yuriy Pylypchuk, Talisha Searcy, and Vaishali Patel. "Adoption of Electronic Health Record Systems Among U.S. Non-Federal Acute Care Hospitals: 2008–2015." *Dashboard.healthit.gov.* The Office of the National Coordinator for Health Information Technology, May 2016. Web.

28. "Clinician Perspectives on Electronic Health Information Sharing for Transitions of Care." *Bipartisan Policy Center Health Information Technology Initiative.* Bipartisan Policy Center, October 2012. Web.

29. Friedberg, Mark W., Peggy G. Chen, Kristin R. Van Busum, Frances Aunon, Chau Pham, John Caloyeras, Soeren Mattke, Emma Pitchforth, Denise D. Ingram Quigley, Robert H. Brook, F. Jay Crosson, and Michael Tutty. "Factors Affecting Physician Professional Satisfaction and Their Implications for Patient Care, Health Systems, and Health Policy." *RAND Corporation.* 9 October 2013. Web.

30. "Health IT Quick Stats." *Health IT.* The Office of the National Coordinator for Health Information Technology, 3 August 2017. Web.

31. Mende, Susan. "The Next Phase of the OpenNotes Movement." *Culture of Health Blog.* Robert Wood Johnson Foundation, 2 February 2016. Web.

32. Livingston, Shelby. "Doctors Are Starting to Let Patients Read Their Notes." *Modern Healthcare.* 31 December 2016. Web.

33. Erickson, Amanda. "What You Need to Know About the Massive Hack That Hit the British Health-Care System and Elsewhere." *The Washington Post.* WP Company, 12 May 2017. Web.

34. Lohr, Steve. "Google to End Health Records Service After It Fails to Attract Users." *The New York Times.* 24 June 2011. Web.

35. Szczerba, Robert J. "If Google Health Failed, Why Will Your Health Portal Company Succeed?" *Forbes: Tech.* Forbes Magazine, 18 June 2014. Web.

36. "Kaiser Health Tracking Poll: The Public's Views on the ACA." *The Henry J. Kaiser Family Foundation.* 22 September 2017. Web.

37. Jacobs, Lawrence R., and Suzanne Mettler. "Liking Health Reform but Turned Off by Toxic Politics." *Health Affairs.* 1 April 2016. Web.

38. Thaler, Richard H., and Cass R. Sunstein. *Nudge: Improving Decisions About Health, Wealth, and Happiness.* Penguin, 2009. Print. pp. 5–6.

39. Loewenstein, George, Joseph Price, and Kevin Volpp. "Habit Formation in Children: Evidence from Incentives for Healthy Eating." *Journal of Health Economics* 45 (2016): 47–54. Web.

40. "WHO Report on the Global Tobacco Epidemic 2017." *World Health Organization.* 2017. Web.

41. Schroeder, Steven A. "Tobacco Control in the Wake of the 1998 Master Settlement Agreement." *New England Journal of Medicine* 350, no. 3 (2004): 293–301. Web.

42. Downs, Julie S., Jessica Wisdom, Brian Wansink, and George Loewenstein. "Supplementing Menu Labeling With Calorie Recommendations to Test for Facilitation Effects." *American Journal of Public Health* 103, no. 9 (2013): 1604–1609. Web.

43. "2015 Employer Health Benefits Survey—Summary of Findings," *The Henry J. Kaiser Family Foundation*, 22 September 2015. Web.

44. Mattke, Soeren, Kandice Kapinos, John P. Caloyeras, Erin Audrey Taylor, Benjamin Batorsky, Hangsheng Liu, Kristin R. Van Busum, and Sydne Newberry. "Workplace Wellness Programs Services Offered, Participation, and Incentives." *Rand Coporation* (2014): *U.S. Department of Labor*. Employee Benefits Security Administration (EBSA) of the U.S. Department of Labor, 2014. Web.

45. De La Torre, Hector, and Ron Goetzel. "From Evidence to Practice: Workplace Wellness That Works." *Harvard Business Review* (2016): Web.

46. Brook, Robert H. et al. "The Effect of Coinsurance on the Health of Adults: Results From the RAND Health Insurance Experiment." *Rand Health Insurance Experiment Series*, 1984. Web.

47. Brot-Goldberg, Zarek C., Amitabh Chandra, Benjamin R. Handel, and Jonathan T. Kolstad. "What Does a Deductible Do? The Impact of Cost-Sharing on Health Care Prices, Quantities, and Spending Dynamics." *The National Bureau of Economic Research (NBER)*. January 2016. Web.

48. Wharam, J. Frank, Dennis Ross-Degnan, and Meredith B. Rosenthal. "The ACA and High-Deductible Insurance—Strategies for Sharpening a Blunt Instrument." *New England Journal of Medicine* 369, no. 16 (2013): 1481–1484. Web.

49. "Community Immunity ('Herd Immunity')." *Vaccines.gov*. U.S. Department of Health and Human Services, January 2017. Web.

50. Chapman, Gretchen B., Meng Li, Jeffrey Vietri, Yoko Ibuka, David Thomas, Haewon Yoon, and Alison P. Galvani. "Using Game Theory to Examine Incentives in Influenza Vaccination Behavior." *Psychological Science* 23, no. 9 (2012): 1008–1015. Web.

51. Chapman, Gretchen B., Helen Colby, Kimberly Convery, and Elliot J. Coups. "Goals and Social Comparisons Promote Walking Behavior." *Medical Decision Making* 36, no. 4 (2015): 472–478. Web.

52. John, Leslie K., and Michael I. Norton. "Converging to the Lowest Common Denominator in Physical Health." *Health Psychology* 32, no. 9 (2013): 1023–1028. Web.

53. Bold, Krysten W., Haewon Yoon, Gretchen B. Chapman, and Danielle E. Mccarthy. "Factors Predicting Smoking in a Laboratory-Based Smoking-Choice Task." *Experimental and Clinical Psychopharmacology* 21, no. 2 (2013): 133–143. Web.

54. Porter, Michael E., and Elizabeth O. Teisberg. *Redefining Health Care: Creating Value-Based Competition on Results*. Harvard Business School, 2006. Print.

55. Porter, Michael E. "What Is Value in Health Care?" *New England Journal of Medicine*. 23 December 2010. Web.

56. Sedrak, Mina S., Jennifer S. Myers, Dylan S. Small, Irving Nachamkin, Justin B. Ziemba, Dana Murray, Gregory W. Kurtzman, Jingsan Zhu, Wenli Wang, Deborah Mincarelli, Daniel Danoski, Brian P. Wells, Jeffrey S. Berns, Patrick J. Brennan, C. William Hanson, C. Jessica Dine, and Mitesh S. Patel. "Effect of a Price Transparency Intervention in the Electronic Health Record on Clinician Ordering of Inpatient Laboratory Tests." *JAMA Internal Medicine* 177, no. 7 (2017): 939. Web.

57. Song, Zirui, Sherri Rose, Dana G. Safran, Bruce E. Landon, Matthew P. Day, and Michael E. Chernew. "Changes in Health Care Spending and Quality 4 Years Into Global Payment." *New England Journal of Medicine* 371, no. 18 (2014): 1704–1714. Web.

58. Clemens, Jeffrey, and Joshua D. Gottlieb. "Do Physicians' Financial Incentives Affect Medical Treatment and Patient Health?" *The American Economic Review*. U.S. National Library of Medicine, April 2014. Web.

59. Fernandopulle, Rushika. "Breaking the Fee-for-Service Addiction: Let's Move to a Comprehensive Primary Care Payment Model." *Health Affairs Blog. Health Affairs*, 17 August 2015. Web.

60. Ibid.

61. See Thaler, Richard H., and Cass R. Sunstein. *Nudge: Improving Decisions about Health, Wealth, and Happiness*. Penguin, 2009. Print.

62. Boynton, Ann, and James C. Robinson. "Appropriate Use of Reference Pricing Can Increase Value." *Health Affairs Blog. Health Affairs*, 7 July 2015. Web.

63. Ibid.

SECTION 3

HOW CONSUMERS CHOOSE

4

The Decision-Making Process

We are all practiced at making decisions—we make dozens every day. Consider, for example, daily decisions regarding what to eat or wear. Though these choices are often repetitive, even monotonous, the idea that we can choose has its own fascination. Psychologists, economists, and philosophers, have studied the drivers behind even the most common human decisions for centuries. Choice is ultimately nestled in the concept of free will, the belief in individual self-determination, autonomy, and liberty. These ideas are codified in religious and moral belief systems, popular culture, and national identity. We assume that individuals can choose freely between right and wrong, good and evil, and that those who act out of malice should be punished by the justice system. Belief in autonomy and choice has driven the American dream—the idea that individuals can succeed if they work hard, seize opportunities, and make the right choices.

All this is to say that we, as humans, like the idea of free will, of choice and control. Thankfully, we live in an unprecedented age of options. From our phones, to our cars, to our fashion decisions, there has never been a wider array of options from which to compare and choose. Improving *per capita* income opens up more consumer options and, thanks to technology, we can more readily compare as well as explore the attributes of different products and services.

This is also true in healthcare. As new provider options have proliferated, consumers have more choices in terms of where to go for care. Consumers can choose between a neighborhood pharmacy clinic, an urgent care center, or a doctor's office. You can see a nurse practitioner or pay to have a premium care experience with a primary care doctor. The Internet now offers an abundance of readily accessible information that permits self-diagnosis and provider selection. More people, especially younger generations, are tracking their health and fitness using wearables. Online communities enable people with the same disease to share insights and recommendations about drug side effects, as well as the impacts of different treatments on overall quality of life.

However, the healthcare system can still appear overly complicated to average consumers. Moreover, we know that, today, many consumers make poor decisions when it comes to their health. They eat unhealthy foods, smoke, or fail to exercise; they select health insurance plans that end up costing them more than alternatives; they do not adhere to their medication regimens; they fail to use price or quality comparison tools—despite having access to them. To understand why consumers make poor choices, we must take a closer look at the consumer decision-making process and consumer behavior.

The principles of consumer psychology are as equally applicable in healthcare decision-making as in any other choice process. When choices are routine, made on impulse, or made under emergency conditions, the decision-making process can be short. But for decisions that are consequential and made infrequently or for the first time, the decision-making process can be lengthy. Consider the decision-making process for an annual flu shot compared to that of undergoing prostate surgery.

The choices involved in obtaining a flu shot are somewhat straightforward: whether or not to get it; where to get it; when to get it; how much to pay for it. A free flu shot may be conveniently offered as an employee benefit at your workplace. Or you might add it on to a visit to your primary care physician for another purpose. If you have to pay out of pocket, you might face a reasonable $15 price when you are in a drugstore and either get the flu shot then and there or plan the necessary 15 minutes into your next store visit.

Even this seemingly mundane decision clearly involves a fair amount of individual decision-making. Unlike childhood vaccinations for polio, measles, and chicken pox, which state and federal policies require children to receive before attending school, the flu shot remains optional for most people. Although a yearly flu shot is recommended for nearly everyone 6 months of age and older and many workplaces and schools offer the vaccination for free, less than half of U.S. adults get vaccinated.[1]

Research has shown that several factors alter the odds of people choosing to receive the shot. For example, we know that people with more positive attitudes are more likely to opt for inoculation.[2] Researchers have also demonstrated that in the workplace (where 20% of all flu shots are administered), people are more likely to receive the flu shot if they walk by the workplace health clinics for reasons other than vaccination.[3] Some people "free-ride" a flu shot, reaping the benefits of herd immunity without ever getting the shot themselves. One study showed that when people hear that others in their community are vaccinated, they are less likely to do so themselves. They can receive the benefits conferred by a more vaccinated population without the hassle or risk of getting the shot themselves.[4]

The decision to obtain the flu shot can be influenced by multiple information sources. You may see a sign in the drugstore advertising flu shots, which reminds you to get one. Or a coworker or email alert at work may remind you of several sessions when the on-site flu shot clinic is available. The fact that you received the flu shot last year and did not get the flu is an additional motivator. To influence consumer behavior more effectively, public health officials need to understand the ways in which various groups of consumers arrive at their decisions, the information sources they use, and their sensitivity to price and convenience.

The decision to screen for and treat a disease like prostate cancer is comparatively more complicated. Prostate cancer is one of the most common types of cancer in men. However, most people develop the disease slowly over time with few symptoms. Detection often occurs from a routine prostate-specific antigen (PSA) test, and many men who receive a positive diagnosis would not have known that they had the disease without the screening. For a long time, it was unclear how beneficial it was to receive the diagnosis and undergo treatment, as opposed to not knowing that you are living with a disease with few symptoms and slow development.[5]

As a result, in 2012, the United States Preventive Services Task Force discouraged routine screening in men who were at, or below, average risk for the disease.[6] The task force feared that the screening test itself could be harmful; a positive result might lead to an unnecessary and uncomfortable biopsy. Ultimately, a false-positive diagnosis might result in unnecessary treatment with severe side effects. For this group of patients, doing nothing at all might lead to similar outcomes.[7] However, in 2017, the panel amended their earlier decision. A newer study had shown that there were fewer deaths and cases of metastatic cancer among men who were screened, compared to those who were not.[8] The task force encouraged men to have a conversation with their physician to decide whether PSA screening is the right decision for them.

When a man receives an early stage, low-risk prostate cancer diagnosis, he has several options. He may choose active monitoring with routine PSA testing, or he may choose treatment. This can range from radical prostatectomy, a surgical procedure that removes the entire prostate gland along with some surrounding tissue, to radiation therapy with or without androgen-suppression therapy (i.e., testosterone-reducing hormone therapy). There are also several other, less common options like cryotherapy, which uses very cold temperatures to freeze the cancer cells and is usually only used after another treatment has failed.[9]

The management of the disease from a clinical perspective has been controversial, because many of the treatments have significant side effects. Furthermore, because the disease is so slow growing, some men die from other causes before the cancer causes mortality.[10] For men who elect a treatment, each type comes with its own inherent risks. Prostate surgery may result in changes to urinary or sexual function. Similarly, radiation therapy has been proven quite effective, but it may cause urogenital side effects like painful or frequent urination, or erectile dysfunction. Sometimes radiation is coupled with hormone therapy, as prostate cancer cells rely on testosterone to grow. Choosing to monitor the disease may be a good personal choice for men who want to avoid the potential side effects of treatment.

For early, slow-growing prostate cancer, the best initial approach has been largely unknown and highly debated. However, in 2016, a set of papers focused on analyzing the long-term outcomes of the different approaches to treatment. The results highlighted that among men with low-risk, early-stage disease, those who received treatment were somewhat less likely to experience metastatic disease or death from prostate cancer 10 years later—irrespective of whether they chose radiation therapy or surgery.[11],[12] However, the authors of one of the papers still cautioned that "men with newly diagnosed, localized prostate cancer need to consider the critical trade-off between the short-term and long-term effects of radical treatments on urinary, bowel, and sexual function and the higher risks of disease progression with active monitoring, as well as the effects of each of these options on quality of life."[13]

Those involved in this complicated individual decision-making process might include a primary care physician, a consulting surgeon, an oncologist, and another surgeon called in to give a second opinion, as well as family, friends, and acquaintances that have had prostate surgery. Websites such as WebMD may be consulted along with disease community sites such as PatientsLikeMe. The American Cancer Society recommends consulting a range of such sources before making a final decision, and it acknowledges that "making such a complex decision is often hard to do by yourself." It recommends men speak not only with family and friends but also with other men who have had the disease. The American Cancer Society also provides a list of questions for men to ask themselves as they consider treatment options (see Box 4.1).

At the end of the decision-making process, the patient may choose to do nothing; more precisely, he may choose to engage with a team of medical experts in watchful waiting, rather than risk the side effects of surgery. In 2016, around 40%–50% of men diagnosed with an early stage of the disease chose this option.[14] In this case, the decision-making process goes on autopilot until the patient's condition or monitoring parameters worsen. Typically, the decision-making process would then be reactivated, and the choice to undergo surgery or radiation would be revisited.

In this prostate cancer example, the decision-making process is likely to continue for months, perhaps years. A final decision to undergo surgery then triggers a series of subsequent choices that need to be made in a relatively short amount of time: what type of surgery is best and to be performed by whom, when, and where. These decisions, in comparison to the flu shot example, are far more likely to require guidance and influence from others. If a man receives the diagnosis and is facing several different options, he might discuss and compare them with his doctors, wife, children, or other trusted family members and friends.

Clearly, most consumer choices come at the end point of a process. This process can be long and complicated. Integral to increasing consumer choice in healthcare is understanding how people make decisions. How do they arrive at their final decisions? Who influences them? Why do they choose as they do? What trade-offs do they make?

In this chapter, we will take a closer look at the consumer decision-making process. We will consider (1) the decision-making process; (2) the individuals and groups that make up the decision-making unit; and (3) other common factors that

---

Box 4.1 **American Cancer Society: Questions to Ask Before Deciding on Treatment**

- Are you the type of person who needs to do something about your cancer, even if it might result in serious side effects? Or would you be comfortable with watchful waiting/active surveillance, even if it means you might have more anxiety (and need more frequent follow-up) in the future?

- Do you need to know right away whether your doctor thinks he or she was able to get all of the cancer out (a reason some men choose surgery)? Or are you comfortable with not knowing the results of treatment for a while (as is the case in radiation therapy) if it means not having to have surgery?

- Do you prefer to go with the newest technology (such as robotic surgery or proton beam radiation therapy), which might have some theoretical advantages? Or do you prefer to go with treatment methods that are better proven and with which doctors might have more experience?

- Which potential treatment side effects (incontinence, impotence, bowel problems) might be most distressing to you? (Some treatments are more likely to cause certain side effects than others.)

- How important for you are issues like the amount of time spent in treatment or recovery?

- If your initial treatment is not successful, what would your options be at that point?

Source: "Considering Prostate Cancer Treatment Options." *American Cancer Society*. 11 Mar. 2016. Web.

---

affect decision-making. How people make healthcare decisions, and how quickly they make them, varies greatly depending on a large range of factors, with cultural, economic, psychological, and social influences affecting the outcome at each step.

The Decision-Making Process

We know that, today, the consumer decision-making process often breaks down in healthcare, leading the consumer to make a poor decision in the end. We will enumerate and analyze some of the reasons why this occurs. Typically, the consumer decision-making process can be broken down into five stages:

- *Problem identification*: The consumer identifies that he or she has a need (in this case, a health or medical one).

- *Information search*: After realizing their need for a product or service, consumers will seek out more information on potential solutions from a variety of sources. This step can be involved and protracted for a new or important purchase, but incidental when the consumer is making an automatic repeat purchase.
- *Evaluation of alternatives*: After or during the process of gathering information, most consumers will compare the alternatives that can satisfy their needs.
- *Decision*: After consumers have compiled information and assessed the alternatives (to the best of their ability), they select their preferred product or service.
- *Post-choice evaluation*: When a consumer selects a product or service, he or she presumes it will meet certain expectations. After purchasing, that person may evaluate its ability to fill those needs (when possible). In other words, the consumer seeks affirmation that his or her choice was correct.[15]

Problem Identification

Often, the consumer journey starts long before any decisions are made. In any consumer buying situation, a person must first become aware of her need for a product or service. Sometimes, a person's health condition alerts her to a potential healthcare need. For instance, a person might notice that she has developed a persistent cough that lasts for several weeks. Other times, it is a family member or friend who notices a change or makes a suggestion. A father might notice that his child has an odd rash, prompting a call to the pediatrician. Sometimes, advertising alerts consumers to a newly available product or service about which they may ask about during their next visit to their primary care physician. We all constantly take in information about health, wellness, and medical options. Direct-to-consumer advertising for prescription drugs means that we often hear about treatment options during advertising breaks as we watch our favorite television shows.

Apart from clear emergencies, it is often difficult for a consumer to understand whether a condition is serious or not. Understanding the importance of a medical concern is no easy task. Some people are stoic, while others trend toward hypochondria, sensing a need where there is none, and ultimately using products and services that are not necessary. The prevalence of hypochondria in the population is estimated at 1%–5%, though it is likely higher among subgroups that interact with the medical system frequently.[16] On the other hand, there are stoic or cavalier people with health or medical needs that they do not attend to. Think of the individual who misses several doses of his daily statin in a row or the person who skips a recommended cancer screening.

Information Search

Throughout the decision-making process, there are many information sources available to consumers. Though information is more readily accessible today, it is sometimes presented in a disorderly manner that is not user friendly. In addition, information can come from a wide range of sources. As a result, it can be difficult for consumers to choose a trusted source they can rely on to make informed decisions. For example, less than half of American consumers report that it is easy to find trusted information on physician quality.[17]

Of course, many people naturally consult family and friends—especially those who are nearby or have experienced a similar health challenge. Word of mouth remains a powerful force in healthcare, where services are still predominantly delivered locally. However, word of mouth can be anecdotal or out of date. As medical know-how and technologies evolve, what your friend or family member did two or three years ago may be obsolete, or now the second-best option.

Word-of-mouth reviews have also moved online to sites like Yelp, where consumers already frequently post reviews about other services, such as restaurants. As the use of Yelp to review hospitals and physicians has increased, physicians have become concerned that such anecdotal reporting may be less helpful to consumers than results from standardized measurement instruments. In a 2016 article, three physicians speculated why this may be the case. Namely, they reasoned that such sites may only attract patients with strong views and "individual reviews may not be balanced, may be deliberately misleading, or may be fake—and the reasons people post on Yelp may compete with the kind of representative sampling that gives crowds wisdom."[18] The authors concluded:

> it is both understandable for health care professions to be concerned about how the public gets its information and natural to expect calls for a more systematic reporting of patient experiences—the kind promised through standardized instruments and the regimented methods of survey firms. Nevertheless, a more feasible and constructive approach to online platform reviews moves past the question of whether patients should pay attention—that seems inescapable—and asks whether physicians and health systems ought to join them in paying attention to these reviews.[19]

Many consumers also seek expert knowledge from their primary care physician or health insurer. A primary care physician's trusted recommendation still wields strong influence over patients who need to visit a specialist. The Advisory Board Company, a healthcare consulting firm, conducted a survey of healthcare consumers and found that 64% of respondents followed a primary care physician's referral when choosing which specialist to visit.[20] However doctor-recommended referrals may have carried greater weight in the past, when people had fewer avenues for finding information about the different specialties and providers they might consult.

As mobile and digital health technology solutions have proliferated, people can glean information from a wider array of sources. Social media and the Internet have made information more readily accessible. However, it is unclear whether this has resulted in longer search processes, where people spend more time looking at a greater number of sources, or shorter processes, because these online searches can increase efficiency. Websites like WebMD enable people to assess their own symptoms and, sometimes, promote self-diagnosis and treatment. All in all, although there are certainly concerns about misinformation or unsubstantiated medical advice from patient discussion forums, the proliferation of such sites has led to a more engaged consumer.

Where a consumer seeks information may depend on what situation she is facing. If the consumer has a new symptom and wants to know whether it is a sign of something more serious, she might conduct a quick Google search and check in the Mayo Clinic Diseases and Conditions guide. If she needs to know how much a procedure will cost, she is more likely to contact her health insurer or use an online tool. If she is worried about a family member's health, she might solicit advice from other family members or friends.

As we will discuss in the next chapter, consumers consider a range of service attributes when making healthcare decisions. Therefore, what information most interests a consumer may depend on his or her own personal priorities. Some consumers will be more interested in cost, while others focus more on the service-related experience or the quality of the care provided.

Evaluation of Alternatives

Although access to information in healthcare has improved, consumers clearly still struggle to compare alternatives. Despite the increasing availability of price and quality transparency tools from health insurers, government organizations, and third-party companies, consumers make little use of them. In general, people put little stock in the healthcare comparison options that are currently available; they have not yet built their credibility. A 2014 survey of consumers showed that only 26% of Americans said that high physician ratings on websites like HealthGrades. com, Yelp, or Angie's List were "extremely" or "very important" to their decision-making process. Additionally, nearly half of those surveyed said that these ratings systems were "not too important" or "not important at all."[21]

Health insurers often offer price estimators so that plan subscribers, especially those with higher deductibles, can find the lowest prices for a particular service within their networks. However, there is limited evidence that such tools reduce spending.[22] A study on the use of one such tool, the Aetna Member Payment Estimator, found that only 1.6% of those eligible used the tool at least once in the first year it was available. In the second year, use increased only modestly to 2.4%.[23] The authors concluded that strong promotion is needed. Their view is that "a campaign to deliver price information to consumers may be important to increase patients' engagement with price transparency tools."[24]

A *New York Times* article in December 2016 documented the challenges associated with price comparisons.[25] The article asserted that "providing more information to consumers doesn't always improve their decision-making." The author offered several explanations for this, as well as discussing how only a subset of health conditions are easy to shop for, and that the system may be overly complex.[26] It also takes time for consumers, who are typically in the market for healthcare services infrequently, to discover more tools and become accustomed to using them.

However, some readers disagreed that consumer behavior was the main reason for the low utilization of such tools. As of early 2017, one popular reader's comment on that *New York Times* article was the following:

> This article does a massive disservice to the cause of a better, more cost-effective health care system. Instead of breezily jumping to fashionable behavioral economics conclusions like "providing more information to consumers doesn't always improve their decision making," a data-driven economist would have investigated the possibility that the price comparison tools were ineffective and provided virtually no price transparency in practice.
>
> I've used a number of these tools and, as other commenters have noted, they are often slow, unfriendly, inaccurate, incomplete, and virtually unpublicized (perhaps in part because they are so low-quality). I don't blame the programmers of the tools—they probably did the best they could with what they were provided from an uncooperative health care establishment.[27]

It is also likely that the tools are not yet enough developed, nor advertised frequently enough, to provide useful comparisons. This seems to be backed up by evidence from The Catalyst for Payment Reform (CPR), a nonprofit group dedicated to improving value in healthcare. Each year, CPR puts out a scorecard on price transparency in each state. Despite policies in all but seven states mandating increased price transparency for healthcare consumers, in 2016, CPR gave 43 states an "F" grade on current price transparency efforts.[28]

Clearly some consumers are neither interested nor able to engage in the process of comparing alternatives. Consumers may not know how to compare options appropriately. Consider comparing quality for pregnancy and delivery, for example. One study found that 73% of women prioritized their selection of an individual physician, rather than the hospital.[29] Women simply go to the hospital where their physician delivers. However, a simple Google search of "Does my OB deliver my baby?" reveals that many women think that doctor will deliver their baby. Though the physician they pick will be their primary caregiver in the months leading up to childbirth, the obstetrician who delivers their baby is usually the one who is on call at the hospital when they go into labor.

The same study found that over half of respondents did not believe that their choice of hospital would affect the quality of their childbirth. However, this assumption is incorrect; in many ways, the quality of their childbirth will be determined by the hospital. The incidence of cesarean sections ("C-sections"),* which can carry risks for both mother and baby, can vary tenfold across different hospitals (from 7.1% to 69.9% in the study).[30] This holds true even among women with lower risk pregnancies, for whom more limited variation might be expected. Because of the risks associated with the unnecessary use of C-sections and other interventions during childbirth, women concerned with quality of care should pay greater attention to hospital-level quality measures, rather than focusing on physician selection.

Finding new ways to advertise price and quality comparison tools, as well as to encourage their use, is critical.

Decision

After a consumer has gathered information and assessed the different choices (to the best of his ability), he selects the preferred product or service. However, just because it is simple does not mean that it is easy. In healthcare, this stage can be filled with indecision. To the consumer, it can often feel as if there is little choice; that opting to select the expert-recommended treatment is the only choice. Just as the consumer has difficulty assessing the severity of his symptoms in the problem identification stage, he may again struggle to understand whether the health product or service is necessary, needed immediately, or associated with hidden risks.

Consider the case of diagnostic medical tests. Often, when physicians prescribe these tests, there is a low likelihood that an abnormality will be found. Further, every test always has false positives, which expose the patient to risks and worries when there is no actual problem. In ordering the test, the physician is motivated by

---

* A C-section is a procedure to deliver a baby surgically through incisions in the mother's abdomen and uterus. C-Sections can be lifesaving when labor is arrested or the baby exhibits signs of distress, such as an irregular heartbeat. However, the use of C-sections for delivery increased rapidly throughout the 2000s, raising alarm among many physicians. Apart from cost concerns (C-sections are more expensive than vaginal deliveries), they also carry risks for both the mother and baby. They can lead to serious complications for mothers, including problems like inflammation of the uterus, hemorrhage, infection, and blood clots. Having a first baby by C-section leaves a woman with an increased chance that subsequent births will also be by C-section. Though rare, C-sections can also pose some risks to babies, including breathing problems and surgical injuries. As the rates of C-sections grew throughout the 2000s, even among low-risk pregnancies, concern grew that physicians were overusing the procedure.

his or her desire to exhaust all possible diagnoses; to miss something serious would reflect poorly on the physician's abilities, possibly resulting in a bad reputation or a malpractice lawsuit, at worst. The patient, who would rather be safe than sorry, most often decides to go ahead with the test for the peace of mind. If the test comes back negative, they both breathe a sigh of relief and move on. But a positive test can be a false alarm. Consumers need to understand these usually hidden risks.

Post-choice Evaluation

When a consumer selects a product or service, she expects it to meet certain expectations. After its purchase and use, the consumer seeks affirmation that her decision was the right one. Often, evaluating a healthcare decision is very difficult. A consumer may assess either immediately or gradually whether she feels better against prior expectations, but often the consumer cannot be sure how she might have felt without intervention.

In a general economic sense, there are several different ways of classifying goods based on how consumers evaluate them. A *search good* is a product or service whose key attributes (i.e., price and quality) are easily observable prior to purchase. A t-shirt is a good example. If you are shopping in person, you can see how it looks, touch it to feel how soft the fabric is, and try it on in the dressing room to appreciate how it looks on you. Although there may be some important attributes that you cannot judge beforehand, such as how it will hold up after several washes, you can make a pretty fair assessment of the product's performance versus its price prior to purchasing it. Few healthcare decisions fall into this category.

Experience goods are those products or services whose value the consumer can only assess by consuming (i.e., "experiencing" them). Foods or drinks are good examples. Although packaging may signal a certain level of quality, evaluation of the product can only happen after consumption. You can probably think of a time when you have selected a new product at the grocery store only to be disappointed when it was not as good as you thought it might be. Many services are experience goods, since they can be difficult to judge prior to consumption. Consider a hotel stay. Although a business traveler might know what to expect at a Westin hotel, much of that assumption is based on brand reputation. For this reason, many experience goods are purchased based on brand image or prior experience.

Credence goods are products and services whose value can never be known with certainty—even after consumption. For example, consider a daily multivitamin. Although you might take the pill each day with the hope that it will improve your overall health, it is very difficult to judge its effect. Even after purchase and consumption, a consumer must believe in the usefulness of the product or its brand reputation. Furthermore, the consumer may not feel better, but he might have felt worse if he had not taken it. Of course, multifaceted products or services may have elements of all three types of goods.

In healthcare, many products and services are credence goods. A typical consumer does not have the level of knowledge necessary to know whether the surgery that was recommended was the right type or what level of service quality she received. Although the physician's credentials, the atmosphere at the clinic, and the testimonials from previous patients may reinforce one's decision, it is very difficult to judge for oneself. However, there are times in healthcare where the quality and necessity of treatment are less ambiguous. Someone with knee pain and dysfunction will know soon whether surgery was a good choice. Anyone who has had a serious infection can tell you that life improves markedly after the first few doses of antibiotics. Your fever starts to come down and pain subsides. The cause-and-effect relationship in this instance is much clearer, and in this example, the product (the antibiotic) and service (your encounter with the physician to receive the prescription for the antibiotic) are more likely to fall into the good experience category.

Factors Affecting the Decision-Making Process

The five-step decision-making process seems simple and intuitive; a person realizes that he has a problem, seeks out information about his options for fulfilling his needs, compares alternatives, makes a decision, and evaluates that decision after the fact. In practice, however, this process is complicated—particularly in healthcare.

Consider the story of Anna, for example. Anna was a talkative, rotund but active, 68-year-old when Dr. Jain saw her for her first medical visit. Accompanied by her daughter Samantha, who was an only child, Anna had diabetes and was a two-pack-a-day smoker. She sourly introduced herself by saying that she had decided, based on the rising premium costs for her supplemental health insurance coverage (that enabled her to avoid paying 20% of her Medicare bills) to change her insurance to a much cheaper Medicare Advantage program. Her face darkened and she said to Dr. Jain, "I had been with my doctor for years. She knew me, and it was convenient to get to her, but my new insurance plan made me come here because you were part of their network, which didn't include my doctor." Her Medicare Advantage HMO plan cost her only an additional $39 a month on top of her basic Medicare—her drug and office visit charges were small and manageable.

She told Dr. Jain that she had been in relatively good health. Dr. Jain concluded that her plan and medications were appropriate. Sheila was doing a good job, with the exception that she had tried, but failed, to take off weight and stop smoking. Over the next three years, she continued to struggle with weight and smoking despite Dr. Jain's best efforts. Then a year ago, Dr. Jain received a call from her hospital's emergency room. Anna had arrived with chest pain lasting a day, accompanied by increasing shortness of breath. It looked as though she had suffered a heart attack. Fortunately, she survived the heart attack without needing coronary surgical intervention. However, during her hospital stay, she remained moderately short of breath and probably had a minor stroke.

Discharging her back to her home without help was out of the question. She needed rehabilitation. More important, her daughter worked, and there was no inexpensive way to secure home help. Her daughter and Dr. Jain spoke about rehabilitation units and skilled nursing facilities (SNFs). Anna wanted desperately to go home, but she needed supportive care and her options were limited to those within her insurer's network, which were primarily institutional.

The social worker in the hospital had more bad news; Anna would need to pay $275 a day for the first five days of her hospitalization. Anna sadly realized that if she had chosen a more costly plan when she enrolled at the beginning of the year, she would have paid less for what she needed now, but there was no changing her plan until the next enrollment period several months away. Samantha pitched in and Anna was transferred to a SNF near her home.

Dr. Jain lost track of Anna because she was unable to serve as her doctor in the rehab facility she chose. Last week, Samantha called to bring Dr. Jain up to date. Sadly, Anna had died, but not before expending all of her savings and those of her daughter. Anna, she said, had gone to the rehab facility but did not do well. She was depressed, and it was hard to get her to participate in her own rehabilitation. After two futile weeks, the social worker talked with Anna and her daughter about long-term care. Anna was bed and chair bound but still alert and able to feed herself and use a bedside commode.

However, the financial consequences were dire. Medicare did not cover long-term care. Moreover, Samantha had received the bill from her insurance company for the five day $275 charge for her hospitalization. The family was strapped for money. Ultimately, it was less expensive to stay in the SNF for the allowable 90 days by making the case that Anna still needed rehabilitation.

The time came when Anna and her daughter had to make a choice. Either pay for a nursing home for long-term care or return home with the minimal home support available through her insurance. Faced with her mother's 24-hour need for support by this time, Samantha asked and received a leave of absence from work to stay home and provide the care. Anna deteriorated quickly at home and after three months Anna took out a second mortgage on her home, which she jointly owned with her daughter. She was not able to get out of bed; she developed bed sores, and gradually became somnolent. After a slow and prolonged decline, she stopped eating, lost consciousness, and died about a week later.

As Anna's story illustrates, the generic decision-making process may appear straightforward, but in real life individual choices are very idiosyncratic. Many factors affect the overall decision-making process. It is rarely simple. Indeed, the complexity of the system can make it hard, especially for people who are sick and financially constrained. In the following section, we will address the five most important factors affecting how and why consumers choose the way they do: (1) the decision-making unit; (2) the individual decision-maker; (3) the healthcare situation; (4) perceived risk; and (5) consumer bias.

The Decision-Making Unit

As in Anna's story, we rarely make healthcare decisions completely on our own—especially when they are difficult, life-threatening, or ongoing medical situations. Family and friends support us, and they often choose to make sacrifices to maintain the health of their loved ones. Parents leave work to attend to a sick child. Adult children accompany elderly parents to their medical appointments. Neighbors stop in to check on friends after a hip replacement. Doctors are involved. These interactions set the stage for how we evaluate care options and make decisions.

The decision-making unit (DMU) includes all of the individuals involved in making a purchase decision about a product or service. There are typically five roles included in the DMU.[31] There are users, influencers, buyers, deciders, and gatekeepers as defined in Table 4.1. In the case of a simple, routine decision like the flu shot, the number of people in the DMU is limited. In fact, the same individual may be the decider, buyer, and user. But, if we are obtaining flu shots for our children, the buyer is no longer the user. Moreover, if we obtain our shot at work, then our employer is acting as the gatekeeper.

In the age of social media and online recommendation, consumers have access to a greater breadth of information. Using the DMU framework can be helpful in a healthcare context because there are often many people and organizations that influence decision-making—from a person's family, to his health insurer, to his clinical care team.

As consumers, we may not always be aware of all of the individuals and organizations who make up the DMU. For example, few consumers make a deliberate decision when in an ambulance about which emergency room to go to. Though a patient can request to be taken to a particular hospital, typically, this decision is made by the paramedics and emergency medical technicians who respond to 911 calls. They route patients to particular hospitals based on proximity, the clinical condition, and available beds.

Understanding the DMU can change how provider organizations, healthcare companies, and public health practitioners frame their interventions. Consider one such example. Victoria Trains in Melbourne, Australia, noticed an uptick in the number of young people playing chicken on train tracks and driving around closed level crossing gates. Reported incidents, near misses, injuries, and even deaths were all on the rise. Public service advertising showing the deadly consequences of such behaviors seemed to make no difference. That is when a new advertising agency took a different approach, choosing a memorable jingle sung by animated cartoon characters and titled "Dumb Ways to Die." Among 16 examples presented in the ad, the last three addressed train safety issues. The ad went viral on social media and even won a prize at a film festival.

The overall success of the advertising strategy could be attributed to the advertising agency's consideration of the DMU. The ad was not targeting the youngsters engaging in the risky behaviors. Rather it was aimed at their peers. The objective was to make these behaviors completely uncool; those engaging in them would not

Table 4.1 **Roles Within the Decision-Making Unit**

Role	Application to Healthcare*
User(s) *The person(s) using the product or service*	• Consumers
Influencers *Those who provide information and help evaluate alternatives*	• Friends and family of consumers • Primary care physicians • Online comparison websites and other advisory information
Buyers *Those who have the formal authority to select the supplier and arrange the terms of purchase*	• Will vary based on the situation • Often, private health insurers or pharmacy benefit managers who negotiate contracts with healthcare service providers and drug companies • Government payers (Medicare/Medicaid) • Consumers (especially in situations when insurance does not provide coverage)
Deciders *Those who have formal or informal power to select or approve the final suppliers (may be the same as the buyer)*	• Will vary based on the situation • Often, private health insurers or pharmacy benefit managers who negotiate contracts with healthcare service providers and drug companies • Government payers (Medicare/Medicaid) • Consumers (especially in situations when insurance is not involved)
Gatekeepers *Those who control the availability of information and services to consumers*	• Government regulators • Private and public health insurers (who limit what is available to consumers)

* Ibid., p. 80.

Source: Kotler, Philip, and Gary Armstrong. *Principles of Marketing*. 17th ed. Pearson, 2017. Print. pg. 80.

be viewed by their peers as brave but as stupid. In addition, the ad targeted other passengers and employees, empowering them to spot and report dangerous behavior, perhaps to caution those involved so as to prevent accidents.

Health and safety are understandably treated seriously by public health professionals in communicating with consumers. Yet we as consumers are most likely to remember ads that are humorous. The Dumb Ways to Die video highlights how public health campaigns can use knowledge of the different actors in the DMU, as well as dark humor, to effectively influence decision-makers by appealing to those around them.

Understanding the influence of others is incredibly important during personal healthcare challenges as well. Family members act as advocates, influencers, and confidants during difficult or trying medical decisions. They may be the ones calling physician offices, transferring medical records, or even making final decisions when a patient is incapacitated. Sometimes family members are the ones footing the bill, making them the "buyer," to use the DMU terminology. The point here is that family members can wield tremendous influence over how people make choices, with the potential to either hurt or help them. For highly emotional decisions, a candid conversation with a sibling or trusted friend may change the medical decision and, ultimately, the outcome.

Expert Opinion

Although family and friends may offer much needed emotional support, one of the most critical influencers in most healthcare decisions remains the clinical expert. Consumers do not have the training and knowledge that the expert does, so they must trust that the expert is acting in their best interests. Currently, healthcare consumers often look to their clinical advisers, primary care physicians, or nurses to fill this role. However, some healthcare consumers may prefer to rely on someone else. Although consumers continue to perceive clinical providers as honest professionals with a high degree of integrity, trust in physicians has waned over the last few decades.[32,33] A 2014, cross-national public opinion survey found that only 58% of respondents in the United States selected "strongly agree" or "agree" to the statement "All things considered, doctors in your country can be trusted." Compare this figure to the country that came out on top; 83% of respondents in Switzerland answered the question affirmatively. This survey placed the United States in the bottom five of the 29 countries surveyed.[34]

This is not a problem specific to healthcare; in many areas of consumer life, we must trust an expert's opinion. We might ask someone at a technology store for assistance repairing a broken phone or a mechanic for help with our car. Car repairs are notoriously expensive, so having a relationship with a trusted mechanic who can fairly present options is important. Likewise, having an adviser in healthcare is often a boon to consumers.

The Individual

Although it is important for healthcare managers and administrators to understand all roles in the DMU, none is more important than the "user"—the consumer, or the person receiving treatment or choosing a health plan. There are several characteristics of individual consumers that are particularly important in shaping their decision-making. These are socioeconomic position, health literacy, cultural background, geographic location, and consumer involvement.

Socioeconomic Position

It is well established that social and economic conditions influence people's decisions about their health, their access to healthcare, and, ultimately, their health outcomes.[35,36] In fact, genetic predisposition is estimated to explain an average of only about 30% of each premature death.[37] The structural and societal conditions that shape an individual's environment (e.g., socioeconomic status, education, access to healthy food) are often referred to collectively as the "social determinants of health," depicted in Table 4.2.

The social determinants of health have an enormous collective impact on the types of decisions consumers face and what they ultimately choose. For example, researchers have shown that urban design and physical environment are associated with physical activity, such as walking and cycling for transportation.[38] Children are more likely to be overweight or obese if they live in unsafe neighborhoods, in poor housing facilities, or have limited access to sidewalks, parks, and recreation centers.[39] Researchers have also noted an increasing disparity in opportunities between children from different socioeconomic

Table 4.2 **Social Determinants of Health**

Category	Examples
Economic stability	Employment, income, expenses, debt, medical bills, support
Neighborhood and physical environment	Housing, transportation, safety, parks, playgrounds, walkability
Education	Literacy, language, early childhood education, vocational training, higher education
Food	Hunger, access to health options
Community and social context	Social integration, support systems, community engagement, discrimination
Healthcare system	Health coverage, provider availability, provider linguistic and cultural competency, quality of care

Source: Adapted from Harry J. Heiman and Samantha Artigas, "Beyond Health Care: The Role of Social Determinants in Promoting Health and Health Equity," The Kaiser Family Foundation, November 4th, 2015.

backgrounds in the United States. Richer children typically have greater access to social support and extracurricular activities, like sports, which teach children valuable skills such as self-discipline, a strong work ethic, and a sense of civic engagement.[40]

Health Literacy

Health literacy is defined as "the degree to which individuals have the capacity to obtain, process, and understand basic health information and services needed to make appropriate health decisions."[41] If someone does not fully understand what her physician or health plan is telling her, she is not able to make a knowledgeable decision about it. In 2010, Dr. Howard Kho authored a "National Action Plan to Improve Health Literacy." In it he wrote:

> Too often, there exists a chasm of knowledge between what professionals know and what consumers and patients understand. Basic health literacy is fundamental to the success of each interaction between health care professionals and patients—every prescription, every treatment, and every recovery. Basic health literacy is fundamental to putting sound public health guidance into practice and helping people follow recommendations.[42]

Many factors affect a consumer's level of health literacy. For example, researchers have shown that women tend to have higher health literacy than men.[43] In families, women usually take on responsibilities related to the healthcare of others, such as older family members and younger children. As a result, they interact with the health system more frequently. Cumulative experience plus involvement (a willingness to learn) builds literacy. Cultural and language barriers can also modify a consumer's ability to understand a physician's advice about, for example, difficult treatment options.

Cultural Background

Culture can affect much more than a consumer's health literacy level. A consumer's cultural background is a lens through which he or she views the world and makes decisions—including those on health and wellness. Our cultural and religious backgrounds touch nearly every aspect of our lives, framing our priorities, values, and beliefs. Therefore, culture can shape how consumers interact with clinicians, how adherent they are to medical recommendations, and even how they think about life and death.

The Agency for Healthcare Quality and Research has outlined the ways in which culture, ethnicity, and religion can impact healthcare access and use:

- *Health beliefs*: In some cultures, people believe that talking about a possible poor health outcome will cause that outcome to occur.
- *Health customs*: In some cultures, family members play a large role in healthcare decision-making.
- *Ethnic customs*: Differing roles of women and men in society may determine who makes decisions about accepting and following through with medical treatments.
- *Religious beliefs*: Religious faith and spiritual beliefs may affect healthcare-seeking behavior and people's willingness to accept specific treatments or behavior changes.
- *Dietary customs*: Disease-related dietary advice will be difficult to follow if it does not conform to the foods or cooking methods used by the consumer.
- *Interpersonal customs*: Eye contact or physical touch will be expected in some cultures and inappropriate or offensive in others.[44]

Researchers have shown, for example, how the cultural construction of illness impacts patients' interpretation of risk and their desire for more aggressive treatment. During breast cancer screening and treatment, women from Western backgrounds are more likely than Asians to emphasize problem-solving and aggressive treatment, ultimately choosing mastectomies, which are invasive and require breast reconstruction. Though lumpectomies with radiation are less invasive and are recommended for early-stage cancer, the women who take this path are more self-confident and control oriented, both of which are culturally engrained. This is layered on top of a medical model that values the most technologically advanced treatment.[45]

Geographic Location

In most markets, location determines available choices. In healthcare, geography is still a limiting factor that affects both the risk of contracting disease as well as the options available for care. For example, there were 88 hospitals in Nebraska in 2015, whereas there were only 36 in Nevada.[46] Although medical tourism and travel may be on the rise—especially for high-cost procedures—most healthcare continues to be delivered locally. For consumers, this means that choices are generally limited to the supply in their home state.

This is not only true for delivery organizations but also for health insurance. Although President Trump has discussed allowing consumers to purchase health plans across state lines, it is not currently practical because state-by-state regulations differ substantially. On the ACA insurance exchanges, this has meant that consumers in some states have a wide range of plans to choose from, while others can select from only one or two available plans.

Consumer Involvement

Consumers vary in how involved they are in thinking about or protecting their health. Most people do not seek care until they need it for themselves or for a family member. Some only confront healthcare issues when they are in critical condition. This behavior is justifiable for the simple reason that few people *want* to consume large amounts of healthcare. When someone does seek out medical care, it is typically because he or she is ill. Low involvement is partly due to bias in rating one's own risk of disease. People tend to view themselves as less likely than others to experience the same health issue.[47] This occurs even among smokers, who often acknowledge that smoking puts people at greater risk for disease but do not feel at greater risk themselves.[48]

The Healthcare Situation

So far, we have focused on the people and organizations involved in decision-making and have addressed how the makeup of the DMU and characteristics of individual consumers can affect the typical decision-making process. While understanding that the individual is critical within the decision-making process, we must also recognize how different circumstances across healthcare situations can result in different decision-making processes. The decision-making process is undoubtedly influenced by factors such as how much time the person has to make the decision, what physical state the person is in, and who else influences the person's decision.

In Chapter 2, we proposed a two-by-two table to help understand the healthcare situations where consumer choice can work and where it is infeasible. Our parameters were medical complexity and urgency, and we argued that in situations where decisions were not inordinately complex, and where there was sufficient time for the decision-making process, consumer choice could be enhanced. In this section, we add another parameter that influences individual decision-making: repeated experiences where the motivated consumer has an opportunity to learn.

Consumer choice thrives when users are knowledgeable. Consumer healthcare decisions encompass everything from general lifestyle choices to primary care physician selection and even end-of-life priorities and planning. There are differences between the processes for a routine decision, such as a monthly prescription refill, and a novel one, such as filling a prescription for a new medication. In the first situation, a consumer might be frustrated that the line at the retail pharmacy cannot move faster. In the latter scenario, he might want to spend extra time speaking with his pharmacist or a physician about possible side effects and dosing. Furthermore, opportunities to learn more about medical care may arise when making a decision regarding health insurance, or when combatting frequently reoccurring conditions such as common infections and minor trauma. Though no consumer or buying situation is the same, there are ways in which a motivated learner can become more autonomous and in control.

Frequency is important because it is a surrogate for how familiar a consumer is with the decision-making process and how much he or she understands about medical issues and ailments. If a decision occurs regularly, consumers are more likely to improve their decision-making through practice over time. Frequency, here, is based on the consumer's experience, not on the clinician's or the healthcare system's perspective. A heart attack may seem commonplace to an ER doctor, but it is infrequent—and terrifying—to the individual who has not experienced one before. Of course, how frequently a consumer interacts with the healthcare system may vary based on the individual and his or her needs. Some consumers may only decide who to enlist as their primary care physician a time or two in their life, while others who change jobs and locations often may have to switch regularly.

Perceived Risk

Knowing the perceived risk tolerance of consumers is critical to understanding how the decision-making process unfolds. Some choices are low in perceived risk. If you had flu shot last year and neither caught the flu nor had an allergic reaction, your perception of the risk associated with repeating the process this year is likely to be minimal. Millions of others get their jab without incident, which gives you further comfort in making this decision. Although you cannot know for sure that the flu shot was the reason you did not get the flu, you are likely to make the attribution.

At the other end of the spectrum, a patient who has been recommended to have surgery will be very worried about all the risks—of the anesthesia, the surgery itself, the rehabilitation, and the risks associated with a bad or good result. An educated consumer will ask about the probability of success, the risk of unintended infection, and complications and side effects, and then calibrate these against the risks of not having the surgery. However, most consumers are not well equipped to accurately weigh risks and probabilities. Savvy consumers may also check that the surgeon (rather than a resident) will perform the surgery and ask who will administer anesthesia and close the wound.

Furthermore, consumers differ widely in their desire as well as their ability to engage in these decisions. Some patients have a high tolerance for risk. They may be unfazed about an illness that would make others deeply fearful. Some patients want to analyze every detail and feverishly evaluate associated risks and benefits. Other patients are unwilling to do so. They may be intimidated, or they may conclude that the time needed to engage in the decision-making process would not improve the outcome. They prefer, therefore, to defer to the expert recommendations of their doctors. It is the path of least resistance, and if anything should go wrong, blame can be attributed to a third party, which causes less anxiety.

Trusted brands help consumers reduce perceived risk. A trusted brand that has been around for a long time gives the consumer confidence and assurance that the quality of the product will meet regulatory standards and consistently deliver what the brand promises. A well-known brand might not be the absolute best option, but it will suffice to a consumer who may be unwilling to spend time conducting his or her own research and evaluations.

Moreover, trusted brands are not a flash-in-the-pan; they take a long time to build and much effort to maintain. Companies live and die by their reputation in the marketplace for quality, honesty, and integrity as well as cost. As a result, it is difficult for new brands to enter a product category where consumers see purchase decisions as high risk, unless they have a powerful value proposition (such as more benefit for the same price, or the same benefit for less).

For example, the decision to buy supplemental health insurance could present a difficult choice. It might be an unwelcome addition to your monthly budget, you would not know if you would ever use it, and you have never bought it before. Yet, depending on your level of savings, and your tolerance for risk, it may give you and your family peace of mind. A Web search reveals a limitless supply of complex information on supplemental health insurance options and how best to decide among them. You ask friends for advice, but their health circumstances may be different from yours. That is when you may take a shortcut by focusing on brands you know and trust.

In this case, a trusted brand can be reassuring. For example, AARP has over 40 million members. They offer a supplemental health insurance plan through the market leader, United Health, which also happens to provide many consumers with health insurance through their employers. You have been a member of AARP for 10 years and you have been pleased to receive their informative monthly newsletters in return for a modest annual subscription. You know that if you buy the AARP plan, it may not be the best and it may not be the cheapest, but it is probably a pretty good option since it is marketed by a major not-for-profit that can probably negotiate pretty good rates. Moreover, should you have problems securing payment on a claim, you know where to go. Instead of conducting a painstaking review of all possible plans, you satisfice rather than maximize and choose a trusted brand or, in this case, two trusted brands. You save time and eliminate the stress associated with trying to make the optimal decision.

Consumers implicitly evaluate returns against risks in healthcare decision-making just as they do in organizing their portfolios of financial investments. Some people are more comfortable with risk and are willing to participate, for example, in trials of experimental drugs—while others are more risk-averse. But that does not mean that the choices made by a consumer who is more comfortable with taking risks will maximize long-term expected value. In the following section, we will discuss some of the heuristics and biases that subconsciously affect decision-making.

Consumer Biases

Although people do explicitly consider multiple factors when making decisions, it is also abundantly clear that they are subconsciously influenced in ways that are not always apparent to them. Daniel Kahneman and Amos Tversky showed how people tend to use heuristics, or mental shortcuts, to make decisions.[49] However, these shortcuts are not always rational, and they often result in cognitive biases or errors in judgment. Before their research, economics was grounded in the underlying principle that people make decisions rationally.

Consider the inaccurate assumptions consumers make with regard to price and their personal risk of a disease. One study found that consumers incorrectly assume that life-saving health goods are priced according to medical necessity rather than by market forces.[50] This leads to the bias that lower medication prices signal more widespread need and thus makes individual consumers feel that their own self-risk is elevated, incorrectly increasing consumption. The reverse is true for higher prices. Higher prices signal a rare and more serious ailment affecting fewer people and therefore falsely lowers the consumer's assessment of their own risk, thus lowering their estimate that they need the treatment. In reality, drugs are not priced this way, yet consumers make inconsistent assumptions about the relationships between price and risk, and disease prevalence and need.

In their seminal work, *Prospect Theory*, Kahneman and Tversky focused on three main heuristics (availability, representativeness, and anchoring and adjustment) while simultaneously laying the groundwork for the growing field of behavioral economics. Prospect theory, a behavioral model, describes how people decide among choice alternatives that involve risk and uncertainty. Kahneman and Tversky demonstrated the prediction bias that occurs because people tend to consider expected utility in relation to a reference point (often the person's current situation or lived experiences). They also showed that people tend to be loss averse, in that they are more influenced by the prospect of loss than gain. Simply put, we typically prefer to keep $20 than to gain $20.

Although the field of behavioral economics has since expanded rapidly, and there are many more identified heuristics and biases than are relevant to our discussion, we review briefly several that are relevant in healthcare contexts in Table 4.3.

Marketers and health promoters can use techniques such as framing and incentives that play into these subconscious biases and heuristics to ultimately encourage consumer choices ranging from buying a type of health insurance to making healthier lifestyle decisions. We will consider how consumers use heuristics and biases to make decisions about health insurance, often leading to poor decision-making.

Table 4.3 **Heuristics and Biases in Behavioral Economics**

Term	*Definition*
Availability heuristic	People estimate how common an event is based on how easily examples come to mind; people tend to rely on readily available information rather than seek out alternatives
Representativeness heuristic	People tend to judge the likelihood of an event by the extent to which it resembles the typical case; they ignore probabilistic likelihoods
Anchoring and adjustment heuristic	The tendency to rely on the first piece of information offered, the "anchor," then adjust away from it to get to a final answer; people adjust insufficiently, resulting in a final guess that is closer to the anchor than it would be otherwise
Loss aversion	The tendency to prefer avoiding losses to acquiring equivalent gains
Endowment effect	Related to loss aversion; people place a higher value on a good that they already own than on an identical good that they do not own
Decision fatigue	The deteriorating quality of decisions made by an individual who makes many decisions in a row
Affect heuristic	A mental shortcut used to make decisions wherein the individual relies on his or her current mood
Gambler's fallacy	The tendency to believe that the outcome of a random situation will be affected by previous outcomes (i.e., that a random process becomes less random as it is repeated; commonly seen in gambling situations)
Choice overload	The tendency to become overwhelmed or have a difficult time making choices when there are too many options

Source: K&T, Baumeister, Roy F. (2003). "The Psychology of Irrationality", in Brocas, Isabelle; Carrillo, Juan D, The Psychology of Economic Decisions: Rationality and Well-Being.

Health Insurance Selection

Today, most people select their health insurance. If you are employed and are receiving employer-sponsored health insurance, you choose from options typically preselected by your employer. If you are buying insurance on the individual market, you select among the available options in your state. If you are eligible for Medicare, you first choose between traditional Medicare and Medicare Advantage plans (Medicare plans managed by private health insurance companies). If you decide to choose a Medicare Advantage plan, you must select from many available options.

Furthermore, you can choose or reject a Medicare Part D plan for prescription drug coverage.

Across all of these situations, an optimal decision-making process for selecting a health insurance plan requires consumers to assess both their level of illness risk and the costs of accessing care. This entails estimating total yearly costs, including both premium costs (the monthly amount the consumer pays to maintain coverage) and out-of-pocket costs (the amount the consumer will be responsible for when she accesses medical services). This process requires that the consumer guess, or estimate, her expected medical use across the year. If the consumer selects a plan with higher monthly premium costs, the plan will likely cover a broader array of providers, as well as reduce the consumer's share of the bill when she accesses medical care. This arrangement is preferable for high utilizers of healthcare services. If they select a lower premium plan with a higher deductible, they are typically on the hook for a greater share of the costs when they need to use medical services, which they do frequently.

Researchers have shown that consumers make poor decisions when they go through the health plan selection process. For example, economists Jason Abaluck and Jonathan Gruber have shown that when consumers choose among Medicare Part D plans for prescription drug coverage, they tend to overemphasize the importance of monthly premium costs and downplay out-of-pocket costs.[51] In other words, consumers base a large portion of their decision-making on the cost of the monthly premium and fail to consider the impact of out-of-pocket costs that might be due at the time of care. As a result, most consumers underestimate the cumulative costs of their yearly out-of-pocket expenditures and thus fail to pick a plan that provides lower costs and better risk protection. Abaluck and Gruber found that the typical senior citizen could save about 30% of his total annual costs through a more appropriate choice of plan.[52] What is more, this effect occurs regardless of age, gender, predicted drug expenditures, or the predictability of drug demand.[53]

Another set of researchers showed similar biased decision-making in employer-sponsored health insurance markets. Janet Schwartz and her coauthors showed that employees choosing among employer-sponsored health insurance options proved most sensitive to the cost of yearly premiums. The results suggested "that people are much more willing to spend marginal dollars on out-of-pocket copayments than monthly insurance premiums despite the fact that the total cost of such plans will be greater for the same medical care."[54]

In addition, these poor choices persist over time as a result of inertia, as well as a preference to avoid recalculating a difficult decision. Simply put, consumers rarely switch plans when they have the opportunity to do so. A study on Medicare Advantage plans investigated decisions during the annual reenrollment when people were most likely to select a new Medicare plan. They found that the selection made when the consumer first became eligible for Medicare persisted over time.[55]

This example highlights barriers to the appropriate consideration of options in the decision-making process. Selecting a new healthcare plan would require a consumer to actively seek out information on the options available, project her own potential needs, and pick a plan that best meets her needs. In reality, many people struggle to estimate their medical care needs for the rest of the year accurately. Moreover, the time commitment and the bureaucracy involved in switching their plans are seen as too onerous relative to their cost savings.

Nevertheless, researchers have shown that these decisions can be improved. In one study, a group of seniors was presented with personalized price information created by entering their drug data into Medicare's Plan Finder website. This group saw the cost of all plans for their personal drug profile as well as how much they would save by switching to the lowest cost plan. Another group of seniors was given only the address of this website where they could access this information. Among the first group, plan switching was 28%; in the latter group, it was only 17%. Additionally, members of the first group had an average $100 decline in predicted consumer cost per year.[56]

Conclusion

The decision-making process may seem simple at first glance, but a closer look reveals that it can vary significantly based upon factors such as the decision-making unit, the healthcare situation, and the characteristics of the individual decision-maker, such as perceived risk and consumer biases. Each step of the decision-making process, from problem identification to the post purchase stage, has several notable barriers that make consumer choice difficult today. We will return to these barriers in Chapter 7, when we address the ways in which our system and the stakeholders within it—including consumers—can improve consumer choice in healthcare.

In this chapter, we have focused on the overall decision-making process. In the next chapter, we will focus on the benefits consumers most frequently seek out when making healthcare choices. Consumers are likely to seek out and consider information on these benefits during the "Information Gathering" stage, or the "Evaluation of Alternatives" stage of the decision-making process. We refer to these benefits as the six E's of consumer choice (Empathy, Economy, Experience, Effectiveness, Efficiency, and Empowerment).

References

1. Beshears, John, James J. Choi, David I. Laibson, Brigitte C. Madrian, and Gwendolyn I. Reynolds. "Vaccination Rates Are Associated With Functional Proximity but Not Base Proximity of Vaccination Clinics." *Medical Care* 54, no. 6 (2016): 578–583. Web.

2. The intention to get vaccinated against influenza and actual vaccination uptake of Dutch healthcare personnel.

3. See Beshears, John, James J. Choi, David I. Laibson, Brigitte C. Madrian, and Gwendolyn I. Reynolds. "Vaccination Rates Are Associated With Functional Proximity but Not Base Proximity of Vaccination Clinics." *Medical Care* 54, no. 6 (2016): 578–583. Web.

4. Ibuka, Yoko, Meng Li, Jeffrey Vietri, Gretchen B. Chapman, and Alison P. Galvani. "Free-Riding Behavior in Vaccination Decisions: An Experimental Study." *PLoS ONE* 9, no. 1 (2014). Web.

5. Ketchandji, Melanie, Yong-Fang Kuo, Vahakn B. Shahinian, and James S. Goodwin. "Cause of Death in Older Men After the Diagnosis of Prostate Cancer." *Journal of the American Geriatrics Society*. U.S. National Library of Medicine, January 2009. Web.

6. Drazer, Michael W., Dezheng Huo, and Scott E. Eggener. "National Prostate Cancer Screening Rates After the 2012 US Preventive Services Task Force Recommendation Discouraging Prostate-Specific Antigen–Based Screening." *Journal of Clinical Oncology*. American Society of Clinical Oncology, 8 June 2015. Web.

7. See Ketchandji, Melanie, Yong-Fang Kuo, Vahakn B. Shahinian, and James S. Goodwin. "Cause of Death in Older Men After the Diagnosis of Prostate Cancer." *Journal of the American Geriatrics Society*. U.S. National Library of Medicine, January 2009. Web.

8. Schröder, F. H., J. Hugosson, M. J. Roobol, T. L. Tammela, M. Zappa, V. Nelen, M. Kwiatkowski, M. Lujan, L. Määttänen, H. Lilja, L. J. Denis, F. Recker, A. Paez, C. H. Bangma, S. Carlsson, D. Puliti, A. Villers, X. Rebillard, M. Hakama, U. H. Stenman, P. Kujala, K. Taari, G. Aus, A. Huber, T. H. Van Der Kwast, S. M. Moss, A. Auvinen, ERSP Investigators, R. H. Van Schaik, and H. J. De Koning. "Screening and Prostate Cancer Mortality: Results of the European Randomised Study of Screening for Prostate Cancer (ERSPC) at 13 Years of Follow-Up." *Lancet*. U.S. National Library of Medicine, 6 December 2014. Web.

9. "Treating Prostate Cancer." *American Cancer Society*. Web.

10. See Ketchandji, Melanie, Yong-Fang Kuo, Vahakn B. Shahinian, and James S. Goodwin. "Cause of Death in Older Men After the Diagnosis of Prostate Cancer." *Journal of the American Geriatrics Society*. U.S. National Library of Medicine, January 2009. Web.

11. D'Amico, Anthony V. "Treatment or Monitoring for Early Prostate Cancer." *New England Journal of Medicine*. 13 October 2016. Web.

12. Hamdy, Freddie C., Jenny L. Donovan, J. Athene Lane, Malcolm Mason, Chris Metcalfe, Peter Holding, Michael Davis, Tim J. Peters, Emma L. Turner, Richard M. Martin, Jon Oxley, Mary Robinson, John Staffurth, Eleanor Walsh, Prasad Bolina, James Catto, Andrew Doble, Alan Doherty, David Gillatt, Roger Kockelbergh, Howard Kynaston, Alan Paul, Philip Powell, Stephen Prescott, Derek J. Rosario, Edward Rowe, and David E. Neal. "10-Year Outcomes After Monitoring, Surgery, or Radiotherapy for Localized Prostate Cancer." *New England Journal of Medicine*. 13 October 2016. Web.

13. Ibid.

14. Kolata, Gina. "More Men With Early Prostate Cancer Are Choosing to Avoid Treatment." *The New York Times*. 24 May 2016. Web.

15. Engel, James F., David T. Kollat, and Roger D. Blackwell. *Consumer Behavior*. Holt, Rinehart, and Winston, 1968. *WorldCat.org*. Web.

16. Magariños, M., U. Zafar, K. Nissenson, and C. Blanco. "Epidemiology and Treatment of Hypochondriasis." *CNS Drugs*. U.S. National Library of Medicine, 2002. Web.

17. "Finding Quality Doctors: How Americans Evaluate Provider Quality in the United States: Research Highlights." *APNORC.org*. NORC Center for Public Affairs Research at the University of Chicago, 2014. Web.

18. Merchant, Raina M., Kevin G. Volpp, and David A. Asch. "Importance of Online Comments and Ratings to Health Care Improvement." *The JAMA Network*. American Medical Association, 20 December 2016. Web.

19. Ibid.

20. What Do Consumers Want From Health Care? Top Findings From Our Three Consumer Choice Surveys." The Advisory Board, 22 June 2015. Web.

21. See "Finding Quality Doctors: How Americans Evaluate Provider Quality in the United States: Research Highlights." APNORC.org. NORC Center for Public Affairs Research at the University of Chicago, 2014. Web.

22. Desai, Sunita, Laura A. Hatfield, Andrew L. Hicks, Anna D. Sinaiko, Michael E. Chernew, David Cowling, Santosh Gautam, Sze-jung Wu, and Ateev Mehrotra. "Offering a Price Transparency Tool Did Not Reduce Overall Spending Among California Public Employees and Retirees." Health Affairs, 1 August 2017. Web.

23. Sinaiko, Anna D., and Meredith B. Rosenthal. "Examining a Health Care Price Transparency Tool: Who Uses It, and How They Shop for Care." Health Affairs 35, no. 4 (2016): 662–670. Web.

24. Ibid.

25. Frakt, Austin. "Price Transparency Is Nice. Just Don't Expect It to Cut Health Costs." The New York Times, 19 December 2016. Web.

26. Ibid.

27. Ibid.

28. De Brantes, Francois, and Suzanne Delbanco. "Report Card on State Price Transparency Laws." Health Care Incentives Improvement Institute. Catalyst for Payment Reform (CPR), July 2016. Web.

29. Gourevitch, Rebecca A., Ateev Mehrotra, Grace Galvin, Melinda Karp, Avery Plough, and Neel T. Shah. "How Do Pregnant Women Use Quality Measures When Choosing Their Obstetric Provider?" Birth Issues in Perinatal Care. Wiley Online Library, 26 January 2017. Web.

30. Kozhimannil, Katy Backes, Michael R. Law, and Beth A. Virnig. "Cesarean Delivery Rates Vary 10-Fold Among US Hospitals; Reducing Variation May Address Quality, Cost Issues." Health Affairs 32, no. 3 (2013). 527–535. Web.

31. Kotler, Philip, and Gary Armstrong. Principles of Marketing. 17th ed. Pearson, 2017. Print. p. 172.

32. Norman, Jim. "Americans Rate Healthcare Providers High on Honesty, Ethics." Gallup.com. Gallup Inc., 19 December 2016. Web.

33. Blendon, Robert J., John M. Benson, and Joachim O. Hero. "Public Trust in Physicians— U.S. Medicine in International Perspective." New England Journal of Medicine. 29 October 2014. Web.

34. Ibid.

35. Heiman, Harry J., and Samantha Artiga. "Beyond Health Care: The Role of Social Determinants in Promoting Health and Health Equity." The Henry J. Kaiser Family Foundation. 4 November 2015. Web.

36. "Closing the Gap in a Generation: Health Equity Through Action on the Social Determinants of Health." Final Report of the Commission on Social Determinants of Health. World Health Organization, 2008. Web.

37. Schroeder, Steven A. "We Can Do Better - Improving the Health of the American People." New England Journal of Medicine 357, no. 12 (2007): 1221–1228. Web.

38. Saelens, Brian E., James F. Sallis, and Lawrence D. Frank. "Environmental Correlates of Walking and Cycling: Findings From the Transportation, Urban Design, and Planning Literatures." The Society of Behavioral Medicine 25, no. 2 (2003): 80–91. Web.

39. Singh, Gopal K., Mohammad Siahpush, and Michael D. Kogan. "Neighborhood Socioeconomic Conditions, Built Environments, and Childhood Obesity." Health Affairs 29, no. 3 (2010): 503–512. Web.

40. Jonas, Michael. "Opportunity Gap." CommonWealth Magazine. 13 October 2015. Web.

41. "National Action Plan to Improve Health Literacy." U.S. Department of Health and Human Services. Office of Disease Prevention and Health Promotion, 2010. Web.

42. Ibid.

43. Cutilli, Carolyn Crane, and Ian M. Bennett. "Understanding the Health Literacy of America Results of the National Assessment of Adult Literacy." *Orthopaedic nursing / National Association of Orthopaedic Nurses* 28, no. 1 (2009): 27–34. PMC. Web.

44. "Consider Culture, Customs, and Beliefs: Tool #10." *Agency for Healthcare Research and Quality.* U.S. Department of Health & Human Services, February 2015. Web.

45. Wong, Nancy and Tracey King. "The Cultural Construction of Risk Understandings Through Illness Narratives." *Journal of Consumer Research* 34, no. 5 (February 2008): 579–594. Web.

46. "Total Hospitals (2015)." *The Henry J. Kaiser Family Foundation.* 30 August 2017. Web.

47. Friedman, Howard S. *The Oxford Handbook of Health Psychology.* 1st ed. Oxford UP, 2014. Print. p. 592.

48. Ibid.

49. Kahneman, Daniel, and Amos Tversky. "Prospect Theory: An Analysis of Decision Making Under Risk." (1979): Web.

50. Samper, Adriana L., and Janet A. Schwartz. "Price Inferences for Sacred Versus Secular Goods: Changing the Price of Medicine Influences Perceived Health Risk." *Journal of Consumer Research* 39, no. 6 (2013): 1343–1358. Web.

51. Abaluck, Jason, and Jonathan Gruber. "Evolving Choice Inconsistencies in Choice of Prescription Drug Insurance." *American Economic Review* (2013). Web.

52. Ibid.

53. Abaluck, Jason, and Jonathan Gruber. "Heterogeneity in Choice Inconsistencies Among the Elderly: Evidence From Prescription Drug Plan Choice." *American Economic Review* 101, no. 3 (2011): 377–381. Web.

54. Schwartz, Janet, Nortin M. Hadler, Dan Ariely, Joel C. Huber, and Thomas Emerick. "Choosing Among Employer-Sponsored Health Plans." *Journal of Occupational and Environmental Medicine* 55, no. 3 (2013): 305–309. Web.

55. Sinaiko, Anna D., Christopher C. Afendulis, and Richard G. Frank. "Enrollment in Medicare Advantage Plans in Miami-Dade County: Evidence of Status Quo Bias?" *Inquiry* 50 (2013): 202–215. Web.

56. Kling, Jeffrey R., Sendhil Mullainathan, Eldar Shafir, Lee Vermeulen, and Marian Wrobel. "Comparison Friction: Experimental Evidence From Medicare Drug Plans." *The National Bureau of Economic Research (NBER).* September 2011. Web.

5

The Six E's of Consumer Choice

In 2017, Ruth was an 89-year-old woman considering the possibility of moving into an assisted living community. Her decision, in which her children were involved, was fraught with indecision. Understanding how Ruth, the healthcare consumer, arrived at this point requires knowing much more about Ruth, the person.

Born in 1928 and raised in a small suburb of Detroit, she had been a bright and precocious child. She had married in her early 20s, and over the course of the next 10 years, she and her husband Tom had four children together. The years passed quickly between work and home life, but they managed to maintain an active social life centered on their community. Long after her children had grown up and started families of their own, Ruth remained energetic and involved in community events. A lifelong learner, she never lost her knack for sharing that passion with others. After she retired, she volunteered at a local museum, giving tours on the weekends. With eight grandchildren, and one great-grandchild, she continued to host large gatherings during the holidays at the home she had owned with her husband, even years after he had passed away from a heart attack.

It was soon after one such celebration, her 87th birthday party, when her children began to notice that Ruth seemed to be reading less frequently. Over the next year, it became clear to them that she was often confused as to what day it was or where she was supposed to be. One day, her daughter visited around 11 AM and noticed that her mother had left the stove on when making tea earlier in the morning. The children discussed the incident together afterward and grew concerned. Two of her children lived nearby and began checking in on her more frequently. They also decided to hire both a housecleaner, who could come in once a week and tidy up, and a home health aide, who visited twice a week, ensuring that Ruth had groceries and that she was taking her medications appropriately. Ruth was grateful for their help, but she felt that she could manage things just fine without it.

After she took a fall walking in her garden in the spring, the kids began suggesting a move to an assisted living community in the neighboring town. She balked. She had lived in her house for over 30 years. It had a large backyard and, when it was warm out in the summer, she liked to sit on her porch. Though the house was a lot to care for at times, the thought of leaving it was gut-wrenching.

In his popular book, *Being Mortal*, Atul Gawande discusses many of these issues, including how attitudes toward aging and dying in the United States have transformed over the last several decades.[1] As families have dispersed and the average life expectancy has increased, more and more old people are living on their own. At the same time, they have a broader array of health issues, and their challenges make living independently more and more difficult. Many families face situations similar to Ruth's. Although she did not have a clear health issue that would require immediate hospitalization, her children were feeling more apprehensive about her living on her own.

Ruth and her family recognized that something needed to change, but they weren't sure what the solution would be. The difficult decisions ahead weighed heavily on the whole family. Though they had lived a comfortable lifestyle, they did not have unlimited savings to fund her care. They wanted to be sure that the facility had the resources to do clinical things like monitor Ruth's medication regimen, but they also wanted her to maintain, at least to some extent, the independence she enjoyed in her home. They hoped they could find a situation that might achieve both, at a reasonable cost. They faced a difficult litany of questions in this quest: What level of care would Ruth need? When would it be time to move to an assisted living community? Should they consider a nursing home? How far away from her current house would it be? How far away would it be from her children's homes? How much would it cost, and what could she afford? Answering these questions involved discussions between Ruth and her family members.

In the last chapter, we reviewed the typical process by which healthcare consumers make decisions, as well as how that process can differ based on the healthcare situation or the individual. In this chapter, we'll take a closer look at what consumers want. Whenever consumers make a choice—in healthcare or in other situations—they do so based on the benefits they anticipate. We'll focus on the most common benefits consumers seek when making health and wellness decisions. Though they may vary in relative importance based upon the healthcare decision at hand, these six commonly sought benefits are economy, effectiveness, empathy, efficiency, empowerment, and experience. In Table 5.1 each benefit is defined and then illustrated through the lens of primary care physician choice.

Benefits and Decision-Making

Before we take a closer look at each of these six benefits, we first need a clear understanding of the role of features and benefits in consumer decision-making. A feature resides within a product or service, whereas a benefit is what the feature delivers to the consumer. Features are observable, concrete attributes, such as design or price, while benefits describe the jobs they perform for consumers. At the end of the day,

Table 5.1 **The Six E's: Benefits Consumers Consider in Healthcare Decision-Making**

Category	General Definition	Example: Primary Care Physician Choice
Economy	The financial costs to the consumer that are associated with the health or wellness intervention	• Monetary costs the patient incurs by utilizing care • Includes the cost of the visit and is affected by health plan coverage
Effectiveness	The health-promoting ability of the intervention; clinical excellence	• The clinical expertise of the care provided; the level of the physician's training or knowledge • Can be measured by clinical outcomes or process-based metrics (e.g., provider adherence to clinical guidelines or standards)
Empathy	The emotional attributes of the healthcare service	• The emotional connection/relationship between the patient-consumer and the provider(s) • Is often established through provider–patient communication, understanding, and emotional/spiritual support
Efficiency	The convenience and timeliness with which services are delivered	• The convenience in appointment-making, wait times at appointments, and ease of communication in follow-up or receipt of results
Experience	The overall level of service associated with the health product or intervention	• How the patient-consumer perceives the overall level of service at the provider • Patient perception may be influenced by facility design, patient safety, and patient–provider or patient–administrator interactions
Empowerment	The extent to which the consumer feels autonomous and in control of decisions regarding his or her health	• How engaged the consumer feels in care decisions • Can be affected by provider-led patient engagement efforts or patient-led empowerment

Source: Mittal, Banwari. *Consumer Behavior: How Humans Think, Feel, and Act in the Marketplace*. First edition. Open Mentis Publishers. March 2007. Print.

consumers choose products and services primarily to solve problems—for their benefits, not for their individual features. As marketing guru Theodore Levitt famously stated: "People don't want to buy a quarter-inch drill. They want a quarter-inch hole!" Or as Charles Revlon, founder of Revlon, said: "At Revlon, we don't sell cosmetics, we sell hope."

Benefits are what consumers seek in the first place. As an example, let's consider a flashy, red toy car for young children. One feature is that it is finished with lead-free paint. But to a concerned father who has young children, the benefit is safety—that his children will avoid any risk of lead poisoning. An advantage of one product over another might be more rigorous safety and quality assurance testing by a third-party company.

Every consumer evaluates benefits when making a purchase decision, yet different consumers approach the benefit evaluation task in different ways. Some may conduct a thorough evaluation of multiple alternatives across the whole array of benefits, weighing in their mind or sometimes on paper the relative importance of each benefit, the degree of perceived difference among the alternatives on each dimension, and the trade-offs they are prepared to make. This thorough process is especially likely to occur when consumers can plan ahead, are heavily involved in the choice, and feel an especially high risk from making a poor selection.

Other consumers may focus on just one benefit as a bellwether for overall value, either to make the selection process easier or because they don't see much difference among the other benefits. Alternatively, the decision may not be regarded as sufficiently significant to warrant a thorough effort, or the information available may not be viewed as reliable enough to justify the extra time.

However, none of this matters if the maker of the product does not articulate these features and benefits to the consumer. Sometimes the benefits will be obvious to the consumer when he reviews the features. Other times, it is the company's role to help the consumer make the connection between feature and benefit. Too often, sellers focus on promoting features, rather than the associated benefits.

Figure 5.1 helps to delineate these tradeoffs. For each consumer, benefits vary not just in terms of their relative importance but also in terms of the degree of

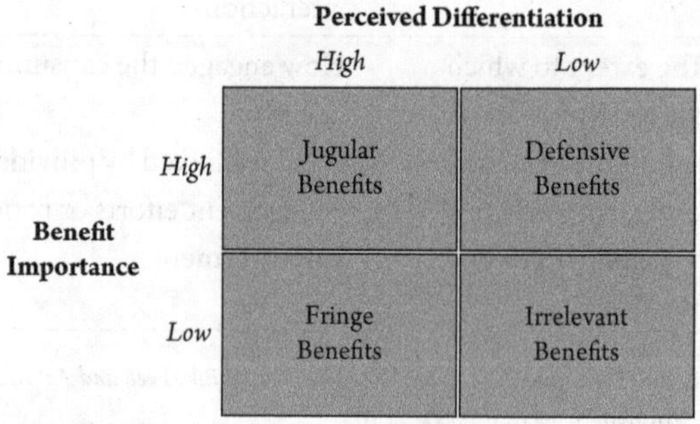

		Perceived Differentiation	
		High	Low
Benefit Importance	High	Jugular Benefits	Defensive Benefits
	Low	Fringe Benefits	Irrelevant Benefits

Figure 5.1 Benefits segmentation.

perceived differentiation among the options. The most likely choice is the one that is superior on the "jugular" benefits, those that are both highly important and on which the options are seen to be differentiated. Of course, it's important that the selected option meet minimum standards on defensive benefits (also known as "must-haves") such as product safety, but superiority on safety factors isn't usually the tie-breaker. Managers who spend time promoting "fringe" benefits are unlikely to succeed. A woman's razor that is the same shape as a man's razor but happens to be colored pink is an example—it's clearly different but on a benefit that's unimportant.

The importance a consumer places on each healthcare decision can be diagrammed within a hexagon. The relative weighting will likely differ depending on the decision. Conceptually, when there are multiple decision-makers, for example, as in the selection of a retirement home or senior living facility, we can map the hexagon for each decision influencer and weight each according to his or her relative influence in reaching the final decision. Figure 5.2a depicts an influencer who values each attribute equally.

Most consumers will attach different weights to different benefits. For example, let's consider the consumer depicted in Figure 5.2b, who has just moved to a new town and is deciding on a primary care physician. The dotted line depicts how he weights the relative importance of the six benefits in contrast to the situation in which all of them are considered equally. He clearly values economy most, followed by efficiency. He isn't as concerned about the experience. A marketer would best

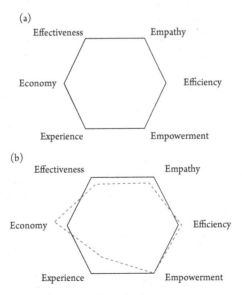

Figure 5.2 Graphic display of consumer benefit choices.

connect to this consumer and others like him by designing an offering and using messaging that highlights value pricing and faster service.

Note that consumer choices based on the benefits of the six E's are choices based on perceptions. The adage "perception is reality" applies here. Consumer perceptions are shaped by prior experience and by the advice of friends or the wisdom of crowds on websites like Yelp. Perceptions of quality are also shaped by tangible evidence. You cannot know for sure how successful surgery is going to be at one hospital versus another. But you can see for yourself whether the foyer is clean, whether the furnishings are modern, and whether the service at the reception desk is responsive. All these factors influence your perception of each hospital's quality. If there are significant differences in your perceptions, you may assume—correctly or incorrectly—that these differences spill over to the likely quality of surgery. The perceived quality of the tangibles influences your impression of the likely quality of the intangibles.

For a consumer to consider every available option against each of the six E's would be very time-consuming, even more so if she decided to research each dimension rather than simply rely on her perceptions. In some cases, such as the choice of a surgeon for critical and risky surgery, consumer involvement would be greater and more time would be devoted to considering other options more thoroughly. In emergency situations, time is not available. If the consumer has thought ahead, she may have established a preference for a particular hospital in an emergency. But if she is traveling away from home, she may have little choice.

At the other end of the spectrum are routine, relatively less important healthcare decisions. You cut your finger in your workshop. Do you go to the emergency room in a teaching hospital nine miles away or an urgent care clinic in a shopping mall one mile away? You've not been to the clinic before but you've heard good things about it from friends, and you remember seeing a large sign on the door indicating that it's open on weekends. You don't pull out a pad of paper and complete a full multiattribute analysis; you use decision shortcuts that focus on the key trade-offs among the six E's.

Although a consumer may consider several or even all of these benefits when making a decision, she can rarely maximize on all six. Consumers use different decision rules to make trade-offs among benefits. One model is to compensate, or balance, among the six Es; this is called a compensatory model. When using this approach, a consumer considers the entire product and service attributes. He then trades off an option's perceived weaknesses on one or more attributes with its perceived strengths on the other attributes. The other model, called non-compensatory, employs shortcuts around the sometimes cumbersome multiattribute compensatory model. There are four types of decision-making shortcuts typically used. These are listed in Table 5.2.

Finally, healthcare providers should also keep in mind that the benefits consumers explicitly state are most important to them are not always the ones that have the

Table 5.2 **Noncompensatory Models of Consumer Decision-Making**

Model	Definition
The Conjuctive Model	• The consumer uses minimum cut-offs for all attributes to compare options. • Each option is then examined on each attribute, and any option that meets the minimum cut-offs on all attributes might be chosen. • If an option fails to reach the cut-off, even on one attribute, it is dropped from consideration. • If all options fail to reach the cut-off levels, then the consumer revises his minimum cut-off levels or uses another decision model. • If more than one option meets all the minimum cut-off levels, the consumer uses another decision model to decide between remaining options.
The Disjunctive Model	• The disjunctive model entails trade-offs between aspects of choice options; the consumer is willing to trade off one feature for another. • The consumer considers the presence or absence of attributes, rather than the degree or amount in which these attributes are present.
The Lexicographic Model	• In the lexicographic model, the consumer rank-orders the product or service attributes in terms of importance. • First, the consumer examines all options on the most important attribute and identifies the option ranking the highest on that attribute. • If more than one option remains, the consumer considers the second most important attribute and repeats the process.
Elimination by Aspect	• The elimination by aspect model is similar to the lexicographic model, but the consumer rates the attributes in order of importance, but also defines the minimum required values. • He or she then examines all alternatives first on the most important attribute, admitting for further consideration only those contenders that satisfy the minimum cut-off level on this most important attribute. • If more than one alternative met this requirement, then the consumer would go to the next step, appraising the remaining alternatives on the second most important attribute, and retaining only those that met the minimum cut-off level on this attribute, and so on.

greatest impact on their overall satisfaction. In 2014, McKinsey's Consumer Health Insights survey showed that there is often a disconnect between what consumers believe matters most and what influences their overall opinions most. The analysts derived this conclusion by mapping the individual factors that hospitalized patients said influenced their satisfaction against their overall reported levels of satisfaction. Although consumers were likely to state that the outcome achieved was the most important influence on their satisfaction, the analysts found that empathy provided by doctors and nurses had a stronger impact on overall satisfaction than outcomes did (see Figure 5.3). Satisfaction levels were also influenced heavily by the information consumers received during and after treatment.

Often, it is necessary in this consumer research to tease out the relative importance of price ("economy" in the six E's model). Consumers tend to say everything is important unless they are forced to make price trade-offs by being asked how much extra they are prepared to pay for a particular benefit. Conjoint analysis is an especially useful methodology when the willingness of consumers to pay for extra benefits needs to be explored. This is a market research methodology in which a respondent is presented with a set of alternative product or service descriptions. Each product or service is identified by its attributes and benefits, and the respondent is forced to make trade-offs between different products. Using these data, the researcher is able to determine the utility the consumer assigns to each benefit. On an aggregate level, this information can feed into a segmentation strategy, as we'll discuss in the next chapter. It is likely that different segments of consumers will share patterns of ranking among different benefits and, ultimately, guide health systems when they are deciding where to prioritize new investments.

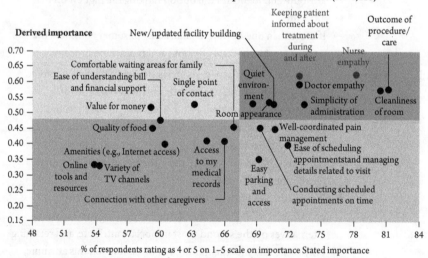

Figure 5.3 Influencers on consumer satisfaction: stated importance versus derived.
Source: Cordina, Jenny, Rohit Kumar, and Christa Moss. "Debunking common myths about healthcare consumerism." McKinsey & Company: Healthcare Systems & Services. December 2015.

Next, we'll review each of the six E's in greater depth. Draw on personal experience as we discuss each of them. Consider which E's might be most important to you as a healthcare consumer and which model of decision-making you might be most likely to use.

Economy

People have limited resources, so perceptions about costs are critical to any consumer decision. Most consumers seek to achieve the greatest value; that is, the most quality for the lowest price. However, price often acts upon consumers as a signal about quality. A higher price can suggest better quality or a more in-demand brand, whereas lower priced items suggest the opposite. Consumers use such assumptions, mental shortcuts, and approximations from past experiences to make decisions.

Despite its importance, many consumers have a difficult time estimating the prices of different products or services—even for common items like groceries, which they purchase regularly.[2] However, in many markets, they rarely need to do the sorting of costs themselves. Third-party companies have filled the void to help improve price transparency and apples-to-apples comparisons. Consider the arduous task of price comparison for air travel prior to websites like Expedia and KAYAK. A person planning a trip might have had to call three or four different flight carriers before finding the best deal. Now, she simply plugs in her destination points online and the best available prices are shown to her.

Just as economy is only one of six benefits discussed in this chapter, so price is far from being the dominant or only differentiating factor consumers consider. For example, although many food retailers know that cost is important, a 2016 Nielsen study reported that consumers rate high-quality produce, convenient location, and product availability above price.[3]

Economy in Healthcare: Definition and Importance

Medical care is pricy. As healthcare costs have increased, about one-third of Americans are overburdened by their medical expenses.[4] For example, we know that many cancer patients burn through their life savings and go into debt while accessing treatment. One study on cancer costs found that one-third of survivors had gone into debt, with 55% of that group owing more than $10,000.[5]

Cost is one of the most frequently confusing elements in healthcare decision-making. Most people view healthcare costs, even when they are minimal, as defeating. Nobody looks forward to spending his hard-earned savings on a hip replacement or MRI. And discussions of healthcare costs can become quite complex, especially because we often consider cost and quality together, referring to the

overall "value" of the product or service. As previously discussed, healthcare services are often credence goods—it is difficult for consumers to judge the impact or
utility of the services, even after consumption. .

As in other markets, higher prices can act as a signal of quality to some healthcare consumers. However, many consumers have a difficult time assessing the relationship between price and quality in healthcare. In 2014, a consumer survey by The
Associated Press–NORC Center for Public Affairs Research found that only about half
of Americans believe that higher quality healthcare comes at a higher cost, and 37%
believe there is no real relationship between quality and cost at all.[6] This finding was
replicated by a Mass Insight consumer survey in 2016 in which 75% of respondents in
Massachusetts indicated that they did not think higher prices for medical procedures
were a sign of higher quality (16% weren't sure and only 9% thought they were).[7]

This confusion about the relationship between price and quality may happen
because, as a consumer, it is difficult to understand the total cost of a procedure,
particularly when one has insurance. The price charged by the healthcare provider
depends on the type of insurance plan the consumer has, and the consumer is rarely
aware of the contracting that occurs between insurers and provider organizations.
Furthermore, if an insurer covers part of the cost, the consumer may receive a bill
for only a portion of the total cost.

Consumers often do not understand their bills. Consider a 2016 study, which
found that patients often face surprise medical charges (i.e., a provider bill that they
did not expect or did not choose) from out-of-network providers.[8] Nine percent of
elective inpatient admissions led to a surprise charge, and, even more significantly,
20% of inpatient admissions that originated in the Emergency Department did the
same.[9] If patients aren't informed that what they're using has an additional cost, or
don't know to ask, how can they possibly make informed decisions?

A lack of comparative information makes this task even more difficult. As we
discussed in Chapter 3, transparency and comparison tools have improved in
healthcare, but they are still in their infancy. Cost estimates must be based on what
services the person needs, as well as her individual insurance plan design. However,
this means that cost information is only available from entities that many consumers
do not trust: health insurers.[10]

Even when comparative data are available, it may not be useful for consumer
decision-making. When Medicare publicly released hospital pricing information
in 2013, many in the media noted the large discrepancies between what different
hospitals charged for the same procedures in the same area. However, hospitals
argued that those prices come from a "chargemaster,"* which is rarely relevant to

---

* A hospital's internal list of prices, which typically includes prices for every service/procedure
offered at the hospital and every supply used. The chargemaster rate is rarely paid by insurers. It serves
as the starting point for negotiated prices, usually far below the stated amount. Consumers without
insurance typically are billed close to the total charge.

consumers. The amount that Medicare actually pays to a hospital is usually far less than what the hospital bills Medicare. At the time of the public release, Carol Steinberg, vice president of the American Hospital Association, was quoted in *The Washington Post* as saying, "The chargemaster can be confusing because it's highly variable and generally not what a consumer would pay. Even an uninsured person isn't always paying the chargemaster rate."[11]

Without delving into the intricacies of hospital–payer contracting, it's safe to say that, in combination, these forces disguise the total expected costs of procedures for consumers. Prices, for the most part, feel arbitrary to consumers, and it's difficult to make any connection between price and quality.

Choosing what health insurance is the best deal for them is not easier. This choice—a decision most consumers must now make annually whether it be through a public exchange, an employer's set of options, or Medicare enrollment. Consumers must consider their need for future risk protection, as well as the economic costs of being insured. Ideally, they would ask themselves the following: What level of coverage do I need? What is the likelihood that I experience a major illness this year? Do I value a wider physician network or will a narrower network plan suffice? How much am I willing to spend on a health plan? What are my projected costs, considering both monthly premium and expected out-of-pocket costs? What other attributes about a plan are important to me?

No one looks forward to reviewing the intricacies of insurance plans. It is an inconvenience. It's also no surprise that, as we discussed in Chapter 4 under Choosing Health Insurance, consumers are biased and make poor decisions when it comes to health insurance. This introduces yet another potential "cost" of care—the effort of planning and arranging. Separate from the direct costs associated with receiving treatment, consumers use time and energy to make decisions about which providers to travel to, which tests to undergo, and what health plan best serves their unique set of needs.

Consumers and Economy: What Consumers Value

Transparency

It has been widely acknowledged that increased price transparency is a significant challenge. To appropriately consider cost in decision-making, people must have better access to accurate pricing information. Additionally, it must be up-to-date, understandable, and available at the time of decision-making.

Lower Priced Options

Obviously, most consumers would prefer to spend less for care. However, this shouldn't be seen as a race to the bottom in terms of quality. Although no one would like to dip below a certain quality threshold, there are ways for provider or-ganizations to reduce the cost of delivering care without sacrificing on quality. The increasing number of retail clinics, urgent care centers, and virtual clinics highlights this trend. Consumers can use these lower priced options for common ailments, like minor infections or stitches, which are much more expensive to deal with in a hospital setting.

Communication About Costs

In an article published in 2014 by oncologists at Duke, the researchers described a young cancer patient who had been receiving a chemotherapy drug as treatment. After receiving the treatment for a period of time, the patient voiced concern about its cost. The physicians were surprised; they didn't realize that the drug wasn't cov-ered by the patient's insurance plan and that he had been paying thousands of dollars in out-of-pocket costs. They switched him to a similar medication, which was covered by his insurance plan; however, the experience left them with the impression that cost-related discussions need to become a greater part of patient care.[12]

Communication with consumers about healthcare costs is often meager if not absent. For example, one group of researchers found 52% of cancer patients wanted to discuss treatment-related out-of-pocket costs with their physicians, but only 19% did so.[13] In another study, researchers identified several physician behaviors that impede open conversations about consumers' out-of-pocket spending.[14] Some physicians never acknowledge financial concerns during the appointment, while others dismiss them too quickly. Other times, physicians fail to resolve uncer-tainty about out-of-pocket expenses or only provide short-term solutions to cost concerns. Many patients would like to discuss not only their clinical concerns but also their social and economic challenges as well.

And to be fair, physicians often don't have the knowledge, training, or time to address these challenges. At the point of care, they may not know the intricacies of a patient's insurance plan or which care option will deliver the most cost-effective choice. Physicians receive little training in health policy or economics during med-ical school, making it challenging for them to discuss costs openly in the same way that they address clinical problems.[15]

Improved Billing and Payment Plans

Too often consumers receive a medical bill that they struggle to understand. In March 2015, the Consumer Reports National Research Center conducted a survey to assess the experience of consumers with private health insurance. It found that in the previous two years, more than a third of those surveyed had received a med-ical bill where they had to pay more than anticipated (i.e., their health insurer paid less than expected).[16] This problem is so pervasive that *The Atlantic* ran an article entitled "The Agony of Medical Bills."[17]

The typical medical bill includes information on the services the consumer received, how much each service cost, and how much the insurer has covered. Of course, it also includes the residual amount that the individual consumer owes. However, because there is no standard for consumer medical expense reporting, consumers receive bills that vary in both content and presentation. To make matters more confusing, people receive bills and explanations of benefits from multiple sources (e.g., provider organizations and health insurers), frequently for the same service encounter. These documents can come at varying times after an episode, within days or even months later.

Meanwhile, consumers are paying most of their other bills very conveniently, frequently online. Offering easy-to-access online payment services, including credit card options, is desirable not only for consumer satisfaction but also for timely payment collection. In addition, many consumers want more flexibility in payment plans. When you go to purchase an expensive new TV, you may be offered layaway, staggered payment, no-money-down, and no-interest options. As consumers become responsible for an ever-growing portion of their medical bills, many need and will request more consumer-friendly payment options.

Some insurers and delivery providers have started to respond to these needs. A number of health insurers offer online payment estimators, which can give consumers a sense of what they might pay before they access care. Delivery organizations are also taking steps to improve billing practices and cost transparency. Some of these actions may take place before the time of service, some at the point of care, and still others will be necessary in follow-up. As we discussed, cost isn't the only factor consumers consider when making decisions; however, it remains an important one.

For example, instead of the traditional practice of billing patients after services are provided, some providers are contacting patients before their appointments to discuss their ability to pay. If issues with payment are expected, financial counselors can set up alternative payment plans with patients to ease the burden of paying a large sum all at once. This helps to mitigate unexpected costs after the consumer has returned home. The Henry Country Health Care Center in Iowa, a 25-bed rural hospital, began using this strategy because of an increase in unpaid bills—even among insured patients, who had previously paid their bills on time. The center also provides a discount for early payment, benefitting both the individual and the center. "Most patients are appreciative that we're telling them up front," said David Muhs, chief financial officer for the hospital.[18] Receiving the estimate leads some patients to skip or delay care, while others use no-interest loans available through the hospital. One caveat is that this might be potentially damaging to long-term outcomes if patients choose to postpone necessary treatment.

After a visit, many consumers struggle when a medical bill arrives that they don't understand. Frustrated or confused consumers may be less likely to pay their bills on time, and bad debt is a very real problem many hospitals and health systems face. Ultimately, it's in the best interest of the provider to bill the patient quickly and accurately, and to minimize the expense of doing it. Unlike digital collection systems linking provider organizations and payers, collecting directly from consumers often entails more work. This wastes time and money and ultimately reduces the net profit associated with payment.[19] Further, there is a strong relationship between the consumer's billing experience and overall satisfaction.[20]

There have also been discussions around improving medical bill presentation. In 2016, a group of partners, which included AARP and The Department of Health and Human Services (HHS), sponsored a challenge called "A Bill You Can Understand." The purpose was simple: to make medical bills more consumer friendly.[21] The winning designs, which focused on enhancing presentation and information, were awarded cash prizes. The first-place design focused on making the bill as concise as possible, while using plain language explanations to put charges in context. It also provided a frequently asked questions section with answers to common questions and definitions of important terminology. The presentation made use of different color segments on the page or screen, making it easy to locate and read specific information.[22] Although the bills are not yet used in practice, the competition stimulated a shift in the *status quo* in billing.

Effectiveness

Effectiveness is "the degree to which something is successful in producing a desired result; success."[23] For something to be seen as effective, it must achieve an outcome that the customer expects. There is no reason to purchase something if it does not produce the desired result. For example, if you take your malfunctioning computer to a repair store, the only effective outcome is to leave with a working computer.

Judging in advance whether a product or service will be effective is inherently difficult when you haven't used it before. This is typically true in credence industries where, as we described in chapter 4, even after the event, the individual consumer can know only if their own problem has improved but not what would have happened if the intervention had not been undertaken. This is especially daunting in industries like healthcare, where the seller is highly skilled in providing the service, and the buyer is not sophisticated about the level of quality. In the end, even quality and a "successful" outcome vary widely in the eye of the beholder. For example, consider an elderly person who has severe pain in her hip, making it difficult to walk around her house. She might find a hip replacement to be effective for improving her mobility within the home and enabling her to maintain independence. For a younger person, such as someone in his 40s or 50s, who is an avid marathon runner but has trouble with his knee, effective treatment would involve more than simply improving mobility; effective intervention would require that he be able to run long distances again.

Effectiveness in Healthcare: Definition and Importance

What benefits does the consumer seek in the domain of Effectiveness? The prospective user first wants to be assured about how likely it is that the action will address their problem. Second they want to be confident about the competence of their caregivers. Effectiveness is assessed with deceptively simple questions: Will the intervention do what I need and want? Is the provider capable? Depending on the situation, when assessing effectiveness, you might ask: Will this prescribed drug lower my risk of disease? Will that surgical procedure alleviate my pain? Is my physician well regarded as effective by her peers?

The consumer who desires the benefits generated in the domain of effectiveness has two options, in a credence industry, for developing their perceptions of effectiveness. The first is to rely on impressionistic information such as brand, anecdotal information from other users or buyers, and externalities such as the demeanor of the doctor and the appearance of the office or hospital. Such information can influence the consumer's perception of effectiveness, which is important but still leaves them not truly informed. The second is to be presented with information based on actual evidence drawn from sound studies of the caregiver's process and outcomes, enabling the consumer to see actual evidence of effectiveness as they consider their own decision.

Effectiveness of a proposed medical intervention is, therefore, best assessed by the study of the results in many patients. This necessitates that providers and insurers create a process to gather evidence about effectiveness. For this reason, the definition of *effectiveness* in healthcare has evolved over time. As discussed in a 2016 blog post in *Health Affairs*, the definition of *effectiveness* has changed over the last 70 years from insurance companies determining medical necessity, to measuring achievement of evidence-based medicine (EBM), and, finally, to assessing if providers have improved the health of the populations they care for. In the 1940s, health insurance companies coined the term "medical necessity" to distinguish between care they would pay for and care they would not (services that were viewed as unnecessary, excessive, or experimental). However, what was deemed necessary or excessive was often at odds with consumer perceptions.

Evidence-based medicine focuses on applying the most current, research-based evidence to clinical decision-making. "Evidence-based medicine" is defined as "the integration of best research evidence with clinical expertise and patient values."[24] Its practical application is through the use by doctors of expert guidelines based on EBM. Effectiveness is assessed by the adherence of providers to guidelines.

Population health added in an additional component of "value" (i.e., level of health outcomes per dollar spent) in defined populations.[25] The Robert Wood Johnson Foundation (RWJF) defined "effective care" as follows:

> Effective care includes health care services that are of proven value and have no significant tradeoffs. The benefits of the services so far outweigh the risks that all patients with specific medical needs should receive them. These services, such as beta-blockers for heart attack patients, are backed by well-articulated medical theory and strong evidence of efficacy, determined by clinical trials or valid cohort studies.[26]

In truth, all of these definitions likely capture separate components of effectiveness. Effectiveness in healthcare speaks to quality, evidence, and, ultimately, outcomes. Quality is consistently listed as the most important attribute consumers consider in medical decisions.[27] And there are many rating systems that seek to assess hospital, physician, and health plan quality. These include Centers for Medicare and Medicaid Services (CMS) star ratings for health plans and hospitals, as well as Vitals, Healthgrades, US News & World Reports, Leapfrog, and Press Ganey (which assesses both patient experience and clinical quality). Hospitals also go through credentialing processes through The Joint Commission to ensure patient safety and meet defined standards.

However, many consumers still struggle to access information on healthcare quality. Despite the plethora of rating systems, only 48% of American consumers report that it is easy to find trusted information on the quality of care provided by different doctors in their local areas; and notably, fewer than a quarter of consumers in 2014 had seen information comparing doctors in the previous year.[28] Even among consumers who have seen information comparing physicians within the last year, most still rely on family and friends for doctor quality ratings. See Table 5.3.

Consumers and Effectiveness: What Patients Value

Accurate Diagnosis and Appropriate Treatment

Consumers desire timely diagnoses and appropriate treatments. When going to a hospital or physician's office, their ultimate goal is, in their minds, to resolve the medical problem that brought them in. Although many consumers will state that effectiveness (i.e., quality) is one of the most important factors in healthcare decision-making, as we discussed above, it's not always clear how to judge it. Many consumers associate their preferred, trusted physicians or medications that they believe are working with effectiveness, and therefore choose a health plan that covers them. For others who receive a difficult medical diagnosis with a risky

Table 5.3 **Consumers' Sources of Quality Information Comparing Doctors (Among Those That Have Seen Comparative Information Within the Year)**

Source	Consumers Who Have Seen Information From That Source*
Friends or family	65%
Newspaper or magazine	50%
Doctor or other healthcare provider	50%
Health insurance company	45%
Ratings website	40%
Online on a community or advocacy group's website	35%
Online on a government website	30%

*Percentages are approximated.

Source: Adapted from data presented in "Finding Quality Doctors: How Americans Evaluate Provider Quality in the United States: Research Highlights." *APNORC.org*. The University of Chicago, 2014. Web.

treatment, many opt for a second—or even third—opinion before undergoing treatment.

Knowledge and Experience

Consumers want, and most believe, their doctors to be well-informed and proficient. In terms of choosing a physician, 80% of consumers say that a doctor's experience with a specific medical procedure, treatment, or surgery is an extremely or very important factor influencing their choices. Similarly, 77% report that board certification in a particular specialty is important. Training, licensure, and well-known brands can act as signals that a physician or healthcare provider is high quality. However, it should be noted that only 48% of consumers report that attending a well-known medical school is important in their choice of doctor.[29]

Consumer Safety

Consumer safety is a prerequisite for overall effectiveness. When consumers visit an outpatient center or a hospital, they anticipate feeling better—not worse—after an appointment. However, there are many ways in which medical care can be unsafe. For example, about 5%–10% of hospital patients will catch a hospital-acquired infection each year, resulting in nearly 100,000 deaths and an estimated $20 billion in additional healthcare costs.[30] These are infections that patients catch while in a clinical setting; they can be transmitted by clinical staff members, other patients, or on equipment. Similarly, medication side effects and interactions can leave a patient worse off than before. A patient fall while in a hospital setting can lead to a longer recovery period. Hospitals, physicians, and pharmacists take many actions to prevent these harmful outcomes.

Empathy

Empathy is "the feeling that you understand and share another person's experiences and emotions."[31] The ability to form and maintain relationships is a cornerstone of human existence. Individuals rely on others for support, comfort, and safety. In many ways, the desire for connection has been biologically engrained in us as a means for survival. This explains why most people feel compelled to comfort others when they are angry or sad. These actions draw upon the concept of empathy, the cognitive and emotional experience of understanding another person's thoughts and actions.

Empathy, kindness, and generosity are highly valued attributes when it comes to any relationship. Psychologists have shown that these characteristics are among the most important when it comes to long-lasting relationship, satisfaction, and happiness in a marriage.[32,33] Although common phrases repeated to children about empathy, such as "put yourself in someone else's shoes" may seem like overused proverbs, they denote a recognition that empathetic, altruistic behaviors are beneficial to both individuals and societies.

Scholars from the fields of psychology, biology, economics, and, more recently, neuroscience have published theories on the definition and development of empathetic behavior. Although these scholars have debated the definition of the word "empathy" since the 1930s, no single definition has prevailed.[34] However, empathy entails some combination of both cognition and emotion; of thinking about another's perspective and experiencing his feelings.

Those who subscribe to the view that cognitive processes are a foundation of empathy, view thinking as the endeavor of acquiring, processing, and understanding another person's perspective.[35] Scholars in this arena argue that empathy requires perspective and role taking, but they place more emphasis on insight as opposed to emotional involvement. In fact, some researchers who subscribe to this belief argue that empathy requires one to understand and assess another's situation without ever making it one's own.[36]

Those who believe empathy is an emotional, or affective, process argue that it is a state of generating identical feelings and sharing emotions among people. The main difference between cognitive and emotional is that the latter emphasizes compassion, whereas the former focuses on insight and understanding. Under an emotional concept of empathy, one need not necessarily understand why another person is suffering.[37]

In some regards, people are biologically wired to be empathetic. Researchers have shown that some people are genetically inclined to be more empathetic than others—even pointing to specific genes that are thought to make one more likely to exhibit prosocial behavior.[38] Another piece of evidence often cited in support of this notion is the discovery of "mirror neurons." Researchers have shown that when someone watches another person take an action, these motor neurons fire as if they had taken the action themselves.[39] If watching an action and performing that action can activate the same parts of the brain—down to a single neuron—then it makes sense that watching could elicit the same reactions.

Empathy in Healthcare: Definition and Importance

In health situations, the importance of empathy is clear. The bedside manner of a clinical provider can either leave a vulnerable patient reassured or more stressed. And when people recount their most harrowing healthcare experiences, such as an unexpected medical emergency or the death of a loved one, they invariably relay the communications exchanged with physicians, nurses, administrators, and other healthcare providers. We can all appreciate the "honest doctor" or "the friendly nurse." However, all too often, patients feel misunderstood by their providers, or they lack trust in healthcare institutions. Such trust gaps can have far-reaching consequences.

There has been growing recognition of the importance of empathy in medical care.[40] Empathy incites prosocial behavior. When levels of empathy are high, people are likely to work together and meet another's needs. In a healthcare context, if patients perceive a higher level of empathy during their appointments, they are more likely to follow their physician's guidance when they are home. Patients feel more motivated by a caregiver who speaks openly with them. Table 5.4 summarizes the findings from multiple studies on the clinical effects of empathy.

Despite the clear evidence that provider empathy can improve outcomes, researchers have shown that empathy declines during medical training. In a longitudinal study in the early 2000s, researchers measured the empathy levels of 450 medical students at five different times during their medical school training.[41] They found that empathy scores did not change significantly during the students' first two basic science years of medical school; however, a decline occurred during the third year and persisted for the rest of their training. The authors noted the irony in the timing of the decline, as the third year of medical school is typically the time when medical education shifts from classroom learning to patient-care activities.

Although female students had higher empathy scores than male students to begin with, both groups saw declines. The researchers also compared the empathy levels of students who chose more "people-oriented" specialties, such as family medicine, pediatrics, and OB/GYN, to those of students in more "technology-oriented"

Table 5.4 **Relationship Between Empathy and Clinical Outcomes**

Study	Patient Population	Findings
The Influence of the Patient-Clinician Relationship on Healthcare Outcomes: A Systematic Review and Meta-Analysis of Randomized Controlled Trials[i]	Patients who were evaluated for a specific disorder (as opposed to a routine visit)	• Researchers analyzed 13 randomized controlled trials (RCTs) in which the patient–clinician relationship was evaluated and healthcare outcomes were either objective, like blood pressure, or validated subjective measures, like pain scores. • They found that the patient–clinician relationship had a positive, statistically significant effect on healthcare outcomes. • Although the effect size was small, the authors pointed out that effect size in medicine is often not large. They stated, "Our meta-analysis indicated that the patient-clinician relationship has a small ($d = .11$), but statistically significant ($p = .02$) effect on healthcare outcomes . . . the effect size for aspirin in reducing myocardial infarction over five years is only $d = .06$; and the effect size for the influence of smoking on male mortality over 8 years is only $d = .08$."
The Relationship Between Physician Empathy and Disease Complications: An Empirical Study of Primary Care Physicians and Their Diabetic Patients in Parma, Italy[ii]	Diabetic patients	• In Italy, researchers studied 20,000 patients and found that patients of physicians with high empathy scores had acute metabolic complications at a rate of 4.0 per 1,000 patients, while patients of physicians with low empathy scores had complications at a rate of 7.1 per 1,000, which was a statistically significant difference.

Table 5.4 **Continued**

Study	Patient Population	Findings
		• The study also assessed the effects of several other factors, including physicians' gender and age, patients' gender, type of practice (solo, association), geographical location of practice (mountain, hills, plain), and length of time the patient had been enrolled with the physician; none were associated with acute metabolic complications.
Physicians' Empathy and Clinical Outcomes for Diabetic Patients[iii]	Diabetic patients	• Researchers in the United States studied nearly 900 diabetic patients over 3 years and showed that 56% of patients with high empathy physicians had good A1c control (A1c < 7.0%), which was significantly greater than then 40% of patients who had physicians with low empathy scores.
		• The authors of that study speculated that "One possible explanation is that greater empathy in the physician–patient relationship enhances mutual understanding and trust between physician and patient, which in turn promotes sharing without concealment, leading to better alignment between patients' needs and treatment plans and thus more accurate diagnosis and greater adherence."

[i] Kelley, J. M., Todd Kraft, L., Schapira, J. Kossowsky, and H. Riess. "The Influence of the Patient-Clinician Relationship on Healthcare Outcomes: A Systematic Review and Meta-Analysis of Randomized Controlled Trials." *PLoS ONE* 9, no. 4 (2014). Web.

[ii] Del Canale, S., Louis, D. Z., Maio, V., Wang, X., Rossi, G., Hojat, M., and Gonnella, J. S. "The Relationship Between Physician Empathy and Disease Complications: An Empirical Study of Primary Care Physicians and Their Diabetic Patients in Parma, Italy." *Academic Medicine* 87, no. 9 (2012). Web.

[iii] Hojat, Mohammadreza, Daniel Z. Louis, Fred W. Markham, Richard Wender, Carol Rabinowitz, and Joseph S. Gonnella, "Physicians' Empathy and Clinical Outcomes for Diabetic Patients." *Academic Medicine* 86, no. 3 (2011). Web.

Source: 2013 Commonwealth Fund International Health Policy Survey in Eleven Countries.

specialties, such as radiology, surgery, and pathology. Although students who chose "people-oriented" specialties tended to have higher levels of empathy at the beginning of their education, both groups saw drops in empathy around the same time. However, the magnitude of the decline in empathy was greater for men and for those in "technology-oriented" specialties. Students who were more empathic at the beginning of training tended to be more empathic at the end.

The researchers conducted follow-up interviews with students to hear their perspectives. Often, students cited the behavior of their superiors, noting their negative attitudes toward patients. Other times, students described patients who were verbally abusive or overly demanding, as well as related issues such as possible malpractice lawsuits, which limit how comfortable doctors feel about speaking openly with patients. The authors contended that students can develop the belief that empathy lies outside the realm of evidence-based medicine and thus is not as important to its practice.

Demands on time can clearly impede empathy. The researchers speculated that, among other causes, the decline was caused by time pressures associated with being a medical student (e.g., high volume of materials to learn and routine exhaustion) and the overreliance on computer-based diagnostic and therapeutic technology. Physicians, especially in urgent care settings, are often tasked with responding to a large number of patients, almost like a short-order line cook, and finding additional time for each patient can be very challenging. One student even said, "I have felt overwhelmingly tired and unempathetic at times—it is the feeling where, upon walking into a patient's room, I am thinking more about getting through the encounter expeditiously than about making a connection with the patient. AND, I have always considered myself an empathetic person."[42]

There are still other barriers to empathy. Physicians are often hesitant to apologize when things go wrong in a surgery or other intervention. Although sincere apologies are commonplace in other industries to restore or maintain a trusted relationship, physicians fear malpractice lawsuits if they admit to error. In one study that analyzed data from early 1990 through 2005, researchers showed that, by the age of 65, around 75% of physicians in low-risk specialties and 99% of those in high-risk specialties had faced a malpractice claim.[43] Though some new policies have encouraged more openness in this realm, physicians in hospital situations may be advised by risk management teams not to discuss wrongdoing.[44]

Many have also noted that empathy can be difficult to foster in increasingly technology-driven medical environments. Although electronic medical records have made it easier to record and track patient health information over time, the ubiquity of computers means that physicians are spending more and more time entering information rather than looking patients in the eye. Time that might have been spent interacting with the patient is instead spent looking at a screen.

In 2016, one physician recounted a recent experience during which a few of his clinical team members reduced their use of computers during patient rounds. He highlighted how this not only affected how care team providers interacted with the patient but also with one another. He wrote, "Freed from the hypnotic power of our screens, we can once again engage with other human beings and pool our knowledge and expertise in satisfying and productive ways. Ultimately, that can't help but benefit our patients. And perhaps our liberation will also lead to more immediate engagement with patients as well."[45]

Although often less obvious than the relationship between clinician and patient, empathy and understanding from healthcare administrators are also important. In accessing healthcare services, consumers interact with many staff members besides clinical providers. Whether it is for medical appointment scheduling, billing, or something else, these interactions can set the tone for consumers' overall perceptions of empathy and whether they are treated as an individual or a number.

The importance of these interactions is arguably amplified for organizations like health insurers, which have fewer, if any, face-to-face touchpoints with the consumer. Unlike health delivery organizations, health insurers invariably interact with the consumer over the phone or through digital channels.

Consumers and Empathy: What Consumers Value

There is ample evidence that patients value empathy and relationships with individual providers, as well as organizations. There are four key components of empathy: open communication, trust, interpersonal warmth, and an ongoing relationship.

Open Communication

A cornerstone of both understanding and compassion is the notion of communication. There is substantial research that highlights the positive relationship between effective communication and health outcomes. Good communication increases adherence to treatment and patient self-management. [46],[47] Further, research shows that a conversation with a provider can even reduce a patient's back pain.[48]

Although physicians are often criticized for their inability to explain complicated medical procedures, communication is a two-way street. Patients often fail to disclose critical information, such as financial concerns that keep them from filling prescriptions and remaining adherent to medications.

Trust

Without trust, communication means little. Although only 39% of people had "a great deal" or "quite a lot" of trust in the medical system as an institution, most trust their individual providers as being honest and ethical.[49] Gallup runs an annual poll that looks at honesty and ethical standards among various professions. Nurses came in at the top of the list, with 84% of the public rating their standards as "high" or "very high," [50] In fact, the top three spots on the list were filled by medical professionals, with pharmacists and medical doctors scoring 67% and 65%, respectively. At the other end of the spectrum were members of Congress, who scored only 8%.[51]

Comparatively few consumers trust health insurers or life science companies (e.g., pharmaceutical and biotech). According to a 2016 Edelman survey about trust, these industries were the least trusted by consumers in the healthcare sector.[52] Instead, many consumers see these organizations as responsible for increasing healthcare costs. A poll by Politico and Harvard in 2016 found that most Americans—Democrats and Republicans alike—hold the pharmaceutical industry responsible for rising costs more than any other healthcare player.[53]

Warmth

A good relationship with their provider makes a big difference in patient satisfaction. In 1995, a factor analysis of patient consultations with general practitioners and specialists found 58% of the variance in patient satisfaction ratings was accounted for by the level of interpersonal warmth and respect and the amount of information communicated by the doctor.[54] In contrast, the researchers found no association between patient satisfaction and either the gender of the doctor or the type of medical practice attended. In another study, researchers analyzed interactions between diabetic patients and dieticians. Dietitians' empathic engagement proved to be predictive of greater patient satisfaction.[55]

Ongoing Relationship

Most people value ongoing relationships with their clinical providers. An important ingredient in creating an empathic, trusted relationship is maintaining such a relationship over time. For example, in one study, researchers analyzed the effects of creating tiers[56]—ranking doctors on quality—on how patients selected their provider and found that it can be difficult to encourage patients to switch their physician.[57] They reported that new patients who did not have a primary care provider were likely to select a physician who was rated higher quality by the insurance company. However, patients who had an ongoing relationship with a primary care provider were unaffected by tiering evidence. Regardless of gender, geographic area, or age, they remained loyal to their physicians.

Efficiency

Efficiency is being "capable of producing desired results without wasting materials, time, or energy."[58] Time is of the essence—or so the saying goes. How quickly a consumer can access products or services is critically important to her satisfaction with them. Speed of service is changing in nearly every market as consumers feel less inclined to wait. Often, it's new companies that step up to meet the demand. Consider the case of ride-sharing apps, like Uber and Lyft. Taxis were a hassle to catch in some cities—you might wait outside in the rain for many minutes throwing your arm wildly in the air, finally hailing a taxi, and then competing with someone else to get in. Instead, many people now call a ride with the simple click of a button. You know the driver's name, license plate, and average rating before he even arrives. You even receive information about when he's likely to arrive and can track his progress to your destination.

The fast food industry has been a model of efficiency from both the consumer and producer perspective. The first fast food chain restaurants appeared in the 1920s, with many offering burgers and other similar comfort foods. McDonald's re-engineered its products, making them less expensive, more standardized, and quicker to get. As concern over the healthfulness of these options grew, meals on the go became healthier in the 1990s with the introduction of "fast casual" restaurants like Chipotle and Panera. As more and more Americans eat on the go, restaurants and snack manufacturers have offered new—and faster—dining choices.

This trend to get what you want when you want it has even affected how we consume TV shows and other entertainment. Years ago, families gathered round to watch the latest, weekly episode of their favorite show. When it ended, they waited another full week to watch the next one. Though traditional cable TV continues to have an audience, more and more people are subscribing to services like Netflix, Amazon Prime, and Hulu. Not only do they often cost less, but these new services also enable people to watch multiple episodes from the same show in one sitting. We even have a term for it now—"binge watching." An article in *Fortune* in early 2017 was entitled "Netflix's Binge-Watching Model Is Set to Take Over TV;" it highlighted how traditional TV networks feel forced to adopt a similar model of releasing a series all at once to compete with these online subscription services.[59]

Efficiency in Healthcare: Definition and Importance

Traditionally, healthcare delivery has been notoriously slow and inefficient from the consumer perspective. We all remember waiting long beyond the scheduled time in a physician's office (if you can't, you're lucky or have blocked it from memory). Vitals, a company whose mission is "to empower people to shop for health care like an expert," has tracked average primary care physician wait times (i.e., time spent in the waiting room before an appointment) in cities across the United States for over five years.[60] Waiting room time varies widely from an average of 14 minutes in Minneapolis to more than 27 in the Bronx.[61] Longer wait times translate to lower patient satisfaction scores and spill over to more negative perceptions of other aspects of care (e.g., the quality of information, instructions, and overall treatment provided by caregivers).[62]

Perception of wait times can often be as important as the wait times themselves. You may perceive wait times differently when you've made a prior appointment versus when you walk in for nonscheduled assistance at the emergency department. However, not everyone perceives wait times in the same way. The perceived appropriateness of a given wait time can be affected by both personal characteristics (some of us are taking time off work or are simply more impatient) and cultural norms. One study found that Asian subgroups and Latinos gave poorer ratings for wait time than non-Hispanic whites, even though there was no difference in wait times across the groups.[63]

Achieving efficiency in healthcare goes beyond minimizing the time spent in a waiting room. It also encompasses other issues related to access and convenience. Healthcare delivery has, traditionally, been spread out across many physical locations. You might go to your primary care physician for an appointment, only to drive across town to complete recommended tests—going to an outpatient lab center for a blood test and a separate outpatient imaging center for an MRI. These services have been set up more for the convenience of the provider than the patient. For people with chronic conditions, who need regular consultation with a range of different providers, the difficulty of going multiple places can be a barrier to achieving good health. For people with simpler conditions, the recent increase in retail and virtual clinics is a welcome improvement that allows for more efficient access to basic services.

Before a consumer can even sit in a waiting room or drive to multiple locations for different types of care, she must be able to make an appointment. This simple task can be daunting. Finding the right number to call and preparing the right information just to make the appointment can be difficult, and often there will be a long waiting period—perhaps several weeks or longer—before an appointment is available. In 2013, The Commonwealth Fund compared wait times for appointments in the United States to those in 10 other countries. It found that the United States performed poorly (see Figure 5.4).

In a 2015 discussion paper presented to the National Academy of Medicine, titled "Innovation and Best Practices in Health Care Scheduling," the authors discussed several of the most difficult challenges in this realm, as well as potential solutions:

> Scheduling in health care is different from that in other industries. The physiologic state of a patient is dynamic, introducing an inherent uncertainty into patient flow. This uncertainty or clinical variability is not consistently addressed in scheduling systems for elective appointments, resulting in an *ad-hoc* method of triage. Most systems can respond to the most acute, emergent patient with the temporary re-allocation of staff to

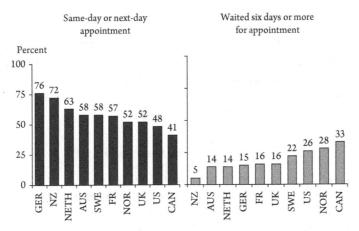

Figure 5.4 Access to doctor or nurse when sick or needed care (2013). Source: Commonwealth Fund International Health Policy Survey in Eleven Countries.

meet unexpected demand. However, for routine or elective visits, acuity is evaluated using disease- or circumstance-specific tools developed within each system with little standardization and few national benchmarks upon which to draw for comparison.[64]

Such delays are common to healthcare insurers as well as providers. Health insurers are often difficult to contact and slow to respond. Long waits on hold are typical responses to phone calls. A mysterious bill may show up months after care, when a person may no longer remember the details of treatment received.

Consumers and Efficiency: What Patients Value

Healthcare does not happen in a vacuum. When you are sick, you still have other responsibilities, such as work, school, and family obligations. Many consumers want healthcare to happen at times other than when the rest of their life is happening—unless it's an emergency.

More Convenient Locations

Consumers are looking for more convenience when it comes to where they go for care. The proliferation and use of drop-in and urgent care clinics in shopping malls, pharmacies, and other high-retail-traffic areas reflect the fact that many consumers are eager to access care near their homes and workplaces, especially when easy parking is available. What's more, the increased use of virtual and telehealth options suggests that many are also willing to consider new technology-enabled solutions if they deliver greater efficiency with sufficient quality when compared to a traditional brick-and-mortar facility.

Easier Communication and Scheduling

Many consumers want to communicate with healthcare providers, administrators, and insurers with greater ease. This means communicating via email, messaging systems, and apps on their phones or tablets. Further, as new market entrants offer same- or next-day appointment guarantees, the standard of acceptable waiting periods for appointments is changing for the better.

Improved Waiting Room Times

Gone are the days when the patient quietly accepts waiting 30 or 40 minutes longer than scheduled for a primary care provider appointment. Many consumers expect shorter wait times, and others want to use waiting room time productively. Many organizations are realizing that they can better meet consumers' needs in the waiting area. When patients have to wait at the physician's office before heading into their appointments, there are efficient ways to use their time. For example, patients with chronic conditions tend to face challenges communicating all of their issues to their physicians in the allotted appointment time. Patients could use this time to prepare for their appointments by checking their medication lists or prioritizing the discussion points they'd like to touch on during the visit.[65]

Not all efficiency improvements are patient facing. Many health systems are using methods from organizational analysis and engineering to redesign physical spaces and improve staffing workflows to better meet demand. At Mayo Clinic Hospital, in Rochester, Minnesota, researchers have redesigned the physical space in the Emergency Department (ED). In this process, the hospital embedded design engineers into the ED to follow staff throughout daily operations. In addition, it used real-time location system and other collection and analysis tools to investigate patient demand patterns in an effort to then match them with ideal staffing levels at different times of the day.[66]

In addition to redesigning spaces and staffing levels, some hospitals have found that relocating physicians can improve efficiency for the patient. When patients with chronic conditions and mental health conditions must meet with multiple types of physicians and access a range of services, situating those services close to each other can make it easier for them to access services and equipment.[67] Instead of asking the patient to go multiple places, different providers come to the patient.

Empowerment

Empowerment is "the process of becoming stronger and more confident, especially in controlling one's life and claiming one's rights." As we have discussed earlier, consumers have gained autonomy and decision-making responsibility across industries. With self-service checkout lines, online shopping, and improved digital services, consumers are doing much more for themselves than in the past. Thanks to search engines, they have efficient access to unprecedented quantities of useful information on the Internet. Norms are changing and expectations are rising for consumer empowerment. Think about how much you value your own autonomy and control in healthcare decision-making.

Empowerment in Healthcare: Definition and Importance

Taking control of one's own healthcare and doing one's part is vital. Few today question the value of consumer empowerment and engagement. Indeed, with 100,000 deaths in the United States each year from avoidable medical errors, your life may depend on it. There is ample evidence that engaged patients have better outcomes and are more satisfied with their care.[68] For example, in a 2017 study, researchers asked patients with advanced cancer to monitor and report their symptoms between doctor visits. Prior to the study, symptoms were only discussed during office visits, unless the patient or a family member contacted the office between visits to discuss new symptoms. During the study, when a patient reported a severe or worsening symptom online, a nurse received an email alert, prompting her to provide symptom management counseling, supportive medications, chemotherapy dose modifications, or referrals. Additionally, when the patient came for his next office visit, the treating oncologist could view a report on the patient's symptom history. Patient self-monitoring in this way was not only associated with better quality of life but also with increased survival rates.[69]

In addition to the clinical benefits, research suggests that increased patient activation is associated with reduced costs. In one study, researchers conducted an analysis of over 33,000 patients at a large healthcare delivery system. They found that patients with the lowest activation levels had average costs that were 8% higher in the base year and 21% higher in the first half of the second year than the group with the highest activation levels.[70]

To measure patient engagement, many healthcare organizations use the Patient Activation Measure (PAM) developed in the early 2000s. Using survey methodology, the measure categorizes consumers into four levels of activation, with level 1 the least and level 4 the most activated. The measure is commonly used for research purposes because it has been found reliable and valid across a range of languages, cultures, demographic groups, and health statuses.[71]

Research studies have shown that consumers who score higher on PAM are more likely to engage in preventive health behaviors, such as screenings and immunizations. Consumers who receive lower scores are three times as likely to have unmet medical needs. Additionally, when consumers with chronic diseases increase their PAM scores, they engage more frequently in healthy behaviors, including regular exercise.[72]

However, enhancing engagement and empowerment is difficult. Engaging patients in their own care is not a new idea; however, it is still very much a challenge. For example, consider medication adherence. Nowhere is the absence of engagement more visible and damaging. Much of healthcare happens at home, work, school, or in the community—not at the physician's office. Healthcare organizations can monitor a patient's drug use in the hospital, but medications are mostly taken independently at home. Medications are a critical component of many treatment plans, yet nonadherence is significant and contributes to increased morbidity and mortality. Even among those suffering from heart failure, a serious condition where medicines can save lives, only 52% of patients, on average, have good adherence.[73] Although estimates vary, between $100 and $300 billion per year of avoidable healthcare costs have been attributed to nonadherence in the United States.[74]

Patients who value empowerment are more likely to adhere to their prescribed regimens.[75] They manage to overcome the common reasons why patients do not take their medicines: a medication might be too expensive, it might be inconvenient to go to the pharmacy and fill the prescription, the medication may cause unwanted side effects that affect the patient's quality of life, or the patient may not sick enough to see any use in taking the medication.

Consumers and Empowerment: What Patients Value

Improved Autonomy and Influence

Studies have demonstrated that consumers value the feeling of control in healthcare and perceive outcomes more favorably when they've had a say in the decision-making process. Refer to Table 5.6 on page 167 in the upcoming "Efficiency" section to see that in a 2015 Deloitte survey healthcare consumer survey, 75% of consumers valued "keeping me informed about my treatment," making it the most frequently rated factor in driving a positive healthcare experience (tied with the quality of the clinician).

Shared Decision-Making

"Shared decision-making" is a model of care that enables consumers to play a greater role in their medical decisions. According to the Agency for Healthcare Research and Quality, the model operates with two premises:

- First, consumers armed with good information can and will participate in the medical decision-making process by asking informed questions and expressing personal values and opinions about their conditions and treatment options.
- Second, clinicians will respect patients' goals and preferences and use them to guide recommendations and treatments.[76]

Shared decision-making is intuitively attractive as a practical approach to help empowered patients engage in their own care and enable them to choose what they want. The most appropriate expression of empowerment is engagement of the patient with her clinical team as a shared enterprise in care. In such a collaborative, team-based effort the patient serves a key role in the delivery of her own care. However, there is only weak evidence that shared decision-making leads to better medical outcomes.[77] Nor is there a single method of shared decision-making that has proven to be best.

Empowerment can also be taken too far. Sometimes autonomy can have unintended negative consequences. Complete autonomy in healthcare is not possible and, even if it were, it would not be prudent when patients can benefit from the trained guidance and interventions of clinicians. Some situations may become too clinically complex, leading the clinician to take charge. In these situations, it's important that the clinician know the patient' goals and preferences so that he can continue to work toward those goals—even if the patient is unable to participate in decision-making in the moment.

Experience

Experience is "the process of doing and seeing things and of having things happen to you."[78] What constitutes an "overall experience"? All of us have myriad experiences throughout our lives—some positive, some negative, and many others, neutral. Every day, we face many different situations, and a variety of factors influence how we perceive them, each as an "overall experience."

In the 1970s, the philosopher Thomas Nagel described the often subjective nature of experience in his well-known essay, "What Is It Like To Be a Bat?"[79] He concluded that each conscious organism's experience is inherently its own. Although one might be able to imagine what it is like to be a bat, one cannot fully experience the bat's perspective.

Similarly, how a customer perceives a business transaction or service experience is based on a wide variety of factors, many of which are deeply personal. The customer's experience reflects the sum of many interactions and often occurs over a period of time, during which a business has several potential and actual touchpoints with the customer. Customer experience experts have long investigated consumers' subjective perceptions of products and services. Providing a unique or fulfilling customer experience is important in building brand reputation, raising customer satisfaction, and motivating repeat purchases.

In a 1998 *Harvard Business Review* article titled "The Experience Economy," B. Joseph Pine II and James Gilmore predicted that a company's success would depend not only on its ability to provide services but also its ability to provide engaging experiences. Failure to do so, they argue, results in minimal differentiation, accelerated commoditization, and consequent low profits.[80] They described four categories: commodities, goods, services, and experiences. Commodities are the least differentiated, and experiences the most. They wrote:

> Economists have typically lumped experiences in with services, but experiences are a distinct economic offering, as different from services as services are from goods. Today we can identify and describe this fourth economic offering because consumers unquestionably desire experiences, and more and more businesses are responding by explicitly designing and promoting them. As services, like goods before them, increasingly become commoditized—think of long-distance telephone services sold solely on price—experiences have emerged as the next step in what we call the progression of economic value.[81]

Pine and Gilmore argue that this is by no means an easy task. Consumers want entertainment or engagement that is personalized and memorable. Consider Starbucks, a company that is so well known for its consumer experience that Joseph Michelli wrote a book in 2006 called *The Starbucks Experience: Five Principles for Turning Ordinary Into Extraordinary*. Although part of Starbucks's allure rests on its ability to create a consistent brand experience across millions of transactions in thousands of stores—think large, comfortable leather chairs and free Wi-Fi—it is equally adept at personalizing experience for individual consumers. When you step up in line, you are encouraged to pick the type of drink, size, and type of milk, among other specifications. Though the long-winded concoctions that result have frequently become the butt of jokes (Huffington Post ran an article in 2013 titled "The Most Obnoxious Starbucks Drink Orders"),[82] they underscore the consumer's ability to create his or her own preferred beverage. Furthermore, instead of giving you a number, as many other fast food restaurants do, the barista writes your name on your cup. All of these opportunities to customize your experience may make you more willing to pay $2 or $3 extra.

One business writer captured his experience of going to Starbucks as follows: "[Starbucks] understand[s] the importance of The Customer Experience and [has] invested a lot of time and money to deliver it. Even though Dunkin Donuts has better coffee according to Consumer Reports, is about $1 cheaper, and is more convenient, I (along with millions of other consumers) will drive a little further, spend a little more time, and spend a little more money for what is promised by this company from Seattle."[83]

Experience in Healthcare: Definition and Importance

Although some service-oriented companies have become customer experience masters, experience has traditionally been an afterthought in healthcare. Many healthcare organizations have prioritized improving objective clinical outcomes and evidence-based care, rather than tackling the subjective experiences of the processes by which the outcomes are achieved. One reason is the inherent difficulty of providing an enjoyable experience during an uncomfortable or stressful situation. Most people would rather avoid most healthcare situations or interactions with health insurers. Doctors poke and prod. Undergoing a medical test can involve painful blood drawing and anticipating the receipt of the results can induce stress.

However, all of that is changing. "Patient experience" is undoubtedly one of the hottest phrases in healthcare today. The term can refer to any number of efforts by healthcare providers to understand and appeal to the subjective experience patients have when accessing or undergoing care. Many have called for more patient-centered care in the past, but the reality was that there was rarely a financial incentive to pursue activities like patient satisfaction.

As the Agency for Healthcare Research and Quality has documented, this shift toward improving the patient experience has occurred for both clinical and financial reasons.[84] Foremost, there is substantial evidence that improved experience often translates to better clinical outcomes. In chronic conditions, better patient experience has been shown to lead to increased adherence to physician recommendations.[85] Beyond clinical benefits, hospitals now have financial incentives to focus on experience initiatives. Negative comments on Internet review sites can influence the choices of future customers. In addition, higher patient experience scores have been associated with lower incidence of potentially expensive malpractice lawsuits.[86] There is also evidence that improved consumer satisfaction goes hand in hand with employee satisfaction, which can further improve productivity and reduce turnover.[87]

In these ways, patient experience has always, to some extent, had the ability to impact health systems' revenues. However, the financial implications have been amplified by the introduction by CMS of the hospital value-based purchasing (VBP) program, which was created under the Affordable Care Act to encourage more than 3,000 hospitals to provide more efficient, high-quality care.[88] Instead of rewarding hospitals solely on the quantity of care delivered, the initiative began adjusting payments (both positively and negatively) starting in 2013, based on the quality of care provided to Medicare beneficiaries. Quality of care is measured using several performance "domains," each of which is given a percentage weight. See Table 5.5 for these domains for three fiscal years, 2016–2018. Whereas the domains change from year to year, consumer and caregiver experience is always a quarter of the overall score.

The VBP program uses multiple measures to assess each domain. Some measures are clinical process-based measures of care, whereas others are outcome measures. To assess the patient experience of care domain, the VBP program uses the Hospital Consumer Assessment of Healthcare Providers and Systems (HCAHPS) survey.[89]

The HCAHPS survey was first implemented in 2006 to enable comparison of hospitals on factors important to consumers.[90] Prior to the development of the survey, many hospitals collected such information on patient satisfaction, but there was no national standard for reporting it.[91] The survey asks 32 questions across

Table 5.5 **Medicare's Measurement of Quality Performance for Fiscal Years 2016–2018**

Fiscal Year	*Applicable Performance Domains and Weights*
2016	• Clinical Process of Care (10%) • Patient Experience of Care (25%) • Outcomes (40%) • Efficiency (25%)
2017	• Patient and Caregiver-Centered Experience of Care/Care Coordination (25%) • Safety (20%) • Clinical Process of Care (30%) • Efficiency and Cost Reduction (25%)
2018	• Patient and Caregiver-Centered Experience of Care/Care Coordination (25%) • Safety (25%) • Clinical Process of Care (25%) • Efficiency and Cost Reduction (25%)

Source: Adapted from data in: Department of Health and Human Services: Centers for Medicare and Medicaid Services. "Hospital Value-Based Purchasing." *CMS website*. 2015. Web.

nine key topic areas: communication with doctors, communication with nurses, responsiveness of hospital staff, pain management, communication about medicines, discharge information, cleanliness of the hospital environment, quietness of the hospital environment, and transition of care. It is given to a random sample of patients 48 hours to 6 weeks after discharge.

The VBP program enhanced focus on patient experience initiatives at many health systems that were already making investments in the area, and it also accelerated broader implementation. There is mounting evidence that such endeavors can financially benefit providers. A 2016 analysis by the Deloitte Center for Health Solutions found that, while investments in patient experience do increase costs, they increase revenue even more. Although the VBP program has led to a newfound focus on patient experience, interestingly, the analysis also found that Medicare VBP incentives accounted for only 7% of the association between patient experience and financial performance.[92] In other words, these hospitals weren't just performing better because they were receiving a higher payment from Medicare. Not surprisingly, the analysis found that the top-performing hospitals tended to have more engaged staff and better employee benefits.

Consumers and Experience: What Consumers Value

Many of the factors that influence consumers' perceptions of experience admittedly overlap with several others of the six E's. In 2015, Deloitte conducted a survey of

Table 5.6 **Main Drivers of Patient Experience**

Driver	Percent of Consumers Designating as Important
Quality of doctors and clinical staff	75%
Keeping me informed about my treatment	75%
Conducting scheduled appointments on time	71%
Ease of scheduling an appointment	70%
Integration of my medical records across of my healthcare providers	68%
Appointment availability for desired date and time	67%
Ease of understanding my bill	66%
Ease of traveling to the facility/parking	59%
Ease of accessing phone support	59%
Postdischarge follow-up and assistance on follow-up appointments	58%
Availability of appointment reminders via phone, text, etc.	49%
Availability of online capabilities	49%
Availability of mobile capabilities	43%
Room appearance and furnishings	39%

Source: Adapted from data in: Betts, David, Andreea Balan-Cohen, Maulesh Shukla, Navneet Kumar. "The Value of Patient Experience." *Deloitte company report*. Downloaded from Deloitte.com. 2016.

healthcare consumers (see Table 5.6) to understand the most important influences on overall patient experience. Especially important were perceptions of high quality staff, good communication with clinical providers, ease of scheduling appointments, and low waiting times.

Communication With Clinical Providers

The Deloitte study clearly shows that measures focused on staff communication and engagement with consumers fall at or near the top of the list. In particular, Deloitte's research showed that patient experience scores related to communication with nurses have the strongest association with hospital financial outcomes.[93] Notice that the top drivers of experience are related to human interaction. Consumers want to work with knowledgeable clinical providers who take their concerns into account. Among many of the top factors, consumers expect clinical providers and administrative leaders to be available to answer questions in person, over the phone, and through email and message systems.

Customer Service

Companies in other industries have long understood that improved customer service—before, during, and after the sale—is one way to differentiate them from the competition. As we have discussed, consumers are beginning to expect the same service elements from healthcare organizations that they enjoy from other industries. Many of these elements are not directly related to clinical care. Consumers will expect more attentiveness, improved product knowledge, better service, and faster response times—particularly from front-line employees. Notice that among the top five factors in the chart, two are related to appointment scheduling and timeliness.

Facility Design

Although changing the physical layout of provider organizations is not always an option because of cost constraints, there are many ways in which design can improve the consumer's experience. For example, many delivery organizations have redesigned their waiting rooms to reduce the stress and anxiety that many consumers feel before an appointment. Other designs facilitate communication and collaboration among clinical providers, who are then better equipped to serve the patient as an integrated team. Still others focus on making something as simple as parking easier, which, for the person who is disabled and struggles with walking long distances, is an essential component of accessing care.

Conclusion

In this chapter we have reviewed the role of benefits in consumer decision-making, highlighting several different models of attribute comparison and decision-making. Whichever model they use, consumers seek out benefits to fulfill their needs. In healthcare, we believe that the six E's model covers the benefits that are most important to consumers. Although the model does not necessarily address every aspect of every healthcare decision, we find it to be a valuable starting point for healthcare organizations and leaders as they think about the range of benefits that are important to consumers.

As we will discuss in the next chapter, segmenting consumers into groups that have similar profiles is a practical necessity. Different consumers will value the different "E's" at different levels of importance and trade off the "E's" in different ways. For some consumers, having the highest quality care will be paramount; for others, a deep and caring relationship with a clinical provider will be most important. Segmentation is a way for organizations to know whom they serve and to differentiate accordingly.

References

1. Gawande, Atul. *Being Mortal: Medicine and What Matters in the End*. New York: Metropolitan Books, Henry Holt and Company, 2014. Print.
2. Anderson, Eric, and Duncan Simester. "Mind Your Pricing Cues." *Harvard Business Review*. September 2003. Web.
3. "Valuable Variables: Consumers Want More Than Low Prices From Retailers." *Nielsen Insights*. 20 June 2016. Web.
4. Hunter, Wynn, Ashley Hesson, J. Kelly Davis, Christine Kirby, Lillie Williamson, Jamison Barnett, and Peter Ubel. "Patient-Physician Discussions About Costs: Definitions and Impact on Cost Conversation Incidence Estimates." *BMC Health Services Research* 16, no. 108 (2016). Web.
5. Banegas, Matthew, Gery Guy Jr., Janet de Moor, Donatus Ekueme, Katherine Virgo, Erin Kent, Stephanie Nutt, Zhiyuan Zheng, Ruth Rechis, and K. Robin Yabroff. "For Working-Age Cancer Survivors, Medical Debt and Bankruptcy Create Financial Hardships." *Health Affairs* 35, no. 1 (2016): 54–61. Web.
6. "Finding Quality Doctors: How Americans Evaluate Provider Quality in the United States: Research Highlights." *APNORC.org*. The University of Chicago, 2014. Web.
7. Data from MassInsight/Opinion Dynamics Survey, 2016.
8. Garmon, Christopher, and Benjamin Chartock. "One in Five Inpatient Emergency Department Cases May Lead to Surprise Bills." *Health Affairs*. 2016. Web.
9. Ibid.
10. White, Kym. "Trust in Healthcare: Warning Signs for Pharma." *Edelman*. 4 May 2016. Web.
11. Kliff, Sarah, and Dan Keating. "One Hospital Charges $8,000—another $38,000." *The Washington Post*. 8 May 2013. Web.
12. Zafar, S. Yousuf, James A. Tulsky, and Amy P. Abernnethy. "It's Time to Have 'The Talk': Cost Communication and Patient-Centered Care." *Oncology* 28, no. 6 (2014): 479–480. Web.
13. Zafar, S. Yousuf, Fumiko Chino, Peter A. Ubel, Christel Rushing, Gregory Samsa, Ivy Altomare, Jonathan Nicolla, Deborah Schrag, James A. Tulsky, Amy P. Abernethy, and Jeffery M. Peppercorn. "The Utility of Cost Discussions Between Patients with Cancer and Oncologists." *American Journal of Managed Care* 21, no. 9 (2015). Web.
14. Ubel, Peter, Cecilia Zhang, Ashley Hesson, J. Kelly Davis, Christine Kirby, Jamison Barnett, and Wynn Hunter. "Study of Physician and Patient Communication Identifies Missed Opportunities to Help Reduce Patients' Out-of-Pocket Spending." *Health Affairs* 35, no. 4. (2016): 654–661. Web.
15. Patel, M. S., M. M. Davis, and M. L. Lypson. "Advancing Medical Education by Teaching Health Policy." *The New England Journal of Medicine* 364 (2011): 695–697. Web.
16. "Consumer Reports Survey Finds Nearly One Third of Privately Insured Americans Hit With Surprise Medical Bills." Consumers Union. 2015. Web.
17. Khazan, Olga. "The Agony of Medical Bills." *The Atlantic*. N.P. 21 May 2015. Web.
18. Mincer, Jilian. "Ballooning Bills: More U.S. Hospitals Pushing Patients to Pay Before Care." *Reuters*. 13 April 2017. Web.
19. Murphy, Brooke. "Beating the Patient-Pay Problem With Three Point-of-Service Collection Strategies." *Becker's Hospital Review*. 1 August 2016. Web.
20. Murphy, Brooke. "10 Thoughts on Improving Hospital Collections." *Becker's Hospital Review*. 6 January 2016. Web.
21. "Challenge Details." *A Bill You Can Understand Challenge*. Web.
22. Ibid.
23. "Effectiveness." *Oxford Dictionary*. 2017. Web.
24. Rosenberg, William, W. Scott. Richardson, David L. Sackett, Sharon E. Strauss, and Robert Brian Haynes. *Evidence-based Medicine: How to Practice and Teach EBM*. Churchill Livingstone, 2000. Print.

25. Ross, Murray. "What's in a Word? The Evolution of *Effectiveness* in Health Care." *Health Affairs Blog*. 26 July 2016. Web.

26. Robert Wood Johnson Foundation. "Quality/Equality Glossary." *RWJF website*. 2013. Web.

27. Betts, David, Andreea Balan-Cohen, Maulesh Shukla, and Navneet Kumar. "The Value of Patient Experience." *Deloitte company report*. Downloaded from Deloitte.com. 2016.

28. "Finding Quality Doctors: How Americans Evaluate Provider Quality in the United States: Research Highlights." *APNORC.org*. The University of Chicago. 2014. Web.

29. Ibid.

30. CDC at Work. "Preventing Healthcare-Associated Infections." *CDC website*. Document No. 119814. Web.

31. "Empathy." *Merriam-Webster.com*. 2017. Web.

32. Gottman, John and Nan Silver. *The Seven Principles for Making Marriage Work*. Harmony, 1999, n.p. Print.

33. Tashiro, Ty. *The Science of Happily Ever After: What Really Matters in the Quest for Enduring Love*. Harlequin, 2014, n.p. Print.

34. Hojat, Mohammadreza. *Empathy in Health Professions Education and Patient Care*. Springer International Publishing, 2016, p. 7. eBook.

35. Dymond, R. F. "A Scale for the Measurement of Empathic Ability." *Journal of Consulting Psychology* 13, no. 2 (1949): 127–133. Web.

36. Hojat, Mohammadreza. *Empathy in Health Professions Education and Patient Care*. Springer International Publishing, 2016. eBook.

37. Ibid.

38. Kogana, Aleksandr, Laura R. Saslowb, Emily A. Impetta, Christopher Oveisc, Dacher Keltnerd, and Sarina Rodrigues Saturne. "Thin-Slicing Study of the Oxytocin Receptor (OXTR) Gene and the Evaluation and Expression of the Prosocial Disposition." *PNAS* 108, no. 48 (2011): 19189–19192. Web.

39. Winerman, Lea. "The Mind's Mirror." *American Psychological Association* 36, no. 9 (2005). Web.

40. Hojat, Mohammadreza. *Empathy in Health Professions Education and Patient Care*. Springer International Publishing, 2016. eBook.

41. Hojat, M., M. J. Vergare, K. Maxwell, G. Brainard, S. K. Herrine, G. A. Isenberg, J. Veloski, and J. S. Gonnella. "The Devil is in the Third Year: A Longitudinal Study of Erosion of Empathy in Medical School." *Academic Medicine* 84, no. 11 (2009): 1616. Web.

42. Ibid., 1189.

43. Jena, Anupam, Seth Seabury, Darius Lakdawalla, and Amitabh Chandra. "Malpractice Risk According to Physician Specialty." *The New England Journal of Medicine* 365, no. 7 (2011): 629–636. Web.

44. Jain, Manoj. "Medical Errors Are Hard for Doctors to Admit, but It's Wise to Apologize to Patients." *The Washington Post*, 27 May 2013. Web.

45. Drazen, Jeffrey. "Hearing Without Listening." *The New England Journal of Medicine* 375 (2016): 1412–1413. Web.

46. Walling, Anne, Nancy Keating, Katherine Kahn, Sydney Dy, Jennifer Mack, Jennifer Malin, Neeraj Arora, John Adams, Anna Liza Antonio, and Diana Tisnado. "Lower Patient Ratings of Physician Communication Are Associated With Unmet Need for Symptom Management in Patients With Lung and Colorectal Cancer." *Journal of Oncology Practice* 12, no. 6 (2016): e654–e669. Web.

47. Heisler, M., R. R. Bouknight, R. A. Hayward, D. M., and Smith, E. A. Kerr. "The Relative Importance of Physician Communication, Participatory Decision Making, and Patient Understanding in Diabetes Self-Management." *Journal of General Internal Medicine* 17, no. 4 (2002): 243–252. Web.

48. Fuentes, Jorge, Susan Armijo-Olivo, Martha Funabashi, Maxi Miciak, Bruce Dick, Sharon Warren, Saifee Rashiq, David Maggee, and Douglas Gross. "Enhanced Therapeutic Alliance

Modulates Pain Intensity and Muscle Pain Sensitivity in Patients With Chronic Low Back Pain: An Experimental Controlled Study." *Physical Therapy* 94, no. 4 (2014): 477–489. Web.

49. "Americans' Confidence in Institutions Stays Low." *Gallup Poll.* 13 June 2016. Web.

50. "Americans Rate Healthcare Providers High on Honesty, Ethics." *Gallup Poll.* 19 December 2016. Web.

51. Ibid.

52. White, Kym. "Trust in Healthcare: Warning Signs for Pharma." *Edelman.* 4 May 2016. Web.

53. Kenen, Joanna. "POLITICO-Harvard Poll: Americans Blame Drug Companies for Rising Health Costs." *Politico.* 28 September 2016. Web.

54. Kenny, Dianna. "Determinants of Patient Satisfaction With the Medical Consultation." *Journal of Psychology and Health* 10, no. 5 (1995). Web.

55. Goodchild, Claire E., T. C. Skinner, and T. Parkin. "The Value of Empathy in Dietetic Consultations. A Pilot Study to Investigate Its Effect on Satisfaction, Autonomy and Agreement." *Journal of Human Nutrition and Dietetics* 18, no. 3 (2005). Web.

56. Tiering is a process by which health insurers rank providers; they usually offer incentives (i.e., lower costs) to their enrollees to visit physicians with better ratings. Tiers are determined by the health plan using quality and cost metrics.

57. Sinaiko, A. D., and M. B. Rosenthal. "The Impact of Tiered Physician Networks on Patient Choices." *Health Services Research* 49, no. 4 (2014): 1348–1363. Web.

58. "Efficiency." *Merriam-Webster.com.* 2017. Web.

59. "Netflix's Binge-Watching Model Is Set to Take Over TV." *Fortune.* January 20, 2017. Web.

60. "About Us." *Vitals Website.* 2017. Web.

61. "Vitals Wait Time Report." *Vitals Website.* 2017.

62. Bleustein, Clifford, David B. Rothschild, Andrew Valen, Eduardas Valaitis, Laura Schweitzer, and Raleigh Jones. "Wait Times, Patient Satisfaction Scores, and the Perception of Care." *American Journal of Managed Care.* 2014. Web.

63. Chung, Sukyung, and Nicole Johns. "Clocks Moving at Different Speeds: Cultural Variation in Satisfaction With Wait Time for Outpatient Care." *Medical Care* 54, no. 3 (2016): 269–276. Web.

64. Brandenburg, Patricia Gabow, Glenn Steele, John Toussaint, and Bernard Tyson. "Innovation and Best Practices in Health Care Scheduling." *Institute of Medicine.* 2015. Discussion paper. Web.

65. Lyles, Courtney R., et al. "User-Centered Design of a Tablet Waiting Room Tool for Complex Patients to Prioritize Discussion Topics for Primary Care Visits." Ed. Gunther Eysenbach. *JMIR mHealth and uHealth* 4, no. 3 (2016): e108. Web.

66. Zimmerman Young, Elizabeth. "Reducing Patient Wait Time and Improving Staff Satisfaction in the Emergency Department." *Mayo Clinic: Advancing the Science Mayo Clinic Medical Science Blog.* 5 February 2016. Web.

67. Rumball-Smith, Juliet, et al. "Under the Same Roof: Co-Location of Practitioners Within Primary Care Is Associated With Specialized Chronic Care Management." *BMC Family Practice* 15 (2014): 149. Web.

68. Hibbard, Judith, and Jessica Greene. "What the Evidence Shows About the Patient Activation: Better Health Outcomes and Care Experiences: Fewer Data on Costs." *Health Affairs* 32, no. 2 (2013). Web.

69. Basch, Ethan, Allison Deal, Amylou Dueck, Howard Scher, Mark Kris, Clifford Hudis, and Deborah Schrag. "Overall Survival Results of a Trial Assessing Patient-Reported Outcomes for Symptom Monitoring During Routine Cancer Treatment." *JAMA* 318, no. 2 (2017): 197–198. Web.

70. Hibbard, Judith, Jessica Greene, and Valerie Overton. "Patients With Lower Activation Associated With Higher Costs; Delivery Systems Should Know Their Patients' Scores." *Health Affairs* 32, no. 2 (2013). Web.

71. Ibid.

72. Ibid.

73. Baicker, Katherine, Y. Zhang, S. Wu, and M. Fendrick. "Variation in Medication Adherence in Heart Failure." *JAMA Internal Medicine* 173, no. 6 (2013): 468–470. Web.

74. Iuga, Aurel, and Maura MacGuire. "Adherence and Health Care Costs." *Risk Management and Healthcare Policy* 7 (2014): 35–44. Web.

75. Hernandez-Tejada, Melba, A., et al. "Diabetes Empowerment, Medication Adherence and Self-Care Behaviors in Adults With Type 2 Diabetes." *Diabetes Technology & Therapeutics* 14, no. 7 (2012): 630–634.

76. Agency for Healthcare Research and Quality. "Shared Decisionmaking." *AHRQ website.* 2013. Web.

77. Légaré, F., et al. "Interventions for Improving the Adoption of Shared Decision Making by Healthcare Professionals." *Cochrane Effective Practice and Organisation of Care Group.* 15 September 2014. Web.

78. "Experience." *Merriam-Webster.com.* 2017. Web.

79. Nagel, Thomas. "What Is It Like To Be a Bat?" *The Philosophical Review* (1974): 435–450. Web.

80. Pine, B. Joseph, and James Gilmore. "Welcome to the Experience Economy." *Harvard Business Review.* 1998. Web.

81. Ibid.

82. "The Most Obnoxious Starbucks Drink Orders." *The Huffington Post.* 6 January 2015. Web.

83. Dollinger, Matthew. "Starbucks, 'The Third Place', and Creating the Ultimate Customer Experience." *Fast Company.* 11 June 2008. Web.

84. "Why Improve Patient Experience?" Agency for Healthcare Research and Quality, Rockville, MD. Content last reviewed April 2016. Web.

85. Zolnierek, Kelly, B. Haskard, and M. Robin Dimatteo. "Physician Communication and Patient Adherence to Treatment: A Meta-Analysis." *Medical Care* 47, no. 8 (2009): 826–834. Web.

86. Fullam, Francis, Andrew Garman, Tricia Johnson, and Eric Hedberg. "The Use of Patient Satisfaction Surveys and Alternate Coding Procedures to Predict Malpractice Risk." *Medical Care* 47, no. 5 (2009). Web.

87. Rave, N., Geyer, M., Reeder, B., et al. "Radical Systems Change: Innovative Strategies to Improve Patient Satisfaction." *Journal of Ambulatory Care Management* 26, no. 2 (2003): 159–174.

88. Department of Health and Human Services: Centers for Medicare and Medicaid Services. "Hospital Value-Based Purchasing." *CMS website.* 2015. Web.

89. Department of Health and Human Services: Centers for Medicare and Medicaid Services. "Hospital Value-Based Purchasing." *CMS website.* 2015. Web.

90. "HCAHPS Fact Sheet." 2009. Downloaded from hcahpsonline.org. Hospital Consumer Assessment of Healthcare Providers and Systems. Web.

91. Ibid.

92. Ibid.

93. Ibid.

RESPONDING TO CONSUMER CHOICE

6

Consumer Segmentation

Larissa shook with nerves. How was she going to tell her mom that she was pregnant? Her mother, Jill, had given birth to her at 17, and she had always warned Larissa about the difficulties of being a young parent. Although Larissa was a bit older at age 20, having a baby now was unplanned. She was enrolled in nursing courses at a nearby community college and was in the process of applying to nursing positions at local hospitals. How would she complete her degree with a newborn? How would she afford having a baby? She was already in debt because of her classes. How would she pay it off if she could not complete her degree? She had been dating her boyfriend for six months, but she had not yet worked up the courage to tell him about the pregnancy. Larissa was not sure how he would react; he also was in school, and they certainly were not ready for marriage. Larissa and her mom had always shared a tight bond, and keeping this secret from her was weighing heavily on Larissa. She knew that she would need her mother's support and advice as she considered what to do. She was scared.

When Sarah saw the two lines appear on the tiny white stick, she began to weep. After a 3-year struggle with infertility that involved a failed trial of Clomid and two rounds of in vitro fertilization, she was finally pregnant. She called her husband, Dan, with the news: "We're pregnant!" she yelled excitedly into the phone. Within a matter of days, the two were eagerly planning every aspect of the next nine months. Sarah went online and purchased seven new books on pregnancy, childbirth, and infancy. Although the infertility treatments were quite expensive, she and Dan were not too concerned about finances. They were both in their mid-30s and had been saving for years with the hope of starting a family. She began drafting her birthing plan and routinely discussed some of the most difficult questions with Dan at dinner each evening. Where was the best hospital in their area to give birth? Should she medically induce labor? Although it was more than five years down the line, she even began researching local elementary schools. Could they afford to move to a better school district? Her excitement was evident to all of those around her.

When Julie found out she was expecting, she felt surprisingly calm. Although they had not planned on having a third child, she and her husband, Rod, knew the drill. She began making appointments with the same obstetrician she had gone to for years and decided she would, again, give birth at the hospital closest to their home. The previous year they had bought a new house; with a new mortgage and two other children, Julie could tell that Rod was nervous about their finances. Their house had only three bedrooms, so they prepared to move their two older daughters into a shared room, selling them on the attraction of bunk beds and countless sleepovers. Beyond that, she really was not thinking about the pregnancy too much. With two daughters under the age of 7, and a busy job in human resources, she could not afford to become distracted. Also, why should she? Both of her prior pregnancies had been uneventful, apart from a rather long labor the first time around. She would follow the advice of her doctor and make sure she set an alarm on her phone to remind her to take her prenatal vitamins.

These three women had entirely different perspectives—they came from disparate socioeconomic backgrounds, had unique health concerns, and dissimilar family situations. However, as they prepared for pregnancy and childbirth, they had many common decisions ahead of them. Some choices were predominantly health related: Do I have an existing relationship with an obstetrician, or do I need to find one? How should I pick an obstetrician or midwife? What should I eat? Which vitamins should I take? Which screening tests should I undergo? Do I need to stop smoking, drinking, or using drugs? Should I receive an epidural[1] during childbirth? Do I want my labor to be induced? Under what circumstances should I consider a cesarean section[2]? Should I breastfeed?

Some concerns were more related to preferences: Should I learn the gender of my child? Where do I want to give birth (e.g., which hospital or at home)? Whom do I want in the room when my child is born? How would I prefer my clinician to communicate with me—via phone, email, or in person?

Still more choices regarding social or financial uncertainties needed to be taken into consideration: Do I have health insurance? What costs will I be responsible for throughout the process? Do I have a partner who will also care for the child? Do I receive paid maternity leave? Can I take time off work, even if it's unpaid?

Of course, many questions traverse all three of these aspects of decision-making—pregnant women must make decisions that will at once affect their health, social, and financial conditions. These questions invariably fall to young, relatively healthy women. In 2014, the average woman's age at the time of her first delivery was 26.3 years in the United States.[1] Unlike older adults with chronic diseases, this group is less experienced in navigating the healthcare system. They may not have a

---

[1] Regional anesthesia that is given through the small of the back; it is the most commonly used method of pain relief for labor.

[2] A surgical operation for delivering a baby by cutting through the mother's abdomen.

regular primary care physician—let alone an established relationship with an obstetrician or midwife.

Different consumers—Larissa, Sarah, and Julie included—will answer these questions differently; there is no one-size-fits-all right or wrong answer. Despite this, healthcare providers, clinicians, and insurers too frequently treat consumers as though they are all alike. In this chapter, we will discuss ways in which healthcare stakeholders can acknowledge and accommodate the differences among healthcare consumers by using a range of segmentation strategies, as well as explain why it is in their best interest to do so. Before we discuss different strategies for consumer segmentation, let us continue to take a closer look at pregnancy and childbirth to illustrate the vast range of different choices open to healthcare consumers and the equally enormous variation in their decisions—even within a condition as common as pregnancy.

A Life-Changing Choice

As almost any parent will tell you, the birth of a child is a life-altering event. A completely dependent human being enters the world, and parents are charged with making an innumerable number of decisions on its behalf. This burden begins long before the child is born. Parents—and women in particular—face a variety of choices when it comes to pregnancy and birthing options. Often, these have health, financial, psychological, and social implications not only for the mother and child but also for other family members and friends.

Although Larissa, Sarah, and Julie all began their pregnancies in 2016, it is important to recognize that pregnancy and childbirth have changed dramatically in the last 200 years. Applying a sociological lens to the process can be helpful for understanding norms, concerns, and superstitions that persist today. Prior to the refinement of medical and surgical techniques, childbirth was largely a private affair that happened in the home. Men were rarely involved and women gave birth only in the presence of female family members and, if they were lucky, a midwife. Women in cities were more likely to have the assistance of a midwife, whereas women in rural areas generally went through childbirth without them.[2]

Despite technical improvements in care, pregnancy remained dangerous up to the 20th century. Though forceps were invented in the 17th century, they were not used frequently until nearly a century later. Around this time in the United States, midwifery became more formally organized; training schools were established and caregiving subsequently improved.[3] It should also be noted that, until this era, childbirth was an incredibly painful experience for most women. Although some early anesthetics had been discovered, labor pains were often perceived to be the will of God, and relieving them was viewed negatively. Obstetrician Sir James Young Simpson introduced chloroform as an anesthetic in the mid-1800s and its use

spread quickly soon after (despite protests from the clergy). Regardless of these significant advances, pregnancy and childbirth still carried grave risks for both mother
and child. Even as late as 1900, the maternal mortality rate in the United States was
more than 800 per 100,000 live births, and up to 30% of infants died during their
first year of life in some urban areas of the United States.[4]

Due to additional advances in medicine (e.g., antibiotics for infection and oxytocin to induce labor), improved physician training (e.g., improved handwashing),
and a shift in birthing location from the home to the hospital setting, the maternal
mortality ratio declined by more than 95% from the early 1900s to the 1990s.[5]
Today, the risk of serious complications or maternal death during childbirth is relatively small. According to the World Bank, the maternal mortality ratio in the United
States was 14 per 100,000 live births in 2015.[6] The infant mortality rate followed a
similar trajectory. As more babies were born in hospital settings in the 1930s and
1940s, more survived.

Advances in medical technology contributed significantly in the vast reduction in maternal and infant mortality rates. Although pregnant women today
are far safer than their counterparts of a century ago, advances in the pregnancy
and childbirth process mean that most women face many challenging choices
throughout the process. The advent of both screening and diagnostic tests has
made it possible to find certain conditions early in a pregnancy. This can raise
a host of difficult moral questions for women, their partners, and their families.
How will they react if they receive the news that a child has a genetic condition or
chromosomal abnormality? Will they consider aborting a pregnancy if an abnormality is detected?

Moreover, medical technology has advanced to a point where pregnancy and
childbirth are treated in the same location and with the same technology as many
diseases. Over time, some have pushed back against this medicalization, arguing
that reproduction is a natural process and should not be treated as a disease. Indeed,
pregnancy and childbirth do differ from most other healthcare situations because
they are not driven by sickness or disease. Childbirth marks the beginning of new
life, and in many ways, it is an altogether more positive experience than most other
healthcare challenges.

Around half of all pregnancies in the United States are unplanned. This does not
necessarily mean that they are unwanted, but it does mean that these women have
less time to choose a physician, decide on appropriate pregnancy care, and plan
for the birth. From the very first moment that a woman learns she is pregnant, she
must confront an initial series of difficult choices; she must choose between abor-
tion, adoption, or raising the child. The woman's family situation, religion, or politics may have a significant influence over the choices she makes regarding these
delicate issues. Some women do not necessarily want to make many firm decisions.
Although there are women like Sarah, at the beginning of this chapter, who plan for
years before becoming a mom, there are many women who do not. Pregnancy and

motherhood are thrust upon them, along with a less-than-welcome set of choices to be made.

Compounding this challenge, they are inundated with advice from a variety of sources—physicians, family members, friends, online communities, and books offer no shortage of guidance on the process. Unlike many conditions, pregnancy is—at a certain point—apparent even to a stranger. For the pregnant woman, this can be helpful as well as overwhelming. It is largely a good thing that people are willing to aid pregnant women—that strangers will give up their seats on buses or open doors. However, once pregnancy is visible, unsolicited advice can come from even a passerby on a street. Recommendations can range from the scientific to the most superstitious wives' tales. Because of these, women can feel judged about the choices they make. Wanting to please everyone from in-laws and spouses to other pregnant friends can be confusing. Whose advice should they follow? How can they know if they are making the right choices?

Figure 6.1 depicts the questions that might come up along a woman's pregnancy patient journey. Notice in this diagram that there are many more financial and social decisions than health or medical considerations. For the average woman with a low-risk pregnancy, many of the most difficult questions will be social and financial. The medical element of the pregnancy largely comprises check-ups and screenings. However, for the minority of women who do experience a complication, this process can easily become far more complex and protracted. Sometimes, these complications are due to preexisting conditions, such as obesity, HIV, or drug use, whereas others develop during the pregnancy, such as when the baby has a genetic condition. In these high-risk cases, women will sometimes schedule additional visits with specialists, such as maternal-fetal experts or perinatologists, who have extra training in high-risk pregnancies. Additionally, among women who know they are pregnant, about 10%–15% who become pregnant will miscarry.[7]

Meeting Individual Needs

How women answer these questions differs significantly These difficult questions surrounding important choices are common to almost all adult women; in 2014, 85% of U.S. women aged 40–44 had given birth to at least one child.[8]. But decision-making in healthcare is highly personalized. It is clear that even with a relatively routine condition such as pregnancy, there are many choices to be made and many ways that consumers go about making them. Moreover, there are significant differences among consumers for nearly any health or medical decision—ranging from the relatively minor to the life altering.

In the past, little time was spent identifying and responding to these differences among healthcare consumers. However, some leading and innovative companies are beginning to do just that. Docent Health ("Docent"), a Boston startup, was

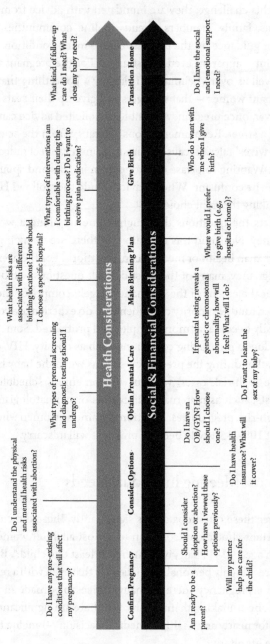

Figure 6.1 Questions Faced on Pregnancy Journey.

launched in 2015 to change the *status quo*; the company helps hospitals and health systems segment healthcare consumers to improve the patient experience. The company works with its clients to map out the patient journey, identifying key inflection points for improving—and personalizing—the process. The company is working with some of the frontrunners in patient experience, such as Dignity Health ("Dignity"), a large health system in California.

In 2016, Docent and Dignity partnered to personalize the pregnancy journey. Docent considers each individual consumer's unique needs, creating "personalized service journeys," and delivering a set of supportive services in line with their preferences. These services are implemented through a combination of human and digital interactions. On the human side, the company employs specially trained staff, called "docents," to support customers throughout the course of their care. The docents, who typically come from service or social work backgrounds rather than clinical, act as support systems for the patient. The company hires them from the communities where their patients are most likely to live, ensuring that they can better understand family and social situations that might arise. Docents also help the health system diverge from its standard service practices when individual consumer needs are unmet.

Docent Health also engages with soon-to-be mothers via its technological platform, which was designed to identify and track patient medical histories, preferences, care goals, and social support needs. The platform then suggests individualized communication and outreach strategies for each patient, and it tailors the communication channel based on the patient's preference—from digital, to phone, to in-person interactions. Targeted communication efforts aim to improve the patient's engagement in her own care. To make the process less intimidating and more supportive, Docent sends education information to expecting mothers about prenatal classes and birthing plans, while also engaging family members during the pregnancy journey.

Rich Roth, chief strategic innovation officer at Dignity Health, commented: "We're focused on caring for the whole person—mind, body, and spirit—and on finding new ways to make the patient journey a better consumer experience. This unique blend of technology and human connection will improve the patient experience for mothers-to-be and their families."[9]

The purpose of Docent Health's initiative is twofold: first, to personalize and improve the experience for individual mothers-to-be. In addition, the plan is to collect data and develop insights on ways to improve experiences for the broader consumer population they want to serve. Docent is analyzing data to determine if a woman's preferences can be predicted based on demographic and usage (i.e., first-time or repeat) profiles even before she has her first appointment.

This work moves Docent Health from the daunting challenge of providing a good experience to everyone regardless of their many differences to a new approach in which Docent understands their own service population's decisions and desires and targets delivery to satisfy that population and its preferences.

This approach depends on one important concept: consumer segmentation. Docent wants to understand the differences among consumers and to change service delivery based on their segmentation. As we will discuss, although this philosophy is critical to creating a consumer-centric healthcare system, very few organizations have implemented it successfully in healthcare. Next, we discuss different approaches to segmentation, as well as why more organizations should follow Docent's lead.

Standardization or Segmentation?

The management expert Peter Drucker once wrote: "The purpose of business is to acquire and retain a customer." Relatively few providers of healthcare services view this as their mission. Their orientation is more toward production than marketing, more frequently stressing cost control than customer satisfaction. Healthcare providers often assume that a one-size-fits-all standardized approach is always the lowest cost solution when, in fact, a tailored solution that targets groups with a similar pattern of consumer preferences might attract more business and even be more efficient.

Consumers are not created equal. We know from our own experiences that different people have different needs and preferences, and place different levels of importance on different product and service benefits. They differ in so many ways: in their demographic profiles; in their attitudes and behaviors; in the information sources they consult, and in what benefits are important to them.

Healthcare analysts and reformers have largely focused on understanding and managing the supply of healthcare rather than the demand. As a result, the healthcare industry has been largely product driven rather than consumer driven. With this mindset, there is an inherent "field of dreams" assumption that if providers create the perfect product or service, healthcare consumers will use it. In such a product-driven culture, consumers are viewed as homogeneous, except insofar as their medical conditions warrant different treatments; to include nonclinical variables would add needless complexity.

However, understanding these nonclinical variables can be valuable in increasing the likelihood of good health outcomes. This is especially the case among patients with chronic conditions, who account for an increasing proportion of healthcare costs. The willingness of these individuals to help themselves is thus critical to success. Some of these patients are motivated by their desire to live as normal a life as possible, whereas others are driven to achieve ambitions not yet accomplished. Every patient's healthcare team members need to customize their approaches to provide maximum support and motivation as choices are made along the patient journey.

Individualization is undoubtedly difficult in an industry that has achieved many successes through standardization. Standardizing has improved care by developing and using treatment guidelines for cardiovascular conditions such as atrial fibrillation (i.e., irregular, often rapid, heartbeat) and myocardial infarction (i.e., heart attack). The American College of Cardiology and the American Heart Association have jointly produced guidelines in the area of cardiovascular disease since 1980 in an effort to help clinicians choose the most evidence-based strategies for treatment.[10] In many such clinical conditions, adherence to the most evidence-based, standardized clinical treatments has undoubtedly saved lives and improved care, and we are by no means discounting these important efforts.

As we think about segmentation, we must recognize that standardization and customization can coexist. For many clinical processes, standardizing to the best possible care will improve overall quality and reduce costs, even while recognizing that there are times when unique conditions require deviating from standard guidelines. There is no conflict between clinical standardization and personalized outreach and interactions with patients. Both are likely to improve patient satisfaction, engagement, and outcomes. There is growing recognition that both concepts are important for patient-centered care. It is critical both to drive toward the most evidence-based interventions, while also acknowledging differences among individual patients, in terms of their values and preferences.

Good Segmentation

A market segment is a group of consumers (not a group of products) with common characteristics. Most successful organizations prefer to focus on the needs of one or two segments and serve them well. The consumer segments that you select define your business strategy. Knowing whom you do not want to serve—and not trying to pretend you can serve them—is equally important.

From a cost management viewpoint, it may be impractical to individualize healthcare completely. But if we can identify segments that cluster individuals together, we can achieve a useful level of customization without completely upsetting an organization's cost structure. This is especially valuable when consumers place a higher value on the customization they experience than it costs the organization to deliver it.

There are various ways to segment markets. Depending on the marketing challenge, some will lead to valuable consumer insights; others will not. For example, you might try to segment your consumers using demographic data; however, you may discover that differences in consumer usage aren't correlated with demographics.

Uncovering a segmentation approach that is actionable is key to success. To illustrate actionable segmentation, consider the case of CancerScan, a Japanese market research company focused on increasing cancer screening rates. CancerScan identified

Table 6.1 **Screening Rates**

	Test Group	*Control Group*
Segment 1	25.5%	7.3%
Segment 2	17.3%	4.7%
Segment 3	13.3%	4.6%

Source: Quelch, John A., and Margaret L. Rodriguez. "Cancer Screening in Japan: Market Research and Segmentation." Harvard Business School Case 514–057, January 2014. (Revised March 2014.)

three segments of consumers who failed to take regular breast screenings. Segment 1 was aware and understood the need for regular testing but did not know where, when, or how to make a screening appointment. Segment 2 was aware of the need to be screened but fearful of the results. Some in this group were fatalistic and did not believe knowing a problem existed could make any difference to the outcome. Segment 3 was unaware of the risks of breast cancer; some of these women were younger and so saw themselves as invincible. CancerScan developed customized direct mail brochures for each consumer segment and achieved significant improvement in screening rates (Table 6.1).

Although the customized mailers were twice as expensive, the health savings from the improved response rates easily offset the extra cost. A problem arose, however, when CancerScan tried to convert these test market findings into a national campaign. Due to privacy concerns, data had not been collected from respondents on their media use profiles. As a result, it was not possible to translate the findings into a more general campaign that used cost-efficient targeting of relevant messages to reach each segment. This example highlights an important caveat in applying consumer segmentation: investing in a segmented marketing approach is only cost-effective if it results in more efficient targeting and increased response rates sufficient to cover the added cost.

Segmentation Improves Marketing

Segmentation is an important component of any organization's overall marketing strategy. It is a valuable tool for organizations because it enables marketers to target specific subsets of customers in meaningful ways. This enhanced consumer targeting ultimately leads to improvements across one or more of four different components of marketing strategy: messaging, distribution, pricing, and product or service design. Before we go deeper into exploring each of these areas, we should note that segmentation should be viewed as mutually beneficial for *both* organizations and consumers. Improved segmentation can enhance the quality of an organization's overall marketing strategy, and better marketing has notable benefits for consumers (outlined in Table 6.2).

Table 6.2 **Marketing's Benefits for Consumers**

Category	Benefits for Consumers
Exchange	• In modern societies, consumers obtain virtually all their goods and most services through voluntary exchanges. • A buyer and seller enter into an exchange because it creates value for both parties; both hope to be better off and both value the freedom of consent.
Consumption	• Consumption is a strong driver of economic growth and has improved societal and individual well-being worldwide. • Marketers have incentives to introduce new products and to make products available to additional segments of the population.
Choice	• The proliferation of products, retail channels, and media has increased options for consumers. • Marketers provide increased alternatives and customization to satisfy individual needs across a diverse consumer population. • However, too many choices can burden and confuse consumers; marketing provides mechanisms to help consumers manage choice.
Information	• Open, accurate, and timely information from marketers allows consumers to make intelligent choices. • Information about consumers enables marketers to target them with appropriate offers. • Information also keeps the market in check; expert opinion and word-of-mouth comments that spread from consumer to consumer often trump corporate advertising.
Engagement	• When marketing engages individuals in the consumer marketplace, they can express their identities, become part of communities, and exercise creativity. • This may not occur with every purchase consumers make, but through those in which they have chosen to be more involved. • Some consumers want deeper relationships with marketers and brands and are willing to pay for a more customized service. • As consumers become more engaged, turning over marketing tasks and functions to them can simultaneously reduce costs and increase their sense of empowerment.
Inclusion	• Consumer marketplaces are naturally inclusive because they benefit from expanding the number of consumers and linking producers and consumers worldwide.

Source: Quelch, John A., and Katherine E. Jocz. *Greater Good: How Good Marketing Makes for Better Democracy*. Harvard Business School, 2008. Print.

A classic example is the market for dishwashing liquid. Procter & Gamble has historically offered three brands: Dawn, Ivory, and Joy. Dawn is formulated to tackle tough dishwashing jobs involving cleaning grease and baked-on food. Every Dawn television advertisement is shot in the kitchen and shows a large family. In contrast, Ivory's key benefit is mildness. A typical Ivory ad shows a mother and daughter playing a piano together, and it is impossible to tell which hands belong to whom. Finally, Joy emphasizes sparkling clean dishes; a typical ad might show spotless fine glassware on the dining room table as the homeowner welcomes guests to a dinner party. Each of these three brands is a good all-round dishwashing liquid, but product formulas and go-to-market approaches have been adjusted to cater to the needs of different consumer segments. It may also be the case that the same consumer might use more than one brand depending on the dishwashing job that needs to be done.

In some ways, segmentation in healthcare is different than in other markets. When marketers segment consumers in other industries, they aim to discover—and then target—the subsegments of consumers who spend the most. This is partly because it is difficult for a single business simultaneously to serve all consumer segments profitably. For illustration, consider the case of a high-end fashion retailer. The marketing team might segment consumers from the past year to understand who bought the most merchandise, how and when they bought it, and ultimately, who might spend the most in the future. After this analysis has been concluded, the business can then stock clothes for the next season based on the preferences of its most valuable consumers during the previous season. In effect, this business serves the needs of its highest value consumer segment and attracts them to become an even higher share of its business in the future.

In healthcare, targeting only the highest revenue consumers does not work in the same way. Insurers pay, rather than the consumer, and reimbursements for services are usually the same across all users. Moreover, for both ethical and financial reasons, provider organizations must look for ways to engage *all* consumers—even those who are not revenue generating. A hospital emergency room cannot, for example, decide that it is no longer going to serve car accident victims because they are less profitable than people who have had heart attacks. In addition, healthcare organizations are increasingly paid through contracts that are based on their shouldering the risks of the costs of providing care. In this reimbursement model, segmentation helps not merely by identifying the most valuable customers in terms of revenue but also by segmenting those who are sicker and thus potentially costly. For health insurers, this means analyzing the consumers with the highest frequency or dollar value of claims. For health delivery organizations participating in these new, value-based contracts, segmenting the population to identify and manage potentially high-cost consumers is equally—if not more—important than to engage the highest value ones.

With this caveat, let us now take a closer look at how segmentation can improve messaging, distribution, pricing, and product/service design in healthcare.

Messaging

Segmentation makes it possible for healthcare organizations and practitioners to tailor their messaging to subgroups of consumers. Tailored messaging is likely to garner higher response rates and better consumer engagement. Therefore, tailored messaging can improve the outcomes of public health campaigns and disease education programs, as well as improve sales and revenue for organizations.

For example, consider the following hypothetical situation. A town requires all five-year-old children to receive several childhood vaccinations prior to beginning kindergarten. This is standard practice, as it protects children from debilitating conditions like polio. However, in recent years, the public health department has noticed more parents are objecting to vaccinating their children. Instead of running a potentially wasteful blanket campaign touting the benefits of vaccination, the department decides to focus on the segment of parents who are not vaccinating their children.

Another arena where segmentation can enhance messaging is when patients leave the hospital. Hospital discharge is an increasing focus for health systems because, under the Hospital Readmission Reduction Program, if a Medicare patient is readmitted to a hospital within 30 days, the health system incurs a penalty. Many health systems recognized that messaging efforts at hospital discharge were falling short, which resulted in many patient readmissions that could have been prevented.

Cedars Sinai, a large health system in California, developed a robust program of care at the time of transition aimed at reducing hospital readmission rates. One component of this program focused on medication literacy and adherence. The system recognized that lack of knowledge about medications could lead to nonadherence, which was a significant contributor to readmissions. The health system's EMR system already flagged high-risk patients upon admission to the hospital. This had already been programmed into the system, so it was a natural group to start with. However, this group was too large for the health system pharmacy department to deliver individual medication counseling at discharge, as well as to conduct a follow-up phone call to every patient. Furthermore, some of these patients understood their medications and were adherent post discharge. The system needed a way to further segment the high-risk population to understand which patients needed additional communication during or after discharge to remain adherent.

The health system's chief pharmacy officer developed the "Medication Adherence and Literacy" tool (known in the system as MedAL). Based on validated measures for both past medication adherence and health literacy, MedAL segments the group of high-risk patients further, so that the pharmacy department can better target its messaging. Those patients who are high in both literacy and past adherence receive less education at discharge, whereas those who are low in both receive a longer education at discharge, as well as a follow-up call from a pharmacist once they are at home. Patients who fall somewhere in the middle receive medication education at discharge, but no follow-up call. This strategy makes it possible for the department to use its resources most efficiently, and ultimately it improves readmission rates, patient outcomes, and financial performance.

Distribution

Distribution refers to how and where consumers access a product or service. Often, there are multiple distribution channels. Consider bottled water, for example. A consumer can buy it at a grocery store, from a vending machine, at a convenience store or drugstore, at a restaurant, or from a food cart. The segment of consumers that buys from each place might differ slightly. Those who purchase water bottles at the grocery story might tend to be more affluent and health conscious, drink mostly bottled water in their homes, and buy in larger sizes on a preplanned basis. Those who buy from a vending machine are purchasing a single serving on impulse when they are on the go. Understanding which consumers buy a product or service from what channel is critical for improving an organization's distribution strategy. An improvement in distribution indicates that the right consumers are being reached at the right time and in the right place.

Using segmentation to improve distribution in healthcare is not a new phenomenon—it just has not always been geared toward consumers. Pharmaceutical companies use highly skilled consultants and complicated models to segment the prescribing physician population for their products. Because physicians are gatekeepers to drug prescriptions and sales, pharmaceutical sales representatives typically target the highest impact prescribers. Although such strategies have engendered significant backlash for the influence they have had over the type of medications that are prescribed, they also highlight the level of analytical rigor that can be applied to improve efficiency in consumer healthcare.

Until recently, healthcare delivery had all but ignored how consumers differ in their preferences for where they access care. Healthcare systems were inflexible behemoths that assumed all consumers would come to them when in need of care. In recent years, it has become clear that, for many healthcare conditions, consumers want to access care that is better or more convenient. Many smaller hospitals have closed and large hospitals have created integrated networks, so that access to their system is distributed widely. New channels for healthcare services have opened, including virtual healthcare service options, retail pharmacy clinics, and urgent care centers. Virtual healthcare services, which are delivered by email, phone, or video conference, have expanded greatly, and research indicates that such appointments are not only replacing existing visits but are also adding new ones. Simply put, healthcare consumers who would not have gone to the doctor are now going because there is a new, lower cost, more convenient distribution channel.[11]

Pricing

Segmenting consumers can improve an organization's pricing strategy, ultimately leading to more customers and enhanced revenues. Different groups of consumers will be willing to pay different prices for the same product, and it is common practice within many service industries to create tiered prices. Airline fares for the same flight can vary greatly depending upon passengers' willingness to commit (nonrefundable fares), timing of purchase (weeks or months in advance), desire for certain service attributes (such as more legroom and priority boarding), and preference for seat location. At entertainment events, seat location is often a differentiator for price, with those wanting to sit closer to the stage paying a higher price.

Consider how this might work for a fitness membership. Someone who has not worked out in a while might be looking for an economical way to start going to the gym once or twice a week. He is not ready to purchase a yearlong gym membership, but purchasing a 1-month membership is an attractive way to try working out again. The gym offers him a 1-month $45 trial membership with the option to renew at a month-by-month cost of $40. By contrast, a gym buff who goes to the fitness center every day before work might be willing to commit to a longer membership. The gym offers her a membership for $30/month for at least 6 months. Both consumers will be using the same gym services, but the second consumer receives a better monthly deal for her willingness to commit over time. Operating two pricing plans benefits both the gym and the two consumers, because each has access to the gym under his or her own terms.

As we have discussed, healthcare consumers have traditionally had difficulty understanding the full cost of a product or service in healthcare. This is because pricing is obscure to consumers, and overall prices are often determined by contracting between organizations. In the case of most employer-sponsored health insurance, pricing segmentation does not occur at the consumer level because the same community rate is charged to an employer's entire employee pool.

We are beginning to see more nuanced pricing strategies in healthcare insurance with different plans offering different prices and services. The Connecticut health insurance exchange, AccessHealth Connecticut, required participating insurers to offer standard bronze, silver, and gold plans so that consumers on different budgets with different price sensitivities could make intelligent apples-to-apples comparisons. Insurers could add additional plans but only after they offered these three.

Product and Service Design

Marketers use consumer insights to create distinct products or services for different segments. This is standard practice in other industries. For example, Target, one of the leading retail stores in the United States, recognized that urban shoppers differed from those in the suburbs. In response, Target created two new store concepts, "CityTarget" and "TargetExpress." Urban consumers using CityTarget often visited the stores on foot and could not carry as much. Bulky items, such as paper towels, needed to be offered in smaller sizes.[12]

In healthcare, consumer segmentation can similarly improve product and service design. Consider how some hospitals have redesigned their services to prevent patient falls, which are more likely among the elderly and those taking certain medications. Patient falls are of particular concern for hospitals. Researchers have shown that a patient fall can increase hospital costs by around $13,000 and length of stay by over 6 days.[13] Around 30% of patients who fall are injured, and since 2008, the Centers for Medicare and Medicaid Services (CMS) has not reimbursed providers for hospital stays that include a patient fall.[14]

In response, hospitals have redesigned processes and even altered the physical environment to aid high-risk patients. In 2012, the University Medical Center of Princeton at Plainsboro opened a new hospital in New Jersey. The planners had created "mock-up" patient rooms at the old location to test the safety of different room designs. The new medical center incorporated several cost-effective safety features specifically for patients at increased risk of falling (e.g., handrails from patients' beds to their bathrooms, bathroom doors that opened easily, patient beds that could be lowered to 16 inches off the floor, and a system for alerting nurses if high-risk patients got up without help).[15]

Segmentation Approaches

There are many ways of segmenting consumers. Some common approaches segment consumers using the following variables:

- Geographic location
- Demographic and socioeconomic data
- Decision-making process
- Past purchase and usage data
- Benefits and their relative importance
- Attitude, interests, and opinions
- Media and information search habits

Often, a marketer will explore multiple segmentation criteria, searching for the one or two approaches that do the best job of differentiating consumer segments. In addition, overlaying analyses can result in richer, more detailed segment profiles or in smaller, more precisely defined segments.

One simple segmentation approach is based on analyzing where customers live and work. An urban shopper might visit a conveniently located store several times a week and be drawn to items in smaller packages that can be carried home on foot or public transport. A suburban shopper might travel by car to a large store and stock up for the coming week. Because healthcare is delivered locally, geographical segmentation is often part of the segmentation approach.

Another common approach segments consumers using demographic data (e.g., education, gender, age, income, occupation, race, or religion). In a healthcare context, these data are often associated with different healthcare risks or behaviors. For example, Dignity Health has developed a standardized Community Need Index (CNI) that enables it to quantify community health risk across the nation.[16] It bases the CNI scores on five socioeconomic barriers that affect overall health: income, cultural/language, educational, insurance, and housing.[17] Dignity has found that CNI scores are positively correlated with hospital utilization, so it uses the scores to develop programs and services aimed to improve health and reduce healthcare utilization.[18] See Table 6.3 for a comparison of CNI scores in high-need and low-need communities.

Table 6.3 **Comparison of CNI Scores for High-Need and Low-Need Communities**

Green Valley, AZ 85614		*Compton, CA 90220*	
Barrier (Variables Measured)	*Barrier Score*	*Barrier (Variables Measured)*	*Barrier Score*
Income		**Income**	
(elderly poverty, children poverty, single-parent poverty)	3	(elderly poverty, children poverty, single-parent poverty)	4
Cultural		**Cultural**	
(non-Caucasian, limited English)	2	(non-Caucasian, limited English)	5
Education		**Education**	
(without high school diploma)	1	(without high school diploma)	5
Insurance		**Insurance**	
(unemployed, uninsured)	2	(unemployed, uninsured)	5
Housing		**Housing**	
(percent renting)	1	(percent renting)	4
↓		↓	
Final CNI Score = 1.8 (Low-Need Community)		**Final CNI Score = 4.6** (High-Need Community)	

Source: Adapted from Dignity Health, "Improving Public Health & Preventing Chronic Disease: Dignity Health's Community Need Index," accessed 2015.

American Family Care (AFC), one of the largest retail urgent care clinic companies in the United States, uses Nielsen's PRIZM system to identify and open new locations. PRIZM is a national database that clusters American consumers into 38 segments with names like "Upward Bound" and "Cruisin' to Retirement." PRIZM identifies the segment profile mix of each U.S. zip code, overlaying rich consumer profiles on top of basic geographic segmentation. AFC knows its level of penetration for each PRIZM consumer segment, so the company can search for new locations where the population mix is similar to the mix served by its most successful, existing clinics. One possible weakness of this approach is that AFC new store location decisions become a self-fulfilling prophecy. Locations are chosen based on where the clinics are currently doing well, but that could simply be a function of where the company was launched rather than the inherent, superior appeal of the AFC concept to those consumers.

Although these approaches can tell us how segments are behaving, they do not tell us *why* they are behaving in a particular manner. For this reason, geographic and demographic segmentation often fall short. A psychographic segmentation strategy divides different populations based on attitudes, interests, opinions, and lifestyles. Employing this strategy can yield insights that explain why consumers behave in particular ways, and it can help managers design more effective communications programs to reach particular segments—particularly if they display different television viewing or social media habits.

Other segmentation approaches divide buyers into segments based on their knowledge of, or usage experience with, a product. Such behavioral data are often used in combination with other classification variables. Deloitte has developed a segmentation approach for healthcare consumers using both behavioral and attitudinal factors to create six distinct consumer segments. See Table 6.4 for Deloitte's behavioral-attitudinal segmentation strategy, along with descriptions and percentage breakdown of consumers who fall into each segment.

Psychographic segmentation can be overlaid on claims data and demographic information to identify segments with high-potential for cost savings and improved outcomes. For example, Humana, the fourth largest health insurance firm in the United States in 2015, uses a behavioral-driven segmentation methodology for its customers.[19] Among the major U.S health insurance companies, Humana has focused the most on improving customer relationships rather than cost reduction. Most consumers suspect healthcare insurers make profits by withholding care, but Humana's 2013 annual report stated: "Our strategy intertwines care delivery, the patient experience and clinical and consumer insights to encourage engagement, behavior change, proactive clinical outreach and wellness. Our primary objective is to help our customers get—and stay—in good health."

With a membership of 14.2 million, it is no surprise that member needs and preferences vary. To increase member engagement, Humana's Consumer Analytics group used deidentified claims and consumer data on 700 variables to cluster

Table 6.4 Deloitte's Behavioral-Attitudinal Segmentation

Segment	Online and Onboard (19%)	Sick and Savvy (11%)	Out and About (8%)	Shop and Save (6%)	Casual and Cautious (34%)	Content and Compliant (22%)
Description	✓ Happy with care but wants to understand options and partner with doctors to make decisions ✓ High use of online resources—wants quality/price details ✓ High use of and interest in health technologies Interested in communicating electronically with doctors	✓ Heavy users of healthcare ✓ High trust in doctors ✓ Partners with doctors to make decisions ✓ Most prepared financially to handle future costs ✓ Some use of online resources ✓ Some use of and interest in health technologies	✓ Independent—tends to rely on self when making decisions but raises questions ✓ Prefers providers who use or integrate alternative medicine and treatment approaches ✓ High use of online resources ✓ Some use of and interest in health technologies	✓ Partners with doctors but raises questions ✓ Actively seeks options and switches plans, doctors, and medications for better value ✓ High use of online resources—wants quality/price details ✓ High use of and interest in health technologies ✓ Saves for future healthcare costs	✓ Least engaged (less need) ✓ Cost-conscious but least prepared financially ✓ Prefers partnering with doctors instead of relying on doctors or self when making decisions ✓ Low trust in and use of information resources ✓ Low use of and interest in health technologies ✓ Least compliant	✓ Happy with plan and providers ✓ High trust in doctors—most likely to rely on doctors to make decisions and least likely to question ✓ Low use of online information resources ✓ Low use of and interest in health technologies ✓ Adheres to treatment recommendations

Source: Adapted from Greenspun, Harry, Sarah Thomas, Gregory Scott, David Betts, "Health care consumer engagement: No 'one-size-fits-all' approach." Deloitte Center for Health Solutions. 2015. Web.

Humana members into 15 "persona" segments. These variables included existing clinical data (insurance claims and prescription fills), socioeconomic information (health, family status, retired/working status, etc.), census data, credit card purchase data, and consumer engagement data (including log-ins on Humana's website, outreach to Humana's call center, and even voting history).

Surveys on attitudes, interests, and opinions were sent to member samples within each segment to detect further commonalities that would add color to the 15 "personas." Level of engagement with their health was the most important variable discriminating among the segments.

Building upon these efforts, Humana tailored its messaging more appropriately, and it determined what incentives would motivate members in each segment to improve their health (thereby lowering Humana's health insurance costs). See Table 6.5. For engaged consumers, a simple email (rather than an expensive call by a nurse) was all that was needed. For less engaged members, outreach through a physician, a caregiver, or a friend was necessary. Humana's consumer experience team aimed to provide each member with a seamless, continuous relationship built on four principles but adjusted to the preferences of each segment. The four principles were as follows: know me; show me you care; make it easy; and help me achieve the best possible health. Humana defined them as the following:

- "Know me:" Have customizable features that understand individual preferences.
- "Show me:" Anticipate people's needs.
- "Make it easy:" Simplify the health and wellness process.
- "Help me:" Give people the tools they need to manage their health successfully.[20]

Table 6.5 **Humana's Behavioral Segmentation**

Segment	Percentage of Humana Beneficiaries	Description	Communication Preferences
Self-engaged optimists (healthy)	15%	"I need to verify it."	Activity on Web: High Inbound calls: High Preventive visits: High
Self-engaged optimists (chronic illness)	9%	"I am inspired to do what is right."	Activity on Web: Low Inbound calls: High Preventive visits: High
Simplicity-seeking followers (healthy)	14%	"I do what's needed."	Activity on Web: Medium Inbound calls: Low Preventive visits: Medium
Simplicity-seeking followers (chronic illness)	10%	"I do what's easy."	Activity on Web: Low Inbound calls: Low Preventive visits: Medium

Table 6.5 **Continued**

Segment	Percentage of Humana Beneficiaries	Description	Communication Preferences
Skeptical control seekers (healthy— group #1)	13%	"I manage my health best."	Activity on Web: Low Inbound calls: Low Preventive visits: Low
Skeptical control seekers (healthy— group #2)	8%	"I'm fine, really."	Activity on Web: Low Inbound calls: Low Preventive visits: High
Skeptical control seekers (chronic illness)	5%	"I'll do it my way."	Activity on Web: Medium Inbound calls: Low Preventive visits: Low
Health services maximizers (healthy)	3%	"I do my part."	Activity on Web: High Inbound calls: High Preventive visits: High
Health services maximizers (chronic illness)	2%	"I'm overwhelmed."	Activity on Web: High Inbound calls: High Preventive visits: High
Autopilot participators (healthy)	6%	"I enjoy life."	Activity on Web: High Inbound calls: High Preventive visits: High
Autopilot participators (chronic illness)	4%	"I need a push to do more."	Activity on Web: High Inbound calls: Low Preventive visits: Medium
Overwhelmed and reluctant reactors (healthy)	2%	"I'd rather not."	Activity on Web: Medium Inbound calls: Low Preventive visits: Medium
Overwhelmed and reluctant reactors (chronic illness)	1%	"I'm losing the battle."	Activity on Web: High Inbound calls: Medium Preventive visits: Low
Support-seeking participants chronic illness)	3%	"I need support."	Activity on Web: Low Inbound calls: High Preventive visits: Medium
Healthy self-sustainers	5%	"I like it on my terms."	Activity on Web: Medium Inbound calls: Low Preventive visits: Low

Source: "Humana's Bold Goal: 20 Percent Healthier by 2020," Nancy M. Kane and Deborah Milstein, Harvard T.H. Chan School of Public Health, 2016.

Back to Benefits

Although many segmentation methods can be useful, benefit segmentation is perhaps the most valuable approach in healthcare. Benefit segmentation measures the relative importance that a consumer attaches to different benefits associated with a product. The product or service is then designed and marketed to appeal to a segment that values that benefit as being especially important.

We believe that benefit segmentation based on the six E's can explain much of the choice in the healthcare sector. Consider how we might segment pregnant women by their preferences across the six E's. How would women like Larissa, Sarah, and Julie perceive their interactions with the healthcare system, and how would they make decisions? What would they want?

Many different benefits come into play. Pregnancy, childbirth, and child rearing are expensive; there are substantial costs associated with pregnancy that must be taken into consideration. For most women, obtaining the very best possible care is the most important driver of decision-making throughout pregnancy and childbirth. Many women also want trusted and secure relationships with their caregivers, preferably those with more experience who can give them sound advice. And yet others may also feel motivated by the level of autonomy they have in making decisions for themselves. As women and their families go through the pregnancy process, they must take many benefits into account and make tradeoffs among them.

For example, each of the three women we described earlier had different priorities. For Larissa, who was young, healthy, and a first-time mother, the cost of services and the relationship with her clinical provider were most important. As a first-time mother, she was scared about what lay ahead and hoped for a reassuring OB/GYN to guide her through the next 9 months. Sarah, who was the most engaged in the pregnancy journey, prioritized the effectiveness of care and empowerment through her extensive research of individual clinical providers as well as hospitals. For Julie, who had been through the pregnancy and birthing process twice before and was busy with work and family life, convenient access to her provider was especially important. These three women are representative of larger segments of consumers seeking similar benefits.

Figure 6.2 shows how the benefit profile for each of the three segments representing our three pregnant consumer types attaches different weights to different benefits. The dotted line depicts each consumer segment's relative importance weights in comparison to the situation in which all benefits are considered equal (depicted by the solid-line hexagon). There may be other segments of pregnant women who value these benefits with other combinations of benefit importance weightings, but these three characters and their respective situations are representative of a large portion of the relevant population.

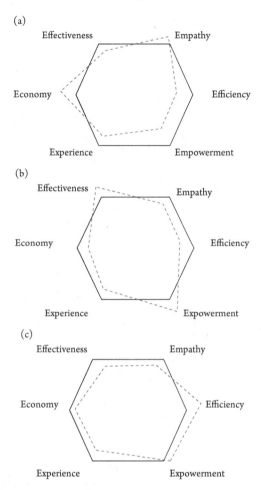

Figure 6.2 Benefit segmentation of pregnant women.

Big Data and Segmentation

Segmentation is ultimately dependent on data and the tools available for analyzing it. For example, consider the range of clinical, financial, and consumer satisfaction data an organization would need to segment pregnant women across the six E's. As the availability of digitized data has expanded across the healthcare industry, and as the cost of data storage and analyses continues to fall, data-driven segmentation is increasingly feasible. Provider organizations store an enormous amount of patient-level clinical information in their EMR systems, while payer organizations have detailed claims data. Pharmaceutical companies have built large databases of research and development data, and the government tracks data from clinical trials and drug approvals.

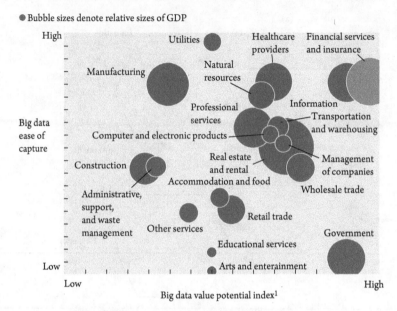

● Bubble sizes denote relative sizes of GDP

[1]Determined by industry average of transaction intensity, amount of data per firm, variability in performance, customer and supplier intensity, and turbulence.

Figure 6.3 Big data's potential by industry. Source: Mole, Kevin, and Nadeau Marie-Claude. "Beyond the Buzz: Harnessing Machine Learning in Payments." *McKinsey & Company*. Sept. 2016. Web.

Data are underutilized in healthcare. A McKinsey study, summarized in Figure 6.3, shows that healthcare providers capture a large amount of data, and there is potential for added value. But, compared to financial services, healthcare is behind. This is due in part to privacy concerns about sharing individuals' data, as well as the closed systems in which much of the information is stored. For competitive reasons, hospitals often do not share patient EMR data beyond their own system, whereas many consumers visit multiple places for care, causing their information to be dispersed among different silos.

We are beginning to see applications of big data and machine learning in healthcare. Some large health systems have organized internal analytics groups to address a range of clinical and business objectives. For example, Carolinas Healthcare System, located in North Carolina, established a dedicated analytics group in 2011 that added value through data-based segmentation studies on a variety of topics. In 2013, it created a "Readmission Predictive Risk Model," which helped clinical teams identify the patients at greatest risk for readmission. The group developed the model from data on thousands of patients who had been previously discharged from a Carolinas facility. Using the model, the group analyzed 600 variables and found that 40 were highly predictive of readmission: these included ED visits, sodium levels, first language, and late-stage renal disease. The model, which was 79%

accurate in predicting 30-day readmission rates, clustered patients into five separate segments, generating unique discharge plans for each.

The Carolinas data analytics group went further. In 2014, they broadened beyond discharge planning and reviewed data on 2.2 million active patients to create a robust segmentation model. The model collected clinical, medication compliance, education attainment, socioeconomic, and consumer spending data for each patient, and in the future, it hoped to obtain data from wearables, such as Fitbit. Creating seven distinct segments, the model helped clinicians identify high-risk patients more quickly, and it made better estimates of the expected *per capita* cost of providing care to patients in each segment. The latter was particularly helpful for improving contract negotiations with payers, who traditionally had access to more and better claims data than the health system did.

Data analytics capabilities are not always internal. Physicians can use decision support tools, like Watson Health, IBM's cognitive computing system, to match the right patients to the right treatments. For one project, Watson Oncology, IBM is partnering with Memorial Sloan Kettering (MSK), a leader in cancer care, to train Watson to interpret clinical information for cancer patients and identify individualized, evidence-based treatment options. MSK stated:

> As Watson Oncology's teacher, we are advancing our mission by creating a powerful resource that will help inform treatment decisions for those who may not have access to a specialty center like MSK. With Watson Oncology, we believe we can decrease the amount of time it takes for the latest research and evidence to influence clinical practice across the broader oncology community, help physicians synthesize available information, and improve patient care.[21]

However, some providers remain reticent about the prospects of such technology one day replacing the diagnosing or treating abilities of a clinician. For the time being, artificial intelligence tools augment the clinical provider's role, rather than supplant it.

Currently, many of these technological tools are focused on health systems and physicians rather than on consumers. In the future, consumer-facing tools that help consumers segment themselves will become increasingly common. Although sites like WebMD allow consumers to look up information on their symptoms, they do not permit consumers to take their personal situations into account or delve into the likelihood of each of many health conditions listed. This can cause anxiety, as consumers with a simple cough begin to think they have a far more serious illness.

Nevertheless, online healthcare consumer platforms such as Buoy Health, a startup health app, began in 2017 with the premise of helping sick consumers diagnose themselves and find the appropriate channel for solving their health issues.

When a consumer logs onto the app, she answers a series of questions about her current condition. The app also accounts for the consumer's gender, age, location, and other factors. The app's algorithm analyzes the answers in real time and decides what to ask next based upon the responses. At the end, it walks the consumer through a detailed analysis of what is most likely ailing her, and importantly, whether she should go to the doctor or not.

We are only just beginning to utilize big data opportunities in healthcare—particularly as they relate to segmentation. For data-driven segmentation to deliver value in healthcare, we will need more nuanced tools, as well as a culture change among clinicians to encourage and accept the more widespread use of open-source data sharing. Enhanced collaboration between clinicians and analysts will further improve the completeness of the data available on each patient.

Conclusion

Consumers are heterogeneous, not homogeneous. A market-oriented healthcare manager recognizes this, respects diversity, invests in consumer research, and develops programs that are tailored to the needs and preferences of different consumer segments. A market-oriented healthcare manager will need to look at many different segmentation approaches to determine which make the most sense to drive improved patient outcomes. The thoughtful application of consumer segmentation requires and reflects a fundamental shift from a production-oriented to a consumer-oriented culture.

References

1. Bichell, Rae Ellen. "Average Age of First-Time Moms Keeps Climbing in the U.S." *NPR*. 14 January 2016. Web.
2. Epstein, Randi Hutter. *Get Me Out: A History of Childbirth From the Garden of Eden to the Sperm Bank*. W. W. Norton, 2011. Print.
3. Porter, Roy. *Blood and Guts: A Short History of Medicine*. W. W. Norton, 2004. Print.
4. "Achievements in Public Health, 1900–1999: Healthier Mothers and Babies." *Center for Disease Control and Prevention*. 1 October 1999. Web.
5. Ibid.
6. "Maternal Mortality Ratio (Modeled Estimate, per 100,000 Live Births)." *The World Bank*. 2015. Web.
7. "Miscarriage." *March of Dimes*. 2012. Web.
8. Livingston, Gretchen. "Childlessness." *Pew Research Center's Social & Demographic Trends Project*. 7 May 2015. Web.
9. "Dignity Health Launches Program Focused on Personalizing the Patient Experience for Mothers-to-Be." *Business Wire*. Berkshire Hathaway, 5 January 2017. Web.
10. January, Craig T., L. Samuel Wann, Joseph S. Alpert, Hugh Calkins, Joseph C. Cleveland, Joaquin E. Cigarroa, Jamie B. Conti, Patrick T. Ellinor, Michael D. Ezekowitz, Michael E.

Field, Katherine T. Murray, Ralph L. Sacco, William G. Stevenson, Patrick J. Tchou, Cynthia M. Tracy, and Clyde W. Yancy. "2014 AHA/ACC/HRS Guideline for the Management of Patients With Atrial Fibrillation." *2014 AHA/ACC/HRS Atrial Fibrillation Guideline: A Report of the American College of Cardiology/American Heart Association Task Force on Practice Guidelines and the Heart Rhythm Society* (2014): 1–124. Print.

11. Ashwood, J. Scott, Ateev Mehrotra, David Cowling, and Lori Uscher-Pines. "Direct-to-Consumer Telehealth May Increase Access to Care But Does Not Decrease Spending." *Health Affairs*. 1 March 2017. Web.

12. "Target Announces Store Growth Plans for 2015." *Target Corporate*. 2 February 2015. Web.

13. Wong, C. A., A. J. Recktenwald, M. L. Jones, B. M. Waterman, M. L. Bollini, and W. C. Dunagan. "The Cost of Serious Fall-Related Injuries at Three Midwestern Hospitals." *Joint Commission Journal on Quality and Patient Safety*. U.S. National Library of Medicine, February 2011. Web.

14. Goldsack, Jennifer, Janet Cunningham, and Susan Mascioli. "Patient Falls: Searching for the Elusive 'Silver Bullet.'" *Nursing2017* 44, no. 7 (2014): 61–62. Web.

15. "How to Design Hospitals With Safety in Mind." *Hospitals & Health Networks*. 14 October 2014. Web.

16. "Improving Public Health & Preventing Chronic Disease Dignity Health's Community Need Index." *Dignity Health*. Web.

17. Ibid.

18. Ibid.

19. Kane, Nancy M., and Deborah Milstein. *Humana's Bold Goal: 20 Percent Healthier by 2020*. Harvard T. H. Chan School of Public Health, 2016. Print.

20. "Using Mobile Apps to Empower People." *Humana.com*. 2017. Web.

21. "Watson Oncology." *Memorial Sloan Kettering*. Web.

7

Making a Consumer Choice "System" Work

In our introduction, we discussed the combination of social, financial, political, and technological forces creating a rising tide of change today. Across all industries, consumers have more choices and are more empowered to seek out information than ever before. This is also true in healthcare, where access to new market entrants like retail clinics, urgent care centers, and virtual medical teams are changing the ways in which consumers interact with the healthcare system. We know that deductibles are rising. As they pick up more of the tab, consumers are paying more attention to the costs of care. Consumers in public and private health insurance marketplaces have been pushed to make important health-related financial decisions many of them have never faced before. Political tensions around the future of healthcare in this country have ignited heated debate, increasing the public's knowledge of and attention to the healthcare system. Furthermore, there are ever more medical advances on offer. Newer, more precise treatments and direct-to-consumer advertising mean that consumers want treatment that is customized to their conditions.

As a result, consumers are more engaged at a time when the system not only offers more options but also pushes them into taking on greater decision-making responsibility. Creating a consumer-centric healthcare system that works for a majority of Americans is no easy task—but we believe it is feasible with careful planning and targeted stakeholder involvement.

Therefore, in the second section of this book, we looked at how consumer choice operates in the broader world and in healthcare. In Chapter 2, we acknowledged the ways in which healthcare differs from other industries. If we, as a society, fail to address these differences, we run the risk of creating a system that does not appropriately support or protect patients. *Caveat emptor ("buyer beware")* is not an acceptable stance in healthcare. If we acknowledge these differences, yet also accept the increasingly consumer-centric nature of healthcare, we believe that we can create a viable consumer marketplace. In Chapter 3, we discussed the six enabling conditions necessary to create this market, as well as why these conditions are currently not met in healthcare today. Motivating change across these six conditions will require an improved understanding of the stakeholder at the core of this book—the consumer.

In Chapter 4, we focused on the individual consumer, presenting the process he uses to make healthcare decisions, and in Chapter 5, we discussed the six E's, the six benefits consumers evaluate when making healthcare decisions. In Chapter 6, we described how organizations, policy makers, and individual clinicians can use this enhanced understanding of consumers to segment their marketplaces, ultimately leading to more targeted messaging and better designed products and services.

In this final chapter, we first present choice from a "systems" perspective by describing a process model for consumer choice, in which producers and suppliers respond to their targeted segments of the population that share common desires and expected benefits. We examine two foundational conditions that are needed to jump-start the healthcare industry to become consumer oriented: incentives and a consumer mindset. We highlight the actions and changes that healthcare providers, insurers, and government—as well as consumers—can play to make consumer choice work. Finally, we reprise why consumer choice is important and propose a way forward.

Strategy for the Supply Side

A "Systems" Model

Initiating and managing change in something as complex as U.S. healthcare is not easy. Many years and countless adaptations have created a system that, while far from perfect, resists change. Trying to achieve large-scale changes quickly in our U.S. political system is especially difficult. Unfortunately, overhauling one or two smaller problems at a time rarely works much better. The writer H. L. Mencken is credited with having warned that for every complex problem, there is an answer that is "clear, simple, and wrong." Fixing a specific problem commonly generates unintended and unforeseen consequences that often lead to failure.

Healthcare is a "system" in a special sense of the word. When we use the term "system" in this chapter, we mean it as a general descriptive term that refers to the way that an enterprise functions as a whole. "Systems" are connected and joined together by a web of interrelationships. A functioning healthcare "system" is more than the sum of its parts; it is a collection of stakeholders as moving parts in a dynamic, interacting process.

Complex systems are most likely to undergo transformation when interventions are directed at a high leverage point that purposely sets off a linked sequence of virtuous changes. Knowing where and how to intervene depends on understanding the system's internal dynamics. With the objective of identifying leverage points, we first proposed, in Chapter 3, six enabling conditions to overcome barriers in our

Figure 7.1 Enabling conditions necessary to spur consumer choice.

current system that disable, block, or slow consumer choice. Few supply-side organizations will be fired up to offer choices without support from an environment in which these six market-enabling elements are present. Figure 7.1 presents the six consumer market-enabling conditions.

We have identified "consumer mindset" and "incentives" as the two enabling conditions most likely to activate healthcare suppliers to deliver consumer-oriented change. These two could generate high impact and are feasible to achieve in today's environment. An organization's shift to a business-to-consumer (B2C) mindset will spur it to develop products with consumer-responsive value propositions. When market incentives are present and active, these early innovators are signaled that they can proceed with confidence that they will be supported and rewarded if their package of benefits gets it right for their target population.

Of the six facilitating conditions, then, an organization's consumer mindset and the presence of incentives are the key drivers in the healthcare sector for jumpstarting system change. A cascade of differentiation, measurement, and transparency is likely to follow from the influence of these two leading conditions. Differentiation will emerge as a result of consumer-oriented incentives that stimulate innovation and new products. Transparency will grow as differentiation and measurement reveal distinctions among product offerings that are important for market success; those that can prove they are better will be sure to promote the data and make consumers aware of the differences. Consumer protection is a *sine qua non*; consumer choices must be safe.

The success of a consumer-centric organization in its marketplace creates a virtuous cycle. As an organization finds that its products bring it more customer approval and business success, it will respond more avidly to the incentives and enhance them. This reinforcing feedback should lead to continuous strengthening of the conditions that favor delivering what consumers want. In the following section we briefly re-examine consumer mindset and incentives, describe why each is important, and identify who is mainly responsible for changing them.

Consumer-Centric Mindset

Consumer centricity is an attitude that inspires organizations to design products and services around consumer needs. Organizations with a consumer-centric mindset want to understand their core users better; they conduct detailed consumer research and use that information to improve the products and services they bring to market. Healthcare stakeholders with a consumer mindset will be highly responsive to incentives that reward them for delivering the six E's of consumer benefits we presented in Chapter 5.

These six benefits, which comprise the patient journey, cover most of the personal preferences that each individual consumer trades off as she engages with the healthcare system. The six E's are economy, effectiveness, empathy, efficiency, empowerment, and experience. In fact, the six enabling conditions and the six benefits generated by that stimulus are closely related. Figure 7.2 shows the complete model, in which an activated consumer mindset, motivated by appropriate incentives, generates the kind of personal patient journey that healthcare consumers desire.

Incentives

Incentives, which we discussed in detail in Chapter 3, are the fuel that fires up suppliers to change and improve. Incentives work because of rewards and penalties built into and across the payer, insurer, and provider interfaces. Incentives are

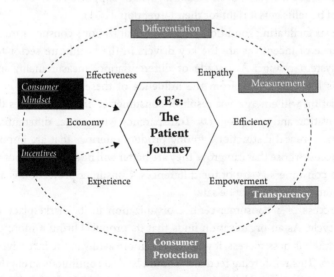

Figure 7.2 The action model to improve the patient journey.

powerful signals that nudge or direct healthcare stakeholders to operate in a certain way. If disabling incentives are left in place, consumer choice will be held back. If these barriers are reduced, progress will be accelerated. Introducing incentives that reward innovators and reduce their risk creates an environment highly likely to deliver the benefits of consumer choice.

Incentives are already very important influences on the behaviors of healthcare consumers when they purchase insurance and use care. Consumer incentives were discussed in detail in Chapter 3. Insurers specify and generally manage incentives like co-payments, deductibles, co-insurance, differential charges for types of services, and tiered pharmacy benefits.

More affirmative consumer-oriented incentives will be needed to stimulate choice. Consumers benefit when insurers offer incentives to nudge them to adopt and maintain healthy behaviors, be more engaged and discerning shoppers, and participate in evaluating the services they receive. Insurers could easily reward good behaviors with discounts, rebates, lower out-of-pocket costs, and social recognition.

Incentives are a multistakeholder enterprise in healthcare. As we have seen with the Affordable Care Act (ACA) and its implementation and repeal attempts, government policy and regulation is a tremendously important force but difficult to achieve or change. In the delivery system, incentives are generally developed and implemented by insurers, carried out by clinical providers, and followed by consumers. Thus, insurers already are the most likely initiators of consumer-oriented incentives focused both on providers and on their insured populations. Why is it they are the leaders? In the United States, insurance companies and The Centers for Medicare & Medicaid Services (CMS), their federal counterpart, are largely responsible for creating supply-side reimbursement policies, including incentives. Their position in the healthcare hierarchy is as middlemen, between payers and providers; their job is to align what payers want to pay with what providers and consumers want delivered. They already employ financial and structural incentives to influence the providers whom they pay. They are already moving into value-based reimbursement to manage costs, and they are the primary source of evaluation data to measure value. They can facilitate competition between the providers of care.

But because they are in the middle, insurers are not completely free to design and use incentives on their own. Therefore, we believe that insurers will need to co-design and collaborate with payers, providers, and patients to design incentives and initiatives that deliver choice to their population segments.

The Six E's and the New Healthcare Value Proposition

The value proposition shifts when organizations compete in a consumer choice system. In Figure 7.3 we present a schematic model of the expanded value proposition delivered in the consumer-oriented patient journey. Producers have traditionally thought about value for their customers in terms of effectiveness (clinical quality)

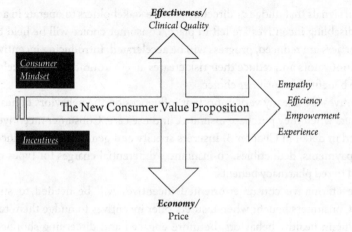

Figure 7.3 The value proposition in the era of consumer choice.

and economy (cost to the consumer). In that framework, quality / cost = value. That traditional value proposition is illustrated by the vertical arrows. In the new value formulation, the four E's comprising service and satisfaction also become important to consumer choice. These benefits encompass how a patient feels about the patient journey he experiences, episode by episode, as he engages with any part of the system, from selecting insurance to making an office visit to being hospitalized. Clinical outcomes and affordability remain very important but no longer dominate the consumer value proposition. Consumers will trade off among quality, cost, and the patient experience to get what each wants. Each healthcare organization should differentiate by delivering the mix of benefits that best serves and satisfies their set of consumer segments.

Stakeholder Roles in Delivering Consumer Choice

Stakeholder roles will change in a more consumer-centric industry. Clinicians, healthcare delivery organizations, insurers, and business will discover new opportunities and face fresh challenges as they create a consumer-centric healthcare system and deliver on the six E's.

Individual Clinicians

Each clinical provider plays a leading role in delivering the patient journey. It is individual clinicians who are most often the face of the healthcare system. They are present in every contact, whether it is by phone, email, or face-to-face visit. They are the most intimately customer-facing of all participants in healthcare, and their effectiveness is critical in creating the experience that consumers want. If they do not deliver the appropriate mix of the six benefits in these interactions, consumer choice will fall short of its potential even if organizations take steps toward consumer centricity.

Physicians and other clinical providers, especially those in primary care, start from a highly regarded position. A survey we conducted in conjunction with Mass Insight Global Partnerships and Opinion Dynamics in 2017 (Figure 7.4) showed that consumers in Massachusetts are generally satisfied with primary care physicians across a wide range of criteria.

Today, patient-consumers generally trust their clinical providers. This relationship is important to maintain. Because patients do not have the scientific or technical knowledge to make many clinical decisions on their own, they depend on clinicians to advise them at their most vulnerable times and help them make difficult decisions. As the healthcare system subjects the consumer to more financial hurdles, the importance of a trusting relationship will only increase.

The roles of clinical providers will shift in many ways. To maintain this trusted advisor role, clinical providers must continue to hone a range of skills—some of which they have focused on for decades and others of which will be new.

First, clinicians will benefit from developing a strong consumer mindset. Their commitment to provide patient-centered, empathetic care is essential to preserve the human relationship on which the best medical care depends. As we discussed, empathy can clearly improve clinical outcomes and patient satisfaction, yet many healthcare providers still struggle to create an empathic environment. In April 2017, *Health Affairs* published an article by a journalist who documented her son's and father's illnesses, as well as her own challenges with Guillain-Barre syndrome. Across all three experiences, she concluded, "After having seen the best and worst of medicine over three generations, I've learned that people suffer needlessly, or

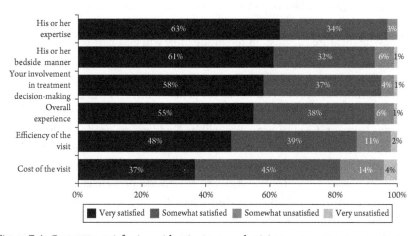

Figure 7.4 Consumer satisfaction with primary care physicians. Source: Data from MassInsight/ Opinion Dynamics Survey, Spring 2017.

pursue new possibilities of healing, based largely on whether they have a healing doctor-patient partnership."[1]

Second, doctors will be rewarded if they can sharpen their ability to discern what benefits are most important to individual patients. For many patients, efficiency is important, whereas for others empathy is key. Some patients will want autonomy and control, whereas others prefer that the doctor make the decisions. Understanding differences between patients will enable doctors to tailor their approach, interacting with patients to improve satisfaction, patient adherence, and good outcomes. Better training in patient interaction is important for doctors, but attitudinal change, targeted measurement, and appropriate rewards are also essential.

Third, caregivers have an obligation to be prepared to discuss financial issues as well as the clinical aspects of care. Successful clinicians will become adept at navigating financial conversations about their patient's costs of care and expected benefits. Today, at the point of care, many physicians struggle to discuss costs with patients. Patients often fail to bring up cost concerns with their physicians. A 2017 study in *Health Affairs* on medical price-shopping behavior showed that a majority of consumers believe price shopping is important; however, one commonly cited reason why consumers fail to compare prices among provider options is that they fear disrupting relationships with their current providers.[2] Physicians will learn to create environments where it is safe to engage in open conversations that address financial concerns, as well as the clinical aspects of care. For example, the University of California, San Francisco implemented a resident-led, case-based cost awareness curriculum for medicine residents.[3,4] Such training programs will become increasingly important to expand their skills and attitudes to support a broader array of consumers' concerns.

Fourth, clinicians should be prepared to participate in professional development that is based on much more rigorous performance assessment than now. They will be measured against a broader array of performance measures to capture the consumer perspective. Today, too many physicians are frustrated with the new metrics they are measured against. In the future, they will be a part of designing those metrics, challenged as a profession to invent the right ways to measure their own performance.

Finally, clinicians will be competing for patients. Insurers will become more selective as they create tighter networks of providers that can satisfy their particular customer segment. Clinical providers will be "bidding" to produce what insurers want for their members. Insurers and provider groups will be specifying clinical process changes, facility redesign, and enhancements of customer service to satisfy the segments they serve. To offer a competitive price, provide excellent care, and deliver the broader benefits is a new clinician challenge.

Despite their stated belief in patient orientation, the medical profession has resisted the idea of their patients being involved in choosing what they want and assessing whether they have received it. Some physicians fear that they will be judged poorly if they open themselves up to measurement and feedback. Perhaps this will be true for a few, but consumers are generally very supportive of doctors and respectful of how difficult their jobs are. We believe that working with, rather than resisting, the consumer choice movement will ultimately make medicine a more satisfying profession.

Several factors also make it relatively easy for service providers to carry off these new functions. First, organizational support for clinicians is stronger than in the past. Provider groups are growing, hospitals are vertically integrating and forming affordable care organizations (ACOs), larger organized managerial entities are taking charge of groups of doctors, and solo or small practice groups are diminishing. Larger groups can plan and implement better. Performance measurement is more meaningful when colleagues take part. Collaboration among doctors makes it easier to learn, change, and monitor how one is doing.

Second, patient orientation is nothing new for clinicians such as doctors and nurses. For centuries, doctors have acknowledged the primacy of patients in their oaths. Hundreds of papers and books have told doctors how important it is to know the patient, to be empathic, and to generate trust. We have taught generations of medical students about the doctor–patient relationship. Our problem in medicine is not misunderstanding the goal of patient orientation and choice; we have simply failed to deliver it well.

Finally, helping consumers and creating a good experience for them is ultimately satisfying for doctors. The role models in medical school are not the surly technician but the caring doctor who relates well to patients. If we can understand better what patients want and learn to deliver it, the result will be emotionally rewarding.

Provider Organizations

Provider organizations—organizations that deliver healthcare services—will be asked by insurers to produce consumer-oriented care for designated populations. Ranging from primary care to specialist groups and hospitals, provider groups will be rewarded for making the patient experience better. Organizational support will make it easier for clinicians to excel. Incentives, measurement, training, structural redesign, rewards, and process improvements will boost their achievement.

Delivery organizations often fall woefully short in creating a consumer-centric environment. Consider the experience of one physician, who in early 2017, published an account of her own harrowing healthcare experience when an occult adenoma in her liver ruptured and she almost bled to death—while 7 months pregnant. Suddenly a patient instead of the treating physician, she recognized all of the lapses in empathy. As she painstakingly documented each of these lapses in sensitivity, she realized, "As a patient, I was privy to failures that I'd been blind to as a clinician. There were disturbing deficits in communication, uncoordinated care, and occasionally an apparently complete absence of empathy. I recognized myself in every failure." Using her experiences as a motivation for organizational change, Henry Ford Health System overhauled its empathy training for both clinical and administrative workers. New employees now receive a training called a "Culture of Caring." During this training, they are taught to recognize both avoidable and unavoidable suffering and to recognize that their role is sometimes just to display empathy when suffering is unavoidable.[5]

Large-scale organizational culture change is often necessary for attitudes to change throughout. Most successful business strategies derive their potency from their organization's underlying ideology and enduring shared values, as described by Collins and Porras in their book *Built to Last*.[6] A healthcare organization with an existing consumer mindset can be a leader in developing new products and processes that enhance choice. Changing to one that takes healthcare consumers seriously requires committed and determined leadership.

The work environment matters. Organizations can create environments in which clinical providers feel that they have the time and support to engage appropriately with consumers. And of course the patient's physical environment is important; better food, attractive surroundings, and willingness to modify disruptive medical routines, such as vital signs at night when they are not needed, can enhance the patient's experience.

Hospitals, especially, must respect consumer preferences and try to accommodate these throughout their hospitalization. Costs might rise as a result but may be offset by improved care and patient loyalty. Hospitals will recognize that they care for diverse patient populations with differing needs and plan accordingly. The very acute, sick, and complicated patients are no longer able to be independent in making choices. There the focus of service shifts toward keeping concerned family and friends engaged and informed. Other patients are competent and functioning, in the hospital for diagnosis and treatment of fairly straightforward conditions. For the latter, giving them choices, better food, and thoughtful service is not only the right thing to do but also makes good business sense. A satisfied consumer is a future customer.

Finally, delivery organizations will want to know more about those they serve and to get better at measuring their experience. Developing data to understand more about who their patients are and what they want, employing metrics to measure their performance in the eyes of consumers, and augmenting information transparency are essential to planning and improving. Before undertaking change initiatives, organizations will see the value of conducting detailed consumer research to understand where they are currently meeting the expectations of their consumers and where they are falling short. For example, a health system could use the six E's model we presented in Chapter 5 to understand which benefits are most important to its target consumer base. Their user audience will likely differ along variables reflecting socio-economic status, the specialty of care that they need, hospital convenience, and appearance and service characteristics of hospital facilities.

Improving consumer centricity means fostering a deep understanding of consumers' needs and preferences and responding to them. A number of healthcare delivery organizations have recognized the importance of such efforts, and these leading organizations are taking system-wide approaches to this task. Many more will feel pressure to follow suit.

Insurers

Among the different types of healthcare organizations, insurers face the greatest disruptions to their business strategy as the system becomes more consumer-oriented. Their industry has been undermined by the growth of employer self-insurance, rising claims costs, resistance from independent-minded and powerful clinicians and hospitals, and their own weak performance in their claims to be managing care. They are an unpopular industry.[7] They take the brunt of anger about rising costs. Their service is seen as poor.

Caught between the interests of provider organizations, employers, government, and consumers, health insurers simply must find a new business proposition to survive. Many realize the importance of offering new products that are oriented toward giving consumers more of the choices they want. Most insurers face the immediate challenge of achieving and sustaining a consumer-driven orientation. Many are still driven by back-room actuaries and see their business as mainly business-to-business (B2B) marketing to employers.

There is some innovation within the insurance industry, although it is not yet dramatic. Some insurers have begun to offer incentives to chronic disease consumers to achieve and maintain healthy behaviors. An example is Vitality, a South African insurance company that is doing well by sharing its profit with patients for doing their part. Professor Regina Herzlinger of Harvard described Vitality as "focusing on consumer-driven health insurance ideas like paying customers to take care of themselves." Vitality has expanded to the United Kingdom and China. She argues that paying consumers for self-care could improve healthcare in the United States as well.[8]

Insurance options will be made much clearer to consumers. Oscar Health, a health insurer that began in 2012 and is expanding now to six states, is trying to focus on making it easier for consumers to do business with them. Health insurance is notoriously complicated, and research has shown that most Americans have a poor understanding of benefit and cost options. In one study, researchers found that only 14% of respondents were correct in answering multiple-choice questions about four basic components of health insurance design (deductibles, co-pays, co-insurance, and maximum out-of-pocket costs). They also found that many respondents struggled to calculate the cost of basic services covered by their plan.[9] Oscar predominantly focused on selling plans to individual consumers via the public marketplaces. As of early 2017, Oscar Health's website boasted its simplicity, clear co-pays (so patients know what they will owe), and concierge services (like talking to a physician about symptoms over the phone for free).[10]

Insurers will become aficionados of incentives, inventing new ones and studying whether and how they work. Incentives are their major tool to shape the consumer experience, upgrade consumerist skills, improve health, and enhance provider performance.

Insurers are best positioned to measure and manage the providers with whom they contract against their targets of consumer service and satisfaction. Insurers will induce their clinicians and hospitals to participate in measuring customer satisfaction as well as clinical performance. Insurers will need to upgrade their skills in selecting the right providers for their performance-based, limited networks.

Insurers will be expected to inform their customers about provider performance. They will need to design metrics and collect the data. Performance measurement must expand to include feedback from users about service and satisfaction, as well as clinical results and costs. Such information should be methodologically rigorous but also presented so consumers will want to read and understand it.

Finally, insurers could become disciplined innovators as they differentiate. Not only will many discover new ways to deliver consumer choice, but they also will become competent investigators, either by themselves or through collaboration. They should become a vibrant locus of research about clinical and consumer effectiveness and organizers, funders, and participants in the emerging field of what has been called delivery science.

Insurers are primed to be the drivers of change toward increased consumer choice. They have the greatest need to change. They are optimally positioned between the payers and the providers to align the two to serve customers better. They have relationships with their insured population, whether or not they have yet used medical care. Stepping up into consumer choice is their big opportunity.

Businesses

Many business stakeholders—especially those outside the healthcare industry—wield enormous influence over the healthcare system. We'll consider two ways in which *all* businesses affect the consumer choice—as payers of insurance and as community members.

Payers of Health Insurance

We must acknowledge the unique role of employers in the U.S. healthcare system. Unlike many other developed nations, which depend wholly on the government either to fund health insurance or provide healthcare services directly to their citizens, much of U.S. healthcare is paid for by employers. According to the Kaiser

Family Foundation, about half of all Americans receive health insurance through their employers.[11] Although employer-sponsored health insurance declined from 67% in 1999 to 56% of the population in 2014,[12] it remained stable during implementation of the ACA. Employers fund around 40%-45% of all healthcare costs in the United States,[13] a sum that the government might be partially responsible for if these individuals did not receive support from their employers. Employer funding of insurance remains a critical part of our system in a way that is different than many other countries.

Employer-sponsored health insurance has a long history in the United States. During and following World War II, factories and other production-focused companies needed workers, so they began offering health insurance as an additional benefit. Federal tax advantages made employer-sponsored health insurance tax-free. From the 1950s to the 1980s, strong labor unions bargained for expanded and better coverage. The 1990s were a time of change, when health maintenance organizations (HMOs) appeared to cut costs for employers. But HMOs limited choice and their popularity declined. Since then, the question of what employer-sponsored health insurance can—and should—look like has been up for debate.

Today, many employers face a penalty if they fail to offer adequate health insurance to their employees. Under the ACA, employers with more than 50 full-time employees were penalized for not offering health insurance coverage to their employees or not offering coverage that met minimum value standards. This provision was created in an effort to maintain the employer-based health insurance market, even as the public marketplaces opened to individuals. If, in a hypothetical situation, the ACA had not required employers to offer coverage, there were fears that employers would stop offering subsidized health insurance coverage and transfer their costs to the government.

So, if the ACA requirement is repealed under the current administration, will employers stop offering subsidized health insurance? The answer is, probably not. There are reasons beyond policy requirements that encourage employers to offer insurance coverage to their employees. Today, many Silicon Valley tech companies and start-ups offer free lunch or unlimited vacation for the same reason that they offer health insurance coverage: to court employees better. With the unemployment rate low, employers might lose out on top talent by providing substandard insurance or pushing employees to the public marketplace. For example, when the ACA passed in 2010, many feared that small employers (i.e., those with fewer than 50 full-time employees) would stop offering health insurance and shift their employees onto the public market. However, this didn't happen for the most part. In fact, employer-sponsored health insurance has remained stable.[14]

Providing better coverage is not only good for a company's hiring; it's also a way to increase productivity and cut costs. Healthier employees produce better work more efficiently, whereas sick employees cost them money. U.S. corporations

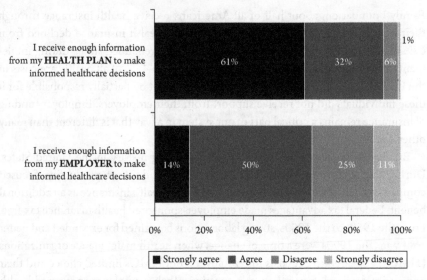

Figure 7.5 Information from health plans versus employers. Source: Data from MassInsight/
Opinion Dynamics Survey, Spring 2017.

lose around $225 billion annually due to absenteeism and "presenteeism"[15]—sick
employees underproducing while at work. Healthier employees also translate to
cheaper health insurance. So, although the structure of employer-sponsored health
insurance might change as regulations shift, it's unlikely that it will go entirely by
the wayside.

Further, there is evidence to suggest that employers could take on expanded
roles in consumer health. Results from the MassInsight survey showed that 61%
of consumers strongly agreed with the statement, "I receive enough information
from my health plan to make informed healthcare decisions," whereas only 14%
strongly agreed when this same statement was made about employers (Figure 7.5).
Employers can give their employees more information about what's included in
their health plan, and they can offer better access to workplace clinics and other
convenient options for care. Making both physical and mental health a key part of
workplace culture can make it quicker and easier for employees to seek out care
when they need it.

As Community Members

Too often, businesses cause unhealthy externalities—negative impacts on society
for which they do not have to pay. For example, most of the world's population buys
food from the private sector, yet very few Americans' diets meet the government's
dietary guidelines.[16] Correcting the consequences of unhealthy food products does
not typically fall to food manufacturers; instead, this responsibility is most often
dealt with by governments and healthcare organizations, not to mention individuals.

We are likely to encourage a broader culture of health within all organizations (including nonhealthcare companies) and in society. The Robert Wood Johnson Foundation (RWJF), the largest philanthropic organization focused on public health in the United States, has pushed for a new societal culture that embraces health and wellness. The organization terms its vision a "Culture of Health" and, with it, seeks to address the underlying determinants of health, encourage cross-collaboration among different kinds of organizations, and improve health equity.[17]

Corporations have an important role to play in implementing this vision. Although rarely discussed, *all* businesses, wittingly or unwittingly through their everyday decisions, lay down a population health footprint based on their cumulative positive and negative effects across four dimensions (see Figure 7.6).

1. *Consumer health*: How organizations affect the safety, integrity, and healthfulness of the products and services they offer to their customers and end consumers.
2. *Employee health*: How organizations affect the health of their employees (e.g., provision of employer-sponsored health insurance, workplace practices, and wellness programs).
3. *Community health*: How organizations affect the health of the communities in which they operate and do business.
4. *Environmental health*: How organizations' environmental policies (or lack thereof) affect individual and population health.

The public's health will no longer be an externality for businesses; ultimately, the effects of poor health hurt every company. Corporations that invest in improving public health stand to reduce costs, increase revenues, and improve their brand

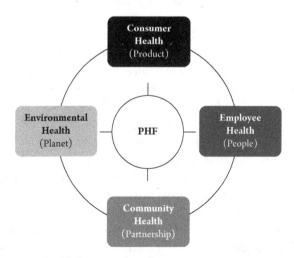

Figure 7.6 Population health footprint (PHF).

image.[18] To do so, businesses—including those outside healthcare—should expand their mission and corporate values to include the health of the public. To achieve a culture of health, corporations must expand their priorities so health is discussed when decisions are made. This new mindset requires a change from seeing health as an expense to seeing it as an investment.

Government

The U.S. government plays two important roles in consumer choice: first, as a funder of health insurance (i.e., Medicare and Medicaid); and second, as a policy-making and regulatory body. As funders of health insurance, government and business share common problems. Both have limited resources and are struggling to contain costs without lowering quality—all while keeping their constituencies happy. The government, now paying for about half of healthcare in the United States, likely has a more urgent problem than business. They face the tougher criticism and have the highest level of accountability—all of elected government can be voted out.

As the country's most powerful legislative body, government can make policy. It creates the laws that determine the design of our healthcare system. They have the power to shape who gets health insurance and what it covers. Government has done exactly this in creating Medicare, Medicaid, and the ACA. It is more than likely they will have to do this again in the future.

With its regulatory authority, the government has other leverage unavailable to business. The executive branch interprets the laws and turns them into regulations. With its authority, government specifies and then oversees the standards that insurers and service providers must meet. Their oversight protects consumers from shoddy products and services that would cause them harm. This oversight will only grow in importance as consumers take on greater decision-making responsibility in healthcare.

Through these powerful tools, government can spur innovation and change among delivery and insurance providers. However, the future of the system remains unclear. When the Congressional Budget Office estimated in May 2017 that the proposed legislation at that time—the American Health Care Act (AHCA)—would result in 26 million fewer people with health insurance in 2026,[19] the majority of Americans considered this an unacceptable solution. Whether the ACA survives repeal attempts by Republicans or not, more work will be necessary to ensure that markets offer affordable options to consumers. Greater public pressure will be exerted politically for government to create a sustainable plan that makes it possible for all Americans to participate in the healthcare system.

In all likelihood, bipartisan political solutions will be necessary to solve the seemingly intractable challenges of health policy reform. There are a few areas where the Left and Right agree (i.e., improved price transparency). However, more often than not, members of both parties cling to partisan ideologies, failing to appreciate potential solutions from the other side. Republicans have long extolled consumer choice and claimed that market forces will improve value. Democrats have proposed solutions focused on access, with many advocating for reforms that more closely resemble single-payer systems in other countries. As we will discuss in our final section of this chapter, both ideas likely have some merit. It will remain a delicate balancing act between supporting a competitive marketplace and maintaining access.

Retail Pharmacies, Urgent Care Centers, and Virtual Clinics

Urgent care centers, retail pharmacies, and virtual clinics are already changing the *status quo* for both consumers and healthcare workforces. They are located conveniently in shopping centers, grocery stores, and pharmacies—places where patients go on a regular basis for other needs. Because of this, many of these retail entities are more familiar and comfortable with operating in a consumer-centric environment today. However, there is still more that they can do to become better promoters of consumer choice.

These new forms of distribution, even by traditional drugstores, are already "disrupters" to the traditional modes of healthcare delivery. These stakeholders are well suited to prioritize and deliver on consumer centricity programs. They tend to have direct interactions with consumers, as well as organizational backing to enact large-scale consumer-oriented change. Much of what we discussed in reference to health delivery providers will be applicable to these less traditional market entrants. These clinics will be challenged to increase their consumer-centric orientation as well. They will need to appoint consumer-oriented leadership, conduct detailed consumer research, and develop and implement new programming based on that research.

Because of their retail lines of business, drugstores interact with consumers directly. In their communities, they often serve as the first place for treatment when a consumer comes down with a simple ailment. We all go to pharmacies to pick up prescriptions or purchase first aid supplies. CVS Health and Walgreens have built on this consumer base to expand their on-site clinical services. Both chains have substantial initiatives underway to develop convenient nurse-led clinical services in their stores. But pharmacists in drugstores could do more to enhance consumer choice. Out of time pressure or ignorance, pharmacists do not offer consumers all the choices that exist behind the counter. Sometimes the generic equivalent of a prescribed drug can cost less than the co-pay—but does the pharmacist tell the consumer? Pharmacies could offer more personalized advice. They can embrace their roles on the front line of healthcare by nudging consumers toward medication adherence and pointing out ways they could save money.

CVS Health has been a leader in consumer support. It has decided to emphasize customer health as a core value. In February 2014, CVS Caremark, as it was then named, announced that it would stop selling tobacco products in its stores by October 2014.[20] It also ran an antismoking campaign. These moves were strategic for CVS. It positioned the company to project a more positive image to both consumers and health delivery providers. It also enabled the company to refocus its efforts on its core business: prescriptions and better health.[21],[22] Soon after, CVS announced that it would be changing its name from "CVS Caremark" to "CVS Health" to reflect its broader commitment to healthcare provision and innovation.[23]

CVS has always focused on helping their customers improve medication adherence. This is good not only for patients but also for business. The company launched the Pharmacy Advisor program, through which patients received face-to-face interventions from pharmacists in retail stores, as well as phone calls from pharmacists. In a 2013 press release about the program, Troyen A. Brennan, the executive vice president and chief medical officer of CVS Caremark, said:

> Pharmacy Advisor offers patients the ability to engage with a pharmacist one-on-one, at the pharmacy or on the phone. The customized, expert care they receive helps change patient behavior over time, making them more likely to take their medications as prescribed by their doctor, leading to better health outcomes long-term. By creating and maintaining positive relationships with patients, pharmacists play a crucial role in monitoring and improving patient adherence.[24]

An article in *Health Affairs* showed that the program increased medication adherence rates by 2.1%. Face-to-face interventions by retail store pharmacists were more impactful than phone consultations, resulting in a 3.9% increase in adherence rates. The return on investment was $3 for every $1 spent on additional pharmacist counseling.[25]

Increasingly, many retail and urgent care clinics have engaged in innovative partnerships with larger health systems. Such partnerships can smooth transitions of care and make it easier for patients to receive care when and where they need it. Consider a recent partnership between Dignity Health, a large hospital and health system, and GoHealth Urgent Care. They've teamed up to offer Uber drivers, who are often on the go, healthcare appointments that work for their schedules. In a Dignity Health press release, Todd Latz, chief executive officer of GoHealth Urgent Care, said, "We believe that the on-demand economy calls for more on-demand services in healthcare. Our simple online check-in feature will give drivers even more control—they can 'wait' before they arrive and be at the front of the line when they do. Our extended hours and broad network of centers—four in the Bay Area today, seven by the end of the year and many more to come in 2017—make care easier to access, and will ensure that drivers with Uber and their families can avoid unnecessary and costly visits to the emergency room."[26]

Virtual care is another increasingly available option for patients. Although digitally supported appointments won't work for every kind of health condition, there are many medical problems where digital options can work in tandem with more traditional appointments. Telemedicine, which offers remote care delivery through telecommunications, has advanced significantly in the last few years and is often offered in place of in-person visits. These types of virtual appointments make it easier for patients to access treatment.[27] Email exchanges with clinicians or other care providers can leave patients assured without a trip to a physical office. For minor infections or the common cold, clinical providers can remotely diagnose and treat based on the patient's description of his symptoms. And often, clinical providers have more than the patient's description of his symptoms. New devices make it possible for patients to measure and record their heart rate, blood pressure, and a range of other vital signs from their homes.[28] They can relay this information to their clinical care team and skip an unnecessary trip to the office if their data show that they are doing well. Though largely begun to manage simpler medical conditions, the technology is now often deployed for chronic or complex conditions as well.

Other Stakeholders (Pharmaceutical, Device, and Electronic Medical Record Companies)

Although we've discussed many of the stakeholders that have direct interactions with healthcare consumers, many others affect consumers' options and experiences indirectly. To be sure, pharmaceutical and device companies provide more and more choices through innovation. However, these sectors are quite concentrated and tend to be protectionist.

Drug and device companies expand consumer choice through their innovation but then limit it in the United States through high pricing that inhibits access. Pharmaceutical companies tend to cross-subsidize lower prices in emerging markets by charging very high prices in the United States, which limits the affordability of choices to U.S. consumers. These pricing policies remain significant drivers in the growth of direct and indirect costs of diagnosis and treatment. Increasingly expensive designer drugs will force insurers to either limit their use or transfer a significant portion of the costs to the patient. In either case, their use will be stifled. To maintain a presence in the vital U.S. market, pharmaceutical companies will no longer be able to load so much of their development costs onto U.S. consumers. Instead, U.S. consumers will force big pharma to develop new drug pricing and development strategies.

Finally, we should consider technology vendors like electronic medical record (EMR) companies. EMR producers do little to support consumer choice today. Like the hospitals they serve, they hide behind data privacy to block seamless sharing of information and consumer-friendly functionalities. EMRs are designed as walled gardens, locking providers and patients into the existing systems. Legacy EMRs, which doctors have learned to use, make it a struggle for doctors to switch to a better competitor. This is a huge barrier for new EMR entrants. However, cloud computing and interoperability of interfaces are already underway. These will facilitate the integration of a patient's data no matter where she obtains treatment and thus stimulate consumer-focused innovation. Competition will increase; eventually innovation will make it easier for doctors to switch suppliers and patients to change from one doctor to another.

Consumers

We must not only improve our system so that it better serves consumers, but we must also *become* better consumers ourselves. Too often, healthcare solutions all but ignore the consumer. They put the onus on healthcare provider organizations, clinicians, and payers to create system-wide change. However, consumers have important roles to play: they must demand change and also become more educated and informed about their own health conditions and skilled at doing their part.

Individuals who use healthcare services do not generally think of themselves as consumers. They are infrequently challenged to act as active participants in the healthcare system. Too often, they lack the health literacy necessary to discuss certain aspects of their care, making them more inclined to defer to their physicians. Furthermore, there is also a substantial level of fear associated with making decisions on one's own behalf. Particularly in high-stakes medical situations, people may not want to know and prefer to defer to the knowledge of the trained clinician.

No one enjoys buying or consuming medical care, and most people prefer not to think about it until they need it. Yet consumers must become informed, get involved earlier, and become less reluctant to take action for themselves. Being your own advocate, or an advocate for a family member, can be difficult. It requires changes ranging from knowing your own diagnoses, allergies, and immunizations to learning how to question the clinical professional: What is that? How much will it cost me? Is there another treatment option?

Physicians and provider organizations should be there to guide and advise the consumer, while acknowledging her autonomy. Likewise, while respecting a clinician's knowledge and ability, consumers should be unafraid to speak up for themselves. This is not at odds with the patient–physician relationship. Many clinical providers recognize the importance of engaged patients and have taken a range of steps to empower them. These include enumerating patients' rights. One of the simplest ways healthcare provider organizations have done so is by stating "Patient Rights and Responsibilities." Many health systems publish these clearly online, designating that patients not only have certain rights during their care but also that healthcare is a two-way street; as such, patients are urged to take on specific responsibilities. Pushing patients to be prepared before their appointments, for example, enables them to be more active in their own care. See Box 7.1 for the "Patient Responsibilities" at Brigham and Women's Hospital.

Box 7.1 **Patient Responsibilities at Brigham and Women's Hospital**

By taking an active role in your own healthcare, you can help your caregivers best meet your needs. That is why we ask you and your family to share with us certain responsibilities. They include:

- Letting us know your expectations about hospitalization and treatment
- Asking questions and making sure you understand any instructions given to you so that you can safely care for yourself when you leave the hospital or doctor's office
- Being open and honest with us about your health history, including all medications you are taking and any legal or illegal addictive substances you use
- Telling us about any situation at home or work that may affect your ability to care for yourself, so that we can direct you to resources that can help
- Letting us know if you feel you cannot follow a plan of care that has been prescribed—or telling us when things do not seem to be going well—so that, together, we can develop the right plan of care for you
- Appointing a healthcare proxy and completing an advance care directive, so that we can know what kind of care you wish to have should you become unable to tell us
- Expressing concerns to your caregivers in a respectful manner. If you need additional assistance or are angry or upset about your care, a Brigham and Women's Hospital Patient and Family Relations or Ethics Committee representative can help you.
- Being honest with us about your financial needs so that we may connect you to resources that can help cover your medical expenses
- Letting us know if you have objections to students or researchers participating in your care. As a teaching affiliate of Harvard Medical School, Brigham and Women's Hospital trains healthcare professionals from all disciplines, and your wishes always determine the extent to which they are involved in your care.
- Following Brigham and Women's Hospital rules and regulations
- Being considerate of Brigham and Women's Hospital staff and property, as well as other patients and their privacy

Source: "Your Responsibilities as a Patient or Family Member." *Brigham and Women's Hospital*. 21 January 2016. Web.

But consumers will need to step up their engagement in order to make a difference. What will consumers need to do? First, it is critical that U.S. consumers learn the rules, respond to incentives, and better understand their insurance options. They will have, as most do now, a number of choices among insurance packages that differ in the narrowness of their networks, the breadth of coverage, and the degree of personal financial risk. The less expensive options will be more restrictive.

Choosing their primary caregivers will be the patients' choice in either the basic or private system. This requires that consumers know what they want from their clinicians and the settings in which they work—independent practices, ACOs, hospital-based, urgent care, or HMO, for example.

Consumers will need to be more involved, better informed, and more action-oriented in their own clinical care. They will face decisions involving critical tradeoffs between costs and benefits of clinical recommendations. These can range from whether to undergo an elective surgery, to accept a specialist referral, or to choose a generic or a branded drug. They should demand and use expert help; not only as they get it today through informed consent before surgery but also with the new decisions that rest on affordability and value to them personally. Traditional "informed consent" to a recommended treatment has been limited mostly to discuss personal risks and benefits, but not cost; that will change.

The first step in involvement is paying attention. Consumers should not only demand that choices are described in terms they can understand, but they should also work hard to make the right personal decisions. This means engaging with the data, examining the alternatives carefully, and seeking help when they are uncertain about how to approach the decision or unclear about the alternative that works best for them.

Consumers have an obligation to do their part in measuring performance. They are asked already for their feedback across many different consumer products; healthcare should be no different. Feedback must be methodologically good enough to drive improvements for everyone. Random feedback is useful, but true assessment of options will require consumers to respond to systematic requests for their opinions of their patient journey and thoughtful assessment of how well their clinical results met their expectations. Performance assessment should be part of the obligation of receiving care; it is where patients do their part to make the system better.

Adding consumer-friendly incentives could enhance feedback. Because measurement is so important, consumers are likely to be rewarded for participating in the collection of data about the performance of providers on clinical results as well as the benefits they consider important. Incentives will help assure that consumers complete surveys, provide direct feedback, and participate in other forms of data gathering, such as focus groups or telephone interviews.

Another example is the use of rewards for patients doing their part in taking care of themselves. Encouraging healthy behaviors helps both the individual and the collective insurance pool. Financial incentives can influence people to eat properly, stop smoking, exercise, take their prescribed medications, meet their preventive screening and immunizations requirements, and avoid dangerous behaviors like failing to wear seatbelts. Adopting healthy behaviors not only helps them stay healthy but also is beneficial for the whole healthcare enterprise. The use of such incentives to positively influence healthy behaviors has been slow to catch on. However, the use of surcharges because of accidents in automobile insurance is widespread and believed to reduce risky behaviors; there is no reason why such incentives wouldn't work to motivate behavior change in healthcare.

Conclusion

Why Is Consumer Choice Important?

An intensifying consumer voice can be a powerful force for improvement in U.S. healthcare. A new, consumer-driven environment is emerging that seeks to personalize choices, promote transparency, and inspire engagement. Products and services are coming to market that are better designed around consumer needs. Why are these solutions so important more broadly and in healthcare specifically? Consumer-oriented changes have the ability to increase consumer satisfaction, improve overall value in the system, and catalyze business innovation.

Consumer Satisfaction

The notion of individual choice is held particularly dear within the U.S. healthcare system. Yet too often, policies and programs in healthcare have failed to include and empower the consumer. We know that empowerment and autonomy are drivers of consumer satisfaction—not only in healthcare but also across many other areas of our lives. More choice can satisfy consumers' varied preferences and needs.

For the vast majority of people, buying insurance and using healthcare are grudge purchases. Few look forward to the transactions with pleasure. Most people would rather spend their money on something else. At the very least, we should seek to make the experience tolerable—minimize the discomfort, make it easier, and provide a more sympathetic experience. Perhaps our consumer choice motto should be "This will only hurt a little" and then to deliver on that promise.

On the other hand, expectations about the experience are already low among healthcare consumers. This leaves a lot of room to exceed them and leave a consumer delighted with an experience that might not be viewed as exemplary in another industry. For example, hospital food is generally terrible. Serving a tasty meal in a hospital would be seen as exceptional service; the same meal in a restaurant would most likely generate critical reviews.

In those services that truly help people feel better, the industry has an opportunity to make the event truly satisfying. Making the delivery of a baby a really wonderful experience, returning function in a hip or a knee so the recipient can resume tennis, and relieving deafness instantly by removing wax from a blocked ear canal are services that are real opportunities to deliver a memorable experience. Healthcare shouldn't miss the opportunity to do these so well that patients are grateful, building up trust that their providers are doing the best they can to draw upon when the outcome is less pleasant.

Overall Value

Consumer choice by itself is not going to fix America's problems with cost or effectiveness, as we have said. However, adding the dimension of choice, measuring service and satisfaction, and activating consumer purchasing power could lift the value of the system regardless of how we ultimately improve cost and quality.

Return for a moment to Sheila, whose story we described at the outset of this book. She was an unsatisfied customer. When she came down with a sore throat, she was willing to try an urgent care center, an option she believed would meet her desire for a quicker service (compared to her traditional primary care doctor). Despite searching for cost information beforehand, she ended up paying $50 more than what she expected for a simple visit. She was confused by the ambiguous information on their web site. Furthermore, the provider's billing office lacked the customer service skills to appropriately address her concerns. Sheila took her complaints to Yelp—and her business elsewhere in the future. Consumers like Sheila will be increasingly common.

We should applaud her effort to find a service that fit her needs. An independent-minded consumer with a problem that she understood, she represents the new consumer. Consumers will, through their choices and loyalty, let the producers of service know whether they are happy with what they are being offered. Armed with improved access to cost and quality information and with their own health data in hand, these consumers will be motivated to push back on services that are poorly designed or delivered. Her actions are what will reward or punish innovative new approaches to delivering and financing care. Multiplied by millions, those like Sheila will deliver a market message about whether an innovation is an improvement worth keeping. Consumers will need to exercise their right to switch when they are dissatisfied. This is a necessary first step in making market forces work to improve value.

Catalyze Business Innovation

Consumer centricity will ultimately permeate much of the healthcare industry. Early-adopter consumers will seek out and enjoy choices and benefits from the leaders. Their favorable experiences will influence other consumers. To stay in business and thrive, other provider organizations will need to emulate the leaders. This shift will involve all directly customer-facing sectors of the healthcare industry. The results of consumer centricity will be to drive innovation and differentiation across the three arms of the consumer value proposition: economy/affordability, effectiveness/quality, and service/satisfaction. Those providers and insurers who succeed will be rewarded.

Figuring out how to make healthcare better is a huge business opportunity. The scale of the market is international. People everywhere want to live longer, happier lives. New technologies are flooding into medical care, some of which are of relatively low yield. Every system in every country is struggling to control costs, improve outcomes, and satisfy its citizens. Because America's healthcare problems are the largest, it may be the best place for new solutions to arise first because where the problem is the biggest, the potential return for innovation is greatest. If Americans invent how to do it better, there is a business opportunity out there for the insurers, providers, and others who figure it out. These methods and models could be a valuable export business for the United States.

Consumer Choice Caveats

The Affordability Challenge

The United States must find a way to deliver effective care that is within peoples' means. In Chapter 2, we argued that all Americans deserve insurance that provides access to good, basic care. But to make this insurance affordable to individuals and the nation, we must control the underlying costs of medical care.

Current efforts at controlling cost and quality are weak. Consumerism by itself is not, in our view, a force strong enough to solve our cost and quality problems. If consumers can be activated and market forces unleashed, consumer choice can help out but not solve this challenge alone. A majority of America's greater cost of healthcare is caused by higher input costs than other nations[29] Theoretically, greater choice and market forces should be able to bring these costs down, but the proof is still lacking. Perhaps this is where our call to increase choice and provide the right market incentives could make a difference.

Nor are we optimistic that providers will control costs at the behest of payers and insurers. Doctors have taken on increasing accountability for managing the costs of care. But provider groups, when given the responsibility, appear unlikely to decrease medical costs far enough to bring deductibles down and lower insurance and out-of-pocket costs into a zone of affordability. To date, the evidence is that cost savings from CMS innovations such as ACOs have been small.[30]

Ultimately, if government decides to give Americans a universal healthcare system that is affordable, it must devise a means to control costs. The international experience in virtually all developed countries tells us that healthcare will grow ever more expensive; new tests and treatments, ageing populations, and surging lifestyle illnesses are all increasing consumption. The collective cost of our current open-ended system, regardless of whether it is paid by government or business, will compete with other important national priorities and undermine our international competitiveness. If it is paid by individual consumers as higher premiums, co-payments, co-insurance, or deductibles, we will have replicated our old system that rationed care by ability to pay rather than by medical need.

We know it is possible for policy makers to design a system with lower costs but ample benefits and excellent results. Other countries have set examples. They achieve better results at amounts much lower *per capita* than what the United States spends. Examples of successful systems that are working well in other countries are readily available. In an *Economist* 2017 article entitled "Health Care: The Expanding Universal,"[31] the authors describe a number of European states that provide cost-effective systems that could serve as models for U.S. healthcare redesign. They conclude that "there are not that many ways to achieve universal health insurance coverage in a country. Fundamentally, U.S. government must either provide it directly, or regulate and subsidize the insurance industry to do it. For any one variant one can imagine, some European country has probably tried it out."

The answer is to create an effective but low-cost, capped system for all but at the same time enable those to pay for it on their own if they wish to buy more. We believe that if healthcare is to be affordable for all, the United States will need to move toward such a type of two-tiered system. The first of the two parts will be an affordable basic insurance package that will cover everyone. It will be limited in benefits to those services that are necessary and be subsidized for those for whom it is still out of reach financially. It will not cover everything that is possible medically and probably will have some caps on expenditures. Choice will be limited, but not absent. It will be a system designed for maximum efficiency and effectiveness but not primarily for choice. But because it is available to all, it satisfies the political requirement of being fair and meets the ethical and moral responsibilities of a nation to provide healthcare for all.

For the second segment, we propose a voluntary top-up system. It would enable those who wish for more, and can afford it, to do so through a private system. In such an open-ended top-up system, choice reigns. In this a discretionary private system, consumers can buy what they want. A private top-up system is also where we could test how strong consumer choice and market forces could be in controlling the growth of costs. As in any consumer market, there will be regulatory constraints to protect the consumers in both systems and keep markets working efficiently.

There are many ways in which the two tiers could be constructed. The two parts could be strictly separated, for example, as is the case in Canada and England. Or it could be one system with choice built in. Examples of this model allow private supplements beyond what standard insurance pays. This approach is in use now in the example of voluntary monthly payments participants pay to be cared for by a concierge practice. Another example is the tiered pricing used by insurers in managing drug benefits.

The latter creates tiers of different out-of-pocket payment for drugs, making the cost-effective parts inexpensive to the consumer and the low-benefit/high-cost drug choices subject to higher co-payments.

There are also ways to achieve universal coverage without opting for a government-run, single-payer system. Herzlinger, Richman, and Boxer suggest that using an individual mandate and significant penalties as leverage could enable America to achieve universal coverage. They point to three other countries—Switzerland, Singapore, and Germany—to illustrate how other countries use mandates and stiffer penalties to nudge consumers toward opting into the system.[32]

Choices We Cannot Have

There are choices we cannot have in a consumer choice system. First, Americans should not be allowed to drop out of universal health insurance. Our current system is far too lenient in allowing people to opt out of participating in the system. In 2014, the first year Americans were required to provide proof of health insurance coverage, 7.5 million people paid a penalty, and another 12 million claimed exemptions.[33] Although there are many ways to inject choice into the U.S. healthcare system, this specific choice is not one we should offer to our populace. If an individual decides not to participate in health insurance, she adversely affects the insurance risk pool. Young people, who do not yet have healthcare needs, opt out. Older people are the only ones left in the risk pool, ultimately driving up premiums.

Other countries have faced these issues before. Princeton health economist Uwe Reinhardt was interviewed in August 2016, at a time when several health insurers had pulled out of the state marketplaces because of continued financial losses. Reinhardt gave a dire assessment of the marketplaces' future given the lack of an enforceable mandate. In the interview, he said:

> The natural business model of a private commercial insurer is to price on health status and have the flexibility to raise prices year after year. What we've tried to do, instead, is do community rating [where insurers can't price on how sick or healthy an enrollee is] and couple it with a mandate.
>
> When you do this as the Swiss or Germans do, you brutally enforce the mandate. You make young people sign up and pay. But we are too chicken to do that, so we allow people to stay out by doing two things: We give them a mandate penalty that is lower than the premium. And we tell them, if you're really sick, we'll take care of you anyhow.[34]

Furthermore, when people who choose not to insure themselves do get sick, most still expect to receive treatment. Because we do not turn people away in emergency situations, there are often challenges of moral hazard. Allowing people to add and drop coverage as they see fit could lead to an inordinate amount of free riding. Someone might add insurance coverage for a year to receive a specific surgery that he has needed for some time, only to drop it the following year.

Second, Americans must accept that the basic healthcare system will not cover everything that consumers want. Not everyone can have a Mercedes. In exchange for a basic system that is effective and equitable, most Americans will need to "pay as they go" when they want services not included in the basic insurance program.

There are inevitable trade-offs in any healthcare system—both at the individual and at the system level. On an individual level, we must all consider our priorities and what we want and are willing to pay for. At the system level, there are *always* trade-offs. This is true in single-payer, government-run healthcare systems and in our more market-based system. As we have discussed, in single-payer systems or its regulated counterpart such as Switzerland, there will need to be some way to reduce low-value tests and treatments; that will constrain consumer choice. There is still a great opportunity to use incentives aligned with desired customer benefits and, at the same time, designed to protect the common resource. A better understanding of consumers—how they use healthcare services and what they want from it—is necessary to continue improving value.

Risks When Consumers Choose

We recognize that there are challenges in arguing for greater consumer choice in the U.S. healthcare system. Patients might hurt themselves by demanding things that don't work or by avoiding things that do. Consumers might find themselves paralyzed with choice when considering a range of options. Research by behavioral economists and psychologists has shown that too much choice can be dissatisfying for consumers, leading to decision errors, regret, and anxiety.[35] When there is legitimate concern about self-harm, when minors are at risk, or when commercial interests are cutting corners or making false claims, regulators are right to step in. It is a delicate balancing act but one that must be joined.

Perhaps the greatest concern in increasing consumer choice is the potential for overutilization. There is a very real risk that giving consumers more choices will lead them to use more services—a challenge that is already an issue here in the United States. Demand for medical care is virtually limitless. If they don't have to pay, people will naturally go for more rather than less care. For example, a 2017 study showed that many women opt to receive double mastectomies when they receive a breast cancer diagnosis, even though there is no proof that doing so significantly reduces the chance of future disease.[36]

In addition, more choice and competition has the potential to increase inefficiency. Markets may fragment as new entrants compete for business. Increased choice may lead to greater questioning of experts and their opinions, resulting in more and longer consultations with physicians. Customization also requires more of providers, who must match the best treatment options for individuals.

Enhancing competition between providers as consumers exercise their choices will lead to losers as well as winners. Healthcare is approaching 20% of the U.S. economy, so choice and competition may have big economic impacts, with disruptions and dislocations. Some sectors may fail, employees will be out of work, and investors disappointed. We may need fewer hospitals; insurers may earn less. But this is the nature of capitalism; if consumers can choose, the producers must adapt or fail. Over our long history, this is the way the United States has prospered.

A Better Future

Readiness for Change

We are trapped in much the same healthcare delivery and financing system that has existed for 50 years. We have had very little innovation that has focused on improving the efficiency and effectiveness of the healthcare system. Yes, the ACA covered more people, as have Medicare and Medicaid. But the way we structure the system, pay doctors and hospitals, buy insurance, and deliver services has changed little. We have advanced the science and technology of medical care, but the latter has come with added costs that are increasingly being transferred to the public. The pressure is rising to fix our insurance, delivery, and financing.

Enhancing consumer power and harnessing competitive market forces are two levers that can help us break away from the *status quo*. Healthcare has been caught in B2B competition that has ignored consumers in favor of products and arrangements that favor the producers—insurers, hospitals, and doctors. With proper incentives and consumer mindset, healthcare suppliers can become more consumer-centric. As it grows, consumer centricity will stimulate insurers and providers to innovate and provide a mix of benefits that is meaningful to its market segments. By exercising their choice, consumers will be better satisfied with what the system provides and will be an engine for making medical care better. Competition to attract the favor of patients in their segment will drive the producers of care toward innovation, improvement, and lower costs.

We are ripe for change. Conditions today are better than ever before for testing the hypothesis that consumer forces can make healthcare better. Consumer power is growing everywhere. We have widespread agreement that our current system needs to change, including in the area of consumer choice. There is little ideological disagreement about the importance of consumer choice in society. We Americans are among the best consumers in the world. Digital transformation is sufficiently advanced to connect, collect, analyze, and assist most of the care processes and engage with participants in the patient journey. We already have identified many of the factors that are holding us back and have the expertise to identify needs, barriers, and opportunities. We have the analytic tools to evaluate how well consumer choice interventions are working. And we are a country that values new ideas.

The Need for Experimentation

We have a desperate need for innovation. We are stifling, rather than inducing, invention in healthcare financing and delivery. We are trapped in our old system, which favors existing players and time-worn structures and in which the financial incentives at work make our problems worse rather than better. We could continue to pour money into healthcare, but if we want more for our money, we need new ideas and experimentation in how to make our system work better. Improvements in financing and consumer-oriented delivery could generate savings, stimulate national productivity, and improve Americans' health. It is outrageous that in a more than $3 trillion industry with extensive national support for biologic research we have so little funding to support delivery system innovation and the development of delivery science research.

A critical question for study is whether and how consumer forces can make a health system better. Despite claims, like ours, that consumer choice can be a force for improvement in healthcare, no one has proven the hypothesis or knows exactly how to make it happen. The proof will be empirical, by evaluating real-life innovation in delivery and financing.

How do we stimulate the right innovation? If we aren't sure what to do to improve our system, instead of pursuing a top-down research and development program that favors what policy makers at the center want, we should be creating an environment that favors entrepreneurship and invention. Innovation generally is most active out in the field. Less top-down and more over-the-transom experimentation is the prescription we propose. Current funding, such as from capital markets, is generally risk averse, and especially so in healthcare.

We are familiar with a model for this kind of research and development environment. It is the Defense Advanced Research Projects Agency (DARPA).[37] DARPA was started by Eisenhower in 1958 in the U.S. Department of Defense as a response to Sputnik. DARPA's mission is to sponsor innovative and transformative research projects in areas of interest to the military through collaborations with universities, industry, and government partners. It is an incubator of innovation. The very successful model for DARPA is that they first specify an area of need and then assist applicants to create, implement, and test ideas. They do so by funding the risks that these expectedly innovative projects take on. DARPA rewards collaboration and quickness. They reduce the financial barriers that deter those with good ideas from coming together to try them out. Two former DARPA directors describe their process as a combination of ambitious goals and flexible, temporary project teams. In their view of the projects, "Their intensity, sharp focus, and finite time frame make them attractive to the highest-caliber talent, and the nature of the challenge inspires unusual levels of collaboration"[38]

There are areas of healthcare that are naturally suited to begin implementing more innovative consumer-oriented policies. We will give two examples, not because they are perfect, but because they highlight what we mean when we call for fresh, creative thinking to engage consumers. These two are end-of-life care and narrowing the scope of health insurance.

Expensive end-of-life care is an area ready for change for a few reasons. First, as Gawande has described in his book *Being Mortal*, many dying Americans are not getting what they want. Here, if anywhere, is a need for personal consumer choice options to be clear and available. Second, for a variety of reasons, it is difficult to curb this expensive sector of its mostly medical spending. Physicians may feel uncomfortable discussing the end of life or the exhaustion of treatment options with a patient, leading to additional and unnecessary treatment. Third, we know that many consumers change their behavior when they are better informed. In one study, researchers showed that end-of-life consumers actually chose less care when they were better informed.[39] Finally, end-of-life medical care is expensive. Typically, in the United States, 25% of Medicare's total cost is consumed by care in the last year of life.[40] Improving education and access to information might not only improve consumer satisfaction and quality of life but could also reduce costs.

What might delivery system innovation look like for end-of-life choice? New insurance products might offer shared savings models. Imagine that, coupled with advance directives, a Medicare patient might choose an expenditure cap or some defined point (e.g., no intensive care or intubation or resuscitation) beyond which medical interventions would be replaced with dignified comfort care in hospice or home. The actuarial savings could be estimated and the cost savings shared with the patients who chose this option, perhaps as reductions in premium costs or even additions to social security payments early enough in their life span to make their elderly years better.

The second example describes how insurance coverage and costs could be reduced selectively for a defined population. Most market-based insurance options focus on comprehensive coverage. Some observers contend that market-based solutions should test more radical benefit mixes. In 2017, after the new healthcare bill was unsuccessfully pulled before Congress could vote on it, Jeff Jacoby wrote an opinion piece in the *Boston Globe* critiquing both the AHCA and the ACA, and arguing for a more consumer-driven system. He wrote:

> The Ryan plan is indeed deeply flawed—not because it obliterates Obamacare, but because it doesn't.... Rather, it's only the latest turn in a long saga of health care "reforms" that have constricted choice, disempowered consumers, banished price awareness, eliminated competition, and discouraged innovation. The results are all around us: skyrocketing medical

costs, mounting economic pressures on employers, employees, doctors, and patients—and a political obsession with providing insurance, rather than with producing good health.[41]

Jacoby goes on in the article to condemn the notion that the only way to pay for healthcare is through health insurance. He argues that Congress is too focused on meeting "the demands of the insurance cartel and the political," and not focused enough on consumers and their needs. He points out that in other markets, such as automobile and homeowner's insurance, insurance is not used for regular expenses. Insurance is reserved for catastrophic events, which keeps the price of insurance down and maintains a consumer-driven market for more regular expenses. For day-to-day home improvements or fixes, the homeowner is on her own to discern what services she needs and to find a good contractor at a reasonable price. Jacoby has argued previously that this sort of model could work in health insurance as well. If consumers were in charge of regular expenses, instead of using the insurance companies as a third-party middleman, they might get a better deal. In the current system, provider organizations have few incentives to compete by offering lower prices because individuals rarely know the full price of care. Often, they remain in the dark about the total cost of care, receiving a notice for only the patient portion of the bill after the insurance company has paid the provider.

Experimentation in this model might bring together a payer, insurer, and collaborating provider. Imagine a self-insured corporation that wanted to try this. The corporation knows its overall costs. If it contracted for and provided catastrophic coverage (which is inexpensive because it is infrequently used) for an employee and family, the company could share part or all of the remainder in a health savings account or as higher employee income, giving the employee and family the ability to manage their own care. Incentives for health behaviors could be built into the requirements as mandates. A large corporation could offer this and then randomly select those to participate. Those who remained in "usual care" would be the control group for a study of the effectiveness of the intervention.

A Beginning, Not an Ending

This book is intended to promote deeper thinking about the details of consumer choice. We hope it helps readers not only to acknowledge the current challenges in the system and understand how consumer markets work but also to understand why and how healthcare differs from other consumer markets. We all need to prepare for consumers who are less passive in this new environment.

We have a lot to learn. If patients are to become good consumers and the healthcare system a better functioning market, we must understand where choice works and where it does not. Healthcare stakeholders must spend more time understanding consumers and how they process decisions. Consumers in healthcare will need to step up their game. And we must protect patients from bad choices and assure that they are safe as they learn to exercise choice.

We have presented a model for a consumer choice-enhanced healthcare system. In this model, healthcare will be moving toward greater consumer orientation. Although future changes in incentives will accelerate this process, the change is already underway. The pace will quicken if payers and insurers adopt a consumer mindset; those who do will remove barriers and provide positive incentives, primarily financial, to induce providers to shift toward a delivery system that does a better job of both helping consumers navigate choice and making their experience better.

This book should serve as the beginning of the conversation—not the end. We need more delivery innovation and improvement research. Those out in the field know best how to innovate to fix our big problems. Payers, insurers, and providers are caught in a tightly integrated dance in today's fraught system. If they can be freed of their bonds, they will find ways to collaborate once they know the target objectives, have the prospect of financial rewards, and receive the resources and legal protection to lower their risks. They have the capacity to work across a range of disciplines to design a better, consumer-oriented system. Payers know what they want, insurers understand benefits and actuarial projections of costs, and clinical providers are well suited to understand the technical research around quality and safety that will be imperative for maintaining effectiveness. If the experience with DARPA is a guide, they will be able to come together and churn out competitive proposals for innovative, consumer choice models. We also need social scientists, such as economists and psychologists, to continue research on the incentives necessary for motivating behavior change. Mostly we need smart entrepreneurs who want to fix healthcare.

In our view, enhancing consumer choice can help change the system for the better. Choice may not control prices by itself, but involving consumers more can certainly help. Even though consumers cannot do this all by themselves, they will be a force for change when the system has positioned itself to stimulate and reward affordability, better health, and innovation.

In this time of turbulence, there is also a very real risk that we miss the opportunity to make the healthcare market work for a majority of consumers. Winston Churchill is said to have originated the admonition: "Never let a good crisis go to waste." We should strive to make our market-oriented system into an asset, where consumer choice could help improve healthcare. We should make choice work better and ensure it gives us a health system we can be proud of and afford.

References

1. Nakazara, Donna Jackson. "How to Win the Doctor Lottery." *Health Affairs* 36, no. 4 (2017). Web.

2. Mehrotra, Ateev, Katie M. Dean, Anna D. Sinaiko, and Neeraj Sood. "Americans Support Price Shopping for Health Care, But Few Actually Seek Out Price Information." *Health Affairs*. 1 August 2017. Web.

3. Moriates, Christopher, Krishan Soni, Andrew Lai, and Sumant Ranji. "The Value in the Evidence: Teaching Residents to 'Choose Wisely.'" *JAMA Internal Medicine*. American Medical Association, 25 February 2013. Web.

4. Ibid.

5. Awdish, Rana L. A. "A View From the Edge—Creating a Culture of Caring." *New England Journal of Medicine*. 5 January 2017. Web.

6. Collins, Jim, and Jerry I. Porras. *Built to Last: Successful Habits of Visionary Companies*. Harper Business, 1994. Print.

7. "Only Nine Percent of U.S. Consumers Believe Pharma and Biotechnology Put Patients Over Profits; Only 16 Percent Believe Health Insurers Do." *Health & Life*. The HarrisPoll, 17 January 2017. Web.

8. Herzlinger, Regina. "Making Health Insurance That Consumers Actually Like." Interview. Audio blog post. *Working Knowledge: Business Research for Business Leaders*. Harvard Business School, April 2017. Web.

9. Loewenstein, George, Joelle Y. Friedman, Barbara McGill, Sarah Ahmad, Suzanne Linck, Stacey Sinkula, John Beshears, James J. Choi, Jonathan Kolstad, David Laibson, Brigitte C. Madrian, John A. List, and Kevin G. Volpp. "Consumers' Misunderstanding of Health Insurance." *Journal of Health Economics*. North-Holland, September 2013. Web.

10. "Health Insurance That Works for You and Your Family." *Oscar: Smart, Simple Health Insurance*. Web.

11. "Health Insurance Coverage of the Total Population." *The Henry J. Kaiser Family Foundation*. September 2017. Web.

12. Long, Michelle, Matthew Rae, Gary Claxton, and Anthony Damico. "Trends in Employer-Sponsored Insurance Offer and Coverage Rates, 1999–2014." *The Henry J. Kaiser Family Foundation*. N.p., 21 March 2016. Web.

13. Cothran, Josh. "US Health Care Spending: Who Pays?" *California Health Care Foundation—Health Care That Works for All Californians*. September 2017. Web.

14. "2016 Employer Health Benefits Survey." *The Henry J. Kaiser Family Foundation*. 14 September 2016. Web.

15. Japsen, Bruce. "U.S. Workforce Illness Costs $576B Annually From Sick Days to Workers Compensation." *Forbes: Pharma & Healthcare*. Forbes Magazine, 12 September 2012. Web.

16. Krebs-Smith, Susan M., Patricia M. Guenther, Amy F. Subar, Sharon I. Kirkpatrick, and Kevin W. Dodd. "Americans Do Not Meet Federal Dietary Recommendations." *The Journal of Nutrition*. American Society for Nutrition, October 2010. Web.

17. Lavizzo-Mourey, Risa. "Building a Culture of Health: 2014 President's Message." *Robert Wood Johnson Foundation*. 2014. Web.

18. Quelch, John A., and Emily C. Boudreau. *Building a Culture of Health: A New Imperative for Business*. Springer, 2016. Print.

19. Antos, Joseph, and James Capretta. "The CBO's Updated Estimate of the AHCA." *Health Affairs*. 6 June 2017. Web.

20. "Message from Larry Merlo, President and CEO." *CVSHealth.com*. 5 February 2014. Web.

21. Stock, Kyle. "The Strategy Behind CVS's No-Smoking Campaign." *Bloomberg.com*. Bloomberg, 5 February 2014. Web.

22. Tabuchi, Hiroko. "How CVS Quit Smoking and Grew Into a Health Care Giant." *The New York Times*. 11 July 2015. Web.

23. "Our New Name." *CVS Health*. 3 September 2014. Web.

24. "CVS Caremark's Innovative Pharmacy Advisor Program Highlighted in New National Report Released by IMS Institute for Healthcare Informatics." *PR Newswire: News Distribution, Targeting and Monitoring*. PRNewswire, 20 June 2013. Web.

25. Brennan, Troyen A., Timothy J. Dollear, Min Hu, Olga S. Matlin, William H. Shrank, Niteesh K. Choudhry, and William Grambley. "An Integrated Pharmacy-Based Program Improved Medication Prescription and Adherence Rates in Diabetes Patients." *Health Affairs.* January 2012. Web.

26. "Dignity Health, GoHealth Urgent Care and Uber Team Up to Offer Health and Wellness Services to Drivers With Uber and Their Families." *Dignity Health.* 19 October 2016. Web.

27. "About Telemedicine." *FAQs—American Telemedicine Association Main.* American Telemedicine Association, Web.

28. Beck, Melinda. "How Telemedicine Is Transforming Health Care." *The Wall Street Journal.* Dow Jones & Company, 26 June 2016. Web.

29. Squires, David and Anderson, Chloe. "*U.S. Health Care from a Global Perspective: Spending, Use of Services, Prices, and Health in 13 Countries,*" The Commonwealth Fund, October 2015.

30. Ginsburg, Paul B., and Kavita K. Patel. "Physician Payment Reform—Progress to Date." *New England Journal of Medicine.* 20 July 2017. Web.

31. "The Expanding Universal: The Fix for American Health Care Can Be Found in Europe." *Economist* 10 (August 2017): 22. Web.

32. Herzlinger, Regina E., Barak D. Richman, and Richard J. Boxer. "Lessons From Three Countries on Achieving Universal Coverage." *JAMA.* American Medical Association, 11 April 2017. Web.

33. Galewitz, Phil. "IRS: 7.5 Million Americans Paid Penalty for Lack of Health Coverage." *NPR. com.* 21 July 2015. Web.

34. Kliff, Sarah. "This Princeton Health Economist Thinks Obamacare's Marketplaces Are Doomed." *Vox.com.* 25 August 2016. Web.

35. Loewenstein, George. "Is More Choice Always Better?" National Academy of Social Insurance's 11th Annual Conference. Washington D.C., 28–29 January 1999. Print.

36. Nash, Rebecca, Michael Goodman, Chun Chieh Lin, Rachel A. Freedman, Laura S. Dominici, Kevin Ward, and Ahmedin Jemal. "State Variation in the Receipt of a Contralateral Prophylactic Mastectomy Among Women Who Received a Diagnosis of Invasive Unilateral Early-Stage Breast Cancer in the United States, 2004–2012." *JAMA Surgery.* American Medical Association, July 2017. Web.

37. "DARPA Homepage." *Defense Advanced Research Projects Agency.* Web.

38. Dugan, Regina E., and Kaighham J. Gabriel. "'Special Forces' Innovation: How DARPA Attacks Problems." *Harvard Business Review.* October 2013. Web.

39. Silveira, Maria J., Scott Y. H. Kim, and Kenneth M. Langa. "Advance Directives and Outcomes of Surrogate Decision Making Before Death." *New England Journal of Medicine.* 1 April 2010. Web.

40. Riley, Gerald F., and James D. Lubitz. "Long-Term Trends in Medicare Payments in the Last Year of Life." *Health Services Research.* Blackwell Science, Inc., Apr. 2010. Web.

41. Jacoby, Jeff. "Ditch Obamacare, and Don't Stop There." *BostonGlobe.com.* 19 March 2017. Web.

ABOUT THE AUTHORS

Gordon Moore, MD, MPH, is a primary care doctor and Professor of Population Medicine at Harvard Medical School. He was educated at Harvard and trained as a specialist in general internal medicine and infectious diseases at the Massachusetts General Hospital. In 1971 he joined the founding group of Harvard Community Health Plan, the country's first academically sponsored HMO, where he eventually became medical director and chief operating officer. He built its first health center in Cambridge, Massachusetts, and practiced there as a front line primary care practitioner for almost 40 years. In his academic work, he designed and started the New Pathway, a new curriculum at Harvard Medical School that has become a worldwide model for medical education. He later became program director of the Robert Wood Johnson initiative to train graduate doctors and nurses in systems thinking and practice improvement. His special interests are primary care delivery and the design, organization, and management of healthcare systems.

John A. Quelch, DBA, MBA, MS, is the Miller University Professor at the University of Miami, Dean of Miami Business School, and University Vice Provost for Executive Education. He holds a joint professorial appointment at Miami Business School and at the Miller School of Public Health Sciences. He served previously as the Charles Edward Wilson Professor at Harvard Business School and held a joint appointment at the Harvard T.H. Chan School of Public Health. His most recent books are *Consumers, Corporations and Public Health* (2016) and *Building a Culture of Health: A New Imperative for Business* (2016) with Emily Boudreau. He is a graduate of Oxford University, the Wharton School of the University of Pennsylvania, Harvard Business School, and the Harvard School of Public Health.

Emily Boudreau, BA, is a PhD student in Health Policy and Management at Yale University. She previously served as a research associate at Harvard Business School, where she coauthored the book *Building a Culture of Health: A New Imperative for Business* (Springer, 2016) and numerous Harvard Business School cases. She has also worked as a senior analyst at The Advisory Board Company, advising hospitals, health systems, and companies in the healthcare industry. Emily graduated *magna cum laude* with distinction from Cornell University, where her thesis on infrastructure and change management within the Veterans Health Administration received the Sherman-Bennett Prize.

INDEX

Tables, figures, and boxes are indicated by an italic *t*, *f*, and *b* following the page number.